T0357717

Advance Praise for *Rise Above*

"Self-actualization is possible for each of us, and there we find a better, happier future. But that means avoiding the traps and barriers we set for ourselves. Scott Barry Kaufman's brilliant new book *Rise Above* is the evidence-based manual we need to be free."

—**Arthur C. Brooks, Harvard professor and bestselling author of**
From Strength to Strength **and** *Build the Life You Want*

"*Rise Above* is a welcome and necessary antidote to the victim narrative that plagues our time. Part memoir, part case study, part scientific tool kit, this book provides both inspiration and practical guidance. A must-read for anyone who wants to move from grievance to gratitude for a more fulfilling life."

—**Anna Lembke, M.D., author of** *Dopamine Nation:*
Finding Balance in the Age of Indulgence

"*Rise Above* is a call to action for anyone who feels stuck in a pattern of anger and blame. We always have another choice—to recognize the ownership we have over our own lives, every day—and Scott Barry Kaufman provides an accessible road map for doing just that. It isn't easy work, but it can be life-changing."

—**Lori Gottlieb, bestselling author of** *Maybe You Should Talk to Someone*

"Scott Barry Kaufman has made so many contributions to research on creativity, positive psychology, and the science of flourishing. In *Rise Above*, Kaufman draws on ancient wisdom and modern psychology to address some of the disempowering ideas and mindsets circulating widely in recent decades. Kaufman shows us all how to stand up and walk through the many doors that are always available."

—**Jonathan Haidt, bestselling author of** *The Anxious Generation* **and**
coauthor of *The Coddling of the American Mind*

"Few things would perplex people from the past—or hopefully the future—more than people today exaggerating their victimhood and thinking of it as what makes them special. *Rise Above* gently but firmly takes us back to the normality of forward-looking resilience."

—**John McWhorter,** *New York Times* **columnist and bestselling author of** *Nine Nasty Words* **and** *Pronoun Trouble*

"A big part of success in business and life is learning how to deal effectively with things that are beyond your control. The secret is called resilience and Scott Barry Kaufman's *Rise Above* is an excellent practical guide for anybody working to build their resilience muscles."

—**Scott Galloway, professor of Marketing at NYU Stern School of Business, cohost of the** *Pivot* **podcast, and author of** *The Algebra of Wealth*

"Scott Barry Kaufman reminds us all of our innate capacity to grow from the challenges we face, even big ones. *Rise Above* leads us beyond our constricted self-perceptions to a far more expansive and empowered sense of possibility that could be ours."

—**Sharon Salzberg, author of** *Lovingkindness* **and** *Real Life*

"A message that needs to be heard today more than ever. No matter how difficult things get, we always have the power to rise above."

—**Mark Manson, bestselling author of** *The Subtle Art of Not Giving a F*ck*

"*Rise Above* is a brilliant blend of science and soul, offering urgent insights for turning life's challenges into opportunities for growth. Scott Barry Kaufman has written the masterful guide we all need to navigate the chaos."

—**Tasha Eurich, organizational psychologist and author of** *Insight* **and** *Shatterproof*

"The perfect book for our times. The victimhood mindset is everywhere, but leading cognitive scientist Scott Barry Kaufman gives us insights and actionable strategies to successfully rise above this pernicious mentality."

—**Kurt Gray, professor of Psychology at UNC Chapel Hill and author of** *Outraged*

ALSO BY SCOTT BARRY KAUFMAN

Choose Growth (with Jordyn Feingold)

Transcend

Wired to Create (with Carolyn Gregoire)

Ungifted

RISE
ABOVE

Overcome a Victim Mindset,
Empower Yourself,
and Realize Your Full Potential

SCOTT BARRY
KAUFMAN, Ph.D.

Tarcher
an imprint of Penguin Random House
New York

t

Tarcher
an imprint of Penguin Random House LLC
1745 Broadway, New York, NY 10019
penguinrandomhouse.com

Copyright © 2025 by Scott Barry Kaufman
Sailboat illustration by Andy Ogden
Chart on p. 158: © Copyright 2004–2024, VIA Institute on Character. Used with permission, all rights reserved.
Penguin Random House values and supports copyright. Copyright fuels creativity, encourages diverse voices, promotes free speech, and creates a vibrant culture. Thank you for buying an authorized edition of this book and for complying with copyright laws by not reproducing, scanning, or distributing any part of it in any form without permission. You are supporting writers and allowing Penguin Random House to continue to publish books for every reader. Please note that no part of this book may be used or reproduced in any manner for the purpose of training artificial intelligence technologies or systems.

Tarcher is a registered trademark of Penguin Random House LLC, and Tarcher with leaf design is a trademark of Penguin Random House LLC

Book design by Angie Boutin

Library of Congress Cataloging-in-Publication Data

Names: Kaufman, Scott Barry, author.
Title: Rise above : overcome a victim mindset, empower yourself, and
   realize your full potential / Scott Barry Kaufman, Ph.D.
Description: New York : Tarcher, 2025. | Includes index.
Identifiers: LCCN 2024044581 (print) | LCCN 2024044582 (ebook) |
   ISBN 9780593715161 (hardcover) | ISBN 9780593715185 (epub)
Subjects: LCSH: Self-actualization (Psychology) | Self-realization. |
   Victims—Psychology.
Classification: LCC BF637.S4 K3949 2025 (print) | LCC BF637.S4 (ebook) |
   DDC 158.1—dc23/eng/20250102
LC record available at https://lccn.loc.gov/2024044581
LC ebook record available at https://lccn.loc.gov/2024044582
p.   cm.

Printed in the United States of America
1st Printing

The authorized representative in the EU for product safety and compliance is Penguin Random House Ireland, Morrison Chambers, 32 Nassau Street, Dublin D02 YH68, Ireland, https://eu-contact.penguin.ie.

I am not what happened to me. I am what I choose to become.

—Carl Jung

CONTENTS

Introduction   xi

PART I: DON'T BE A VICTIM

1. Don't Be a Victim to Your Past   3

2. Don't Be a Victim to Your Emotions   28

3. Don't Be a Victim to Your Cognitive Distortions   58

4. Don't Be a Victim to Your Self-Esteem   77

5. Don't Be a Victim to Your Need to Please   120

PART II: EMPOWER YOURSELF

6. Find the Light Within   151

7. Channel Your Gifts of Sensitivity   169

8. Harness Your Underdog Motivation   201

9. Live Gratefully   216

10. Help Empower Society   232

    Acknowledgments   265

    Notes   267

    Index   309

Introduction

Listen.
I wish I could tell you it gets better.
But, it doesn't get better.
You get better.

—*Joan Rivers*

My entire career has been an attempt to discover our greatest potential and show people what's truly possible—to help people break out of their imprisoning labels and show that *diagnoses aren't destiny*. But somehow in the past few years, this idea has become controversial.

It's almost as if we've stopped believing in our potential for growth and development. Life's challenges now seem insurmountable, and we've begun to cling to diagnostic labels (sometimes even inventing them for ourselves) so strongly that we can't see ourselves as anything else. Our obstacles have become so ingrained in our self-concept that we don't recognize what we could become. And we don't see that these obstacles are, in many cases, our *path to our potential*—that we become our greatest self because of, not in spite of, life's challenges.

To be fair, we weren't exactly getting it right before, either. Society largely overlooked the very real challenges people faced. We were in many ways discouraged from sharing our struggles, and that certainly wasn't healthy. It's still true that we have real problems to work through, and the things we're facing can be extremely hard to overcome. Yet somewhere along the way, we overcorrected. Our solution has become a problem, too. We're living in a time where we identify so strongly with our victimhood that our potential has taken a back seat to our pain.

Hey, I get it—life can be a total shitshow. But life can be other things, too. It can also be full of moments of beauty, joy, wonder, awe, meaning, intimate connections, and, potentially, the realization of your full creative and humanitarian possibilities.

Look: It takes work to embrace the messiness of life. It's hard to summon the courage to take responsibility for your whole complex human self and engage in the trial-and-error required to navigate it all with self-compassion and self-connection. But holy moly will developing that skill set lead to a life you never even imagined could be possible.

So much is already there within you. But to access it, you have to stop fixating on what's "wrong" and start doing some cognitive reframing. You've got to expand your perception to include not just your obstacles but the opportunities they bring. I realize this may sound like I'm telling you to simply put on a happy face, but nothing could be further from the truth. This isn't about magical thinking; it's about making a very real shift in your mindset from one that will keep you perpetually feeling like a victim to one that will unleash your ability to overcome.

I say all of this as a cognitive scientist, author, professor, and self-actualization coach who has spent the last twenty-five years of my career formally studying the mysteries of human intelligence, creativity, personality and neurodiversity, and how to unlock human potential. What in the world do these topics have to do with a victim mindset? As I've discovered, a whole lot.

THE VICTIMHOOD TRAP

Heads up: In this book I'm going to be using some words and phrases that will probably feel uncomfortable, at least at first. I'm talking about terms like *victim mindset*, *narcissism*, and *neuroticism*. Usually when we encounter these phrases, we welcome them to the extent that they're used to describe someone else—typically someone you already don't like very much (for example, "My ex-husband was *such* a narcissist!" or "Those snowflakes have *such* a victim mindset!"). Rarely do we look inside and contemplate whether this applies to us—even just a little. It's our sensitivity to these words that makes us not want to see such behaviors or characteristics in ourselves. Yet I pretty much guarantee you that at least in some circumstances, you lapse into these patterns of thinking and behaving. That's because at one time or another we all do.

Narcissism, like many of the other characteristics and behaviors I'll talk about in this book, occurs on a continuum, and it's nothing to be afraid of. It's simply a personality trait, and we pretty much all exhibit some degree of it now and then. Yes, some of us more than others, but the extremes are the outliers. As I mentioned a moment ago, it's really important to not seize on words like these and view them as concrete diagnoses or adhere them to our identity. As we'll explore in these pages, self-diagnosing and overmedicalizing natural human behaviors and experiences is one of the biggest challenges we face these days when it comes to realizing our potential.

One of my primary goals with this book is to help you develop a more flexible identity. I want to help you see that a little dysfunction here and there is totally normal and not something to get hung up on. I also aim to convince you that whatever is true in this moment can change. Who we are is not static. That's why I generally prefer phrases such as *people who score high in narcissism* over *narcissist*. The latter sounds so labeling and set in stone. It's true that there are some aspects of ourselves we can't totally shift, but as I'll show you, we actually have a remarkable ability to steer our outcomes. So when you encounter these words, phrases, and ideas, please hold them gently; don't point them at yourself like weapons. They're meant to help you gain understanding to fuel your growth, not give you ammunition to judge yourself (or others).

Take the phrase *victim mindset*. Without judging, honestly look at these features of a victim mindset and think through how they apply in your own life:

Having a victim mindset means:

- You tend to blame your problems on external circumstances—whether it's that life dealt you a bad hand, or that a person or even an entire group of people have it in for you and are holding you back.

- You attribute all or most negative outcomes or challenges in your life to your past or "that one thing that happened to you."

- You're often distrustful of people and wonder what people want from you if they give you something positive.

- You rarely give people the benefit of the doubt if they seem mean to you. You tend to take things personally.

- You believe you don't need to take responsibility for your actions or reactions because of past trauma.

- You tend to feel entitled to good things in life because you've suffered or are suffering.

- You tend to feel entitled to behave aggressively or selfishly because of your suffering.

- You often believe your suffering is more important than anyone else's suffering.

- You seek recognition of your victimhood beyond healthy sharing. For instance, you are quick to tell your story to total strangers or at inappropriate times.

- You often feel a sense of moral superiority and accuse others of being immoral, unfair, or selfish while seeing yourself as moral and ethical.

- You often lack empathy for the pain and suffering of others (unless perhaps they are part of *your* identity group).

- You can't stop ruminating about your past victimization. You may even fixate on how to enact revenge, and you rarely think about solutions or ways of moving forward with your life with hope and purpose.

I bet it's easier now to see how pretty much all of us end up engaging in a victim mindset at some point. Even if you don't hang out there a lot, there can still be that one issue or circumstance that can get you stuck in what I refer to as the *victimhood trap*. It's a trap because the more you dwell in that headspace, the more you will continue to dwell there, making it harder to eventually get out and move forward with your life. Also, just to be clear . . .

Having a victim mindset does NOT mean:

- You were never a victim of a terrible life circumstance.

- You've never had real pain.

- You aren't suffering right now.

- You should stop fighting for justice.

- You should ignore systems that have a powerful effect on our psychology.

Being or having been a victim is not synonymous with having a victim mindset. You can also not have been a victim and still have a victim mindset. That's right: Having a victim mindset can be independent of actual victimization. This is so important!

Having a victim mindset can be independent of actual victimization.

For those among us who have been victimized, you absolutely should not be blamed for what's happened, and no one should criticize you for having a victim mindset. Again, this isn't about shaming and blaming. Yet in spite of your past experiences, you can still take responsibility for how you show up in this world and what you're doing to help yourself cope with future uncertainties and challenges. To me, and I hope to you too, that's what real empowerment looks like.

And for those who haven't been victimized but still claim victim status? Well, there's hope for you too! For reasons I'll unpack in these pages, these days people are often encouraged to highlight their perceived victimhood. But while that may garner attention in the short term, it works against your long-term growth.

Before we get this party started, I'd be remiss if I didn't cover a concept that's critical to this discussion, and that's vulnerability.

LET'S TALK ABOUT VULNERABILITY . . .

Generally speaking, I am a big fan of vulnerability. For instance, I despise how men are often treated as weak if they are generally more emotional and sensitive people. (As you'll see, this is something I've struggled with myself.) I believe that authentically expressing your thoughts and emotions can be incredibly healing and can help form deeply intimate and healthy connections with others. Brené Brown has done a great job showing us that there is a power to vulnerability.[1] But we've created a monster!

These days it seems like the reward itself is the attention we get from sharing—not the growth it enables. We're applauding people for broadcasting their experiences at every opportunity, and ignoring vulnerable people who get stronger through adversity—as if personal empowerment is simply not an option for most people. (As we'll explore in the pages that come, a lot of this has to do with social media.)

To be sure, vulnerability is a powerful tool that can be deployed thoughtfully. In that spirit, I think it's worth distinguishing between *performative vulnerability* and *healthy vulnerability*. Performative vulnerability (or as my friend Mark Manson calls it, "TikTok vulnerability") is vulnerability in the service of greater attention, social status, rewards and privileges, and being treated as special. Healthy vulnerability is vulnerability in the service of connection, growth, and development as a whole person.

Learning to practice healthy vulnerability is a major goal of this book. And one realization on your path to healthy vulnerability is understanding that you are not a completely passive vessel on this planet. Instead, you can create the conditions of your life far more than you may think.

You can create the conditions of your life far more than you may think.

I can personally attest to this. Growing up, I was an extremely anxious and sensitive soul who also happened to have an auditory processing disability. That was a tough combination. It was hard for me to hear things in real time and it was especially hard for me to process auditory directions in real time. To all outward appearances, I was decidedly *ungifted*.[2] As a result, I was placed in special education, which only caused me greater anxiety and a pervasive sense of shame.

In some ways special education was helpful because I received a lot of extra resources, some of which I truly needed—at least at first. At the same time, I found that I enjoyed getting all sorts of extra accommodations and being treated as "special." Again, at first.

Over time I started to notice that I really didn't need as many accommodations. I mean, a little extra time on a test, fine—but *unlimited* time? Also, the way the teachers spoke to me felt patronizing and demeaning. A fire started burning in my belly to do more with my life—to show people I had a lot more potential than anyone was giving me credit for. I just wasn't sure how to do that, so I retreated into a quiet, introverted world with my computer. (In fact, I became a really good computer hacker and actually impressed a lot of other nerds in the international hacking community.)

Then, one day toward the start of high school, we had a new special education teacher who was covering for our regular teacher. I had never seen her before, and she had never seen me. She had no history of expectations about my performance. Having noticed my frustration and snarkiness, after class she took me aside.

She looked at me and it was like she was peering into my soul.

Finally, she tilted her head and said, "I *see* you. I can sense your frustration. What are you still doing here?"

Her question rang in my ears. It quickly shifted to Yeah, what *am* I still doing here?

A jolt of inspiration shot through my entire body as I ran to the pay phone and called my mom. "I'm not reporting to special ed anymore!" I declared. Hearing this, she shrieked and asked what had happened to me. Fearing that I wouldn't be able to handle the rigors of a regular classroom, she was concerned. But I wasn't having it. The horse had already left the barn, and with that, I became the first special ed student in my school's history to break out of the program by myself. That's right—I scheduled a meeting with all the special education teachers and school administrators and took myself out, determined to see what I was capable of.

For one, I decided to learn cello. My grandfather had retired after spending fifty years playing cello with the Philadelphia Orchestra, and he was delighted to teach me. But I didn't stop there. I joined the school choir and earned a spot in the all-regional choir. I became a Latin scholar. Of course, I also sucked at a lot. (I dropped out of *West Side Story*. That dancing? No way.) But that's not the point. When I expanded my horizons, my entire world opened up. I was in a better position to see what I was truly capable of, which turned out to be very different from what *others* had told me I was capable of. I was so much more than my disability identity had reduced me to.

In the beginning, my diagnosis was useful—it put a name on what I was struggling with and helped me get support I genuinely needed. But over time, seeing myself only through that one lens became precisely the thing that was holding me back. And I'm not the only one. This is a lot more widespread than you may think.

HOW YOUR VULNERABLE ENTITLEMENT IS HOLDING YOU BACK

When I started my career, I expected to find that the biggest inhibitor of self-actualization would be a person's intelligence, or at least the ways we think about intelligence.[3] But it turns out that while the ways we measure, identify, and cultivate intelligence are important (especially in early childhood education), it wasn't the whole story, or even the most important part of the self-actualization story.

Among my various research interests, I have more recently been studying a form of narcissism that has generally gone under the radar. (There's that word! Remember, it's only one trait of many, and it exists on a continuum.) We all know about *grandiose narcissism*; it's hard to miss. Chest thumping, bragging, overconfidence, and entitlement are its central features. However, when someone scores high in narcissism, the entitlement takes the following form: "I deserve all the special privileges in life because I'm inherently superior to everyone else." Yet there's another type of entitlement we can experience, and that belongs to a different beast.

It goes by many different names—vulnerable narcissism, hypersensitive narcissism, closet narcissism, or, Taylor Swift's preferred term, covert narcissism.[4] I'll use the term *vulnerable narcissism* (sorry, TayTay).[5] A core feature of vulnerable narcissism is *vulnerable entitlement*.[6] Put simply, vulnerable entitlement can be defined as a stable and pervasive sense of entitlement that the person justifies by their past suffering or their self-perceived fragility. Again, we're likely to look at this in its most extreme manifestations, but pretty much all of us exhibit some degree of vulnerable narcissism and some entitlement, as you're about to discover. I know—no one wants to see themself this way, but we all show these qualities now and again.

I'm going to give you twelve statements and I want you to be as honest as possible in rating how much you agree with each one from "Nope, not me at all" to "Wow, that is so me."

Ready? Let's go!

1. If I were on a sinking ship, I would deserve to be on the first lifeboat to make up for all my hardships.

2. I honestly feel I'm just more deserving than others because I've experienced worse outcomes than others.

3. Things should go my way because life has been too hard on me.

4. I get angry when criticized.

5. It irritates me when people don't notice how good a person I am.

6. I like to have friends who rely on me because it makes me feel important.

7. Sometimes I avoid people because I'm concerned they won't acknowledge what I do for them.

8. I often fantasize about being recognized for my accomplishments.

9. I dislike sharing the credit of an achievement with others.

10. I am secretly "put out" when other people come to me with their troubles, asking me for my time and sympathy.

11. I wonder why more people aren't more appreciative of my good qualities.

12. I have problems nobody else seems to understand.

These are scientifically validated statements that measure a person's average levels of vulnerable narcissism and vulnerability-based entitlement.[7] (My personal favorite is the *Titanic* one.) Wherever you scored on this test, it's important to recognize that while this is a measure of average personality functioning, we all have our moments. We ebb and flow on these items throughout the course of our day. Also, whether you identified strongly with any of these statements or not, I promise there is material in this book for you. On close analysis, we all uncover ways and times when we play the victim—when we feel like we deserve more than others because it's our turn or we've suffered more. To be clear, my goal isn't to pathologize narcissism—that's very much already been done. There's enough shaming and blaming going around to last us into the next millennium! The thing is that it's natural to land in the victim mindset at least once in a while; you just don't want to take up residence there.

What's interesting is that this mindset is paradoxical. (We can refer to it as the *entitlement paradox*.) On the one hand we feel like we're worthless and broken deep down because we're wounded. On the other, because we're wounded, we feel that we're special—entitled to special privileges precisely because of our woundedness.

To be clear, I'm not referring to entitlement that results from a specific situation ("I'm entitled to Social Security because I paid into the system"). Rather, the sense of entitlement I am referring to here is one that's experienced across situations.[8] Social life is full of ambiguities and human imperfections. Sometimes people will be too busy to text you back right away. Sometimes your new date just won't be all that into you. Sometimes that busy barista won't return your smile. We're referring here to a sense of entitlement that pervades all of life. Do you overcome ambiguous and challenging situations in life constructively and resiliently, or see yourself as a perpetual victim of life, deserving more than others because of it?

Also, it's important to distinguish between a "sense" of entitlement rather than actual entitlement, because what we're talking about in this book is someone believing they deserve things that other people don't for an inadequate reason.

Of course, there are things that certain people are genuinely entitled to. Sometimes entitlements are justified based on past injustices. Let's say someone has illegally discriminated against you in the past (for example, the U.S. government refusing loans to Black farmers based on race, such as in the *Pigford* case). In that case you are legally and/or morally entitled to some kind of recompense. But when we say "He's so entitled," no one thinks we might mean that he's done amazing things and therefore deserves something special. Everyone knows we mean that he thinks he deserves special treatment for no good reason.

A key element of entitlement is the belief that your desires take precedence over others'. You think you deserve things that other people don't. The fact that you feel stressed or anxious or depressed means that everyone else has to do exactly what you want. You fail to consider that someone else might be similarly stressed or anxious. Also, you may feel entitled to act aggressively and selfishly.[9]

Psychologist Emily Zitek and her colleagues undertook an interesting study that shed light on this phenomenon. As they describe in their paper "Victim Entitlement to Behave Selfishly," they prompted some participants to recall a time when they felt their lives were unfair, and others to recall a time when they felt bored. Afterward, the scientists asked the participants to help the researchers with an extra task they described as "pilot testing for another project." Those who'd recalled a sense of unfairness were more likely to decline this extra request than those who'd simply recalled a time when they were bored. They were also more likely to engage in a number of selfish behaviors. For instance, in one of their studies, those who lost at a computer game for an unfair reason (they were told there was a computer glitch) asked to be paid more for a future task than participants who lost the game for a fair reason. Those with a higher sense of entitlement (for example, "I deserve more things in my life" and "things should go my way") were even more likely to act selfishly.

Zitek and her colleagues propose that entitlement can be thought of as a "dynamic mindset." Our sense of entitlement varies over the course of the day—even from moment to moment—based on what past experiences are at the forefront of our minds. When opportunities for selfish behavior emerge, how we act depends on which memories are most salient at the time. The researchers argue that entitlement is a mindset that can be activated (dare I say *triggered*) whenever one is wronged or even, in the absence of current victimhood, by "merely reminding individuals of a time when they were wronged." What's more, they suggest that injustice and poor treatment can have a "ripple effect" that goes beyond the initial incident:

> *Not only does wronging lead to unhappiness on the part of the victim, but it can potentially hurt a third party if the victim ends up behaving selfishly as a result of the wronging. To the extent that the*

*people affected by the first victim's selfish behavior in turn feel
wronged, one can imagine a domino effect of increased selfish behavior (or decreased prosocial motivation) ad infinitum.*[10]

What I've found in my research, and what I aim to demonstrate
in this book, is that living with a perpetual victim mindset goes hand
in hand with a perpetual sense of entitlement. And together, *they will
hold you back in life.*

A healthier mindset would be to perceive that we deserve things
because we're inherently worthy, because we earned them, or because we have agency—because we have authentic pride in our
strengths, what we've accomplished, and our ability to make a positive contribution to society. In other words, an *empowerment mindset.*

HARNESS YOUR EMPOWERMENT MINDSET

Regardless of your life circumstance, I believe that you can cultivate
an empowerment mindset. This requires Yes/And thinking, where
we acknowledge our struggles but also understand that this isn't the
end of our story. We both embrace the reality of our experiences or
our obstacles *and* maintain a belief that life holds more for us! If you're
familiar with improv, you understand Yes/And thinking.[11] An improv comedian must accept whatever setup they're given, no matter
how challenging, and work with it. Over time, they become more
adept at steering the skit where they'd like it to go.

Someone with an empowerment mindset thinks like this about
their life experiences:

- Yes, something happened and it has affected me, *and* it
  doesn't define me.

- I have deep reservoirs of resiliency within me and can handle
  difficult situations.

- I don't want to be reduced to the worst thing that has happened to me. Instead, I'd like to be seen as a whole person—

that includes my strengths as well as what has happened
to me.

- My reactions are within my control.

- I am aware that I am not the only one on this planet who has
  suffered or who is suffering.

- I am not a victim to my feelings—I can learn techniques and
  strategies to regulate my emotions.

- There's a lot of wisdom I can learn from my adverse life experiences to become a better human being.

- I can develop strengths because of my adversity.

- I don't expect everyone to walk on eggshells around me or
  open doors for me just because of the adversity I've experienced.

- I strive for empathy and understanding of others who are
  suffering but who may seem very different from me.

For most of us, it's not easy to shift from a victim mindset to one
centered on empowerment, and that's why I wrote this book! I want
to help you get there, no matter your life experiences. At the same
time, I won't ignore or downplay your circumstances. This book will
attempt to avoid *toxic agency* (the idea that you can achieve anything
just by lifting yourself up by your bootstraps) as well as *toxic passivity*
(the belief that you are completely helpless and hopeless because your
circumstances suck).

Remember when it was considered a great thing to overcome
your challenges, conquer your demons, have a positive attitude, be
kind to others despite your life circumstance, and positively contribute to society? The fact is that, for many of us at least, stories of overcoming are still extremely popular and inspiring. That means that we
haven't lost sight of the value of rising above our past. But instead of

letting that notion simmer on the back burner, let's bring it front and center!

WELCOMING HONEST LOVE

All of these insights into the victim mindset are well and good, but communicating about them brings its own challenge. People typically take one of two tactics. On one end there's *tough love*. It's people saying things like "Look at all those lazy snowflakes complaining all the time. They need to shut up and toughen up!" But I don't see how that helps anyone. When people are genuinely suffering, they probably already feel a lot of shame for how they feel. Why make them feel worse?

Yet I don't find the other end particularly useful, either. I see an awful lot of what can best be described as *coddling*. Like "It's totally okay that you're an asshole to everyone—you have trauma and so it's completely justified. Just follow me on Instagram and I'll keep telling you all the things you're not responsible for!"

Both extremes make me cringe. That's why this book offers something different. In these pages I've done my best to offer a heaping dose of what I call *honest love*. The love part is acknowledging real suffering and pain. I sincerely believe that the best starting point to being a caring, compassionate human is to acknowledge that another being is having their own experiences of life, and that it's just as valid as your own experiences.

But the honest part means we don't stop there. I'm not here to placate you or to make you feel better than others only because of the challenges you may have faced. I take a *humanistic* approach to psychology.[12] In this school of thought we focus on common humanity, self-acceptance, life-acceptance (a term I just made up), vitality, and whole-person growth. I believe all of these things are compatible with each other. We can love and accept ourselves for who we are, and also want to learn and grow.

So in this book I will repeatedly encourage you to be as honest as you can be about yourself and your maladaptive patterns of thinking and behaving and also believe in your higher potential. I fully under-stand that asking you to take a step back and look at yourself with as honest and open a mind as possible is enormous, but I can promise you that it comes with an equally enormous payoff.

So, why wait? Let's get started facing reality right now! We'll kick it off with the acknowledgment that those special hurdles you've faced? Well, many of them are just part and parcel of a thing we call *life*.

WARNING: YOU MIGHT HAVE A CASE OF LIFE

We've got to stop operating with this idea that life is not supposed to be hard, and if it is hard, something is wrong. Or the world did wrong by us. One of the saddest aspects of this whole victim mindset cul-ture we've got going is how much it isolates us from one another.[13] But the fact is—in spite of what so many people would have you believe—we're all more alike than we are different. However, we each deal with the "givens of existence" in our own way:*

- We all want to feel safe from harm in our environment.

- We all want a sense of control over our lives.

- We all want to feel connected to ourselves.

- We all want to feel connected to others.

- We all want to matter.

- We all want to contribute something positive to society.

- We all want to find a higher purpose or meaning to our lives.

- We're all afraid of dying with unrealized creative potential.

- We all yearn for the freedom to be ourselves.

---

* The phrase "givens of existence" was coined by the existential psychotherapist Irvin Yalom to describe the existential facts of life. Yalom, I. (1980). *Existential psychotherapy*. Basic Books.

Sure, there are exceptions. Some of us focus more on one of these needs than others, and some of us really aren't interested in some of these things at all. For instance, psychopaths tend to not care as much about intimate connections with others.* But taken together, I think this is a pretty good list of what it means to be human.† This perspective allows us to feel a sense of connection with our fellow humans for wanting what we want out of life. And we can call this movement toward growth and development our quest for *self-actualization*.[14] This book adopts my main framework for self-actualization to help you in your journey of healing and growth.[15]

In my book *Transcend* I revised Maslow's famous hierarchy of needs.[16] You know that pyramid displayed in endless psychology textbooks and flashed on slideshows during motivational presentations? Well, it turns out Maslow never actually drew a pyramid—that was created by management textbook illustrators.[17]

To more appropriately capture what I believe Maslow intended, I created a new metaphor—a sailboat. This metaphor captures our basic, shared yearnings and categorizes them as *security needs* (which stabilize the boat and allow it to move) and *growth needs* (which allow us to open our sail and move in our most valued and purposeful direction).

In life, we're all just doing our best to captain our own ship amid the windswept seas of life. And the thing is, we all encounter storms. Sure, some of us encounter a minor tropical depression here and there, while others are like George Clooney clinging to the decks in a Junger-esque disaster, but no one encounters entirely smooth sailing. (And as I'll demonstrate in this book, a lack of adversity can actually be counterproductive to growth.)

---

* But note that it doesn't follow that all people who don't seek out intimacy are necessarily psychopaths!

† On Irvin Yalom's original list of givens are death, freedom, isolation, and meaninglessness. I incorporated his ideas into my own list, which also adds other basic human needs into the mix to round out the list. See Yalom, I. (1980). *Existential psychotherapy*. Basic Books.

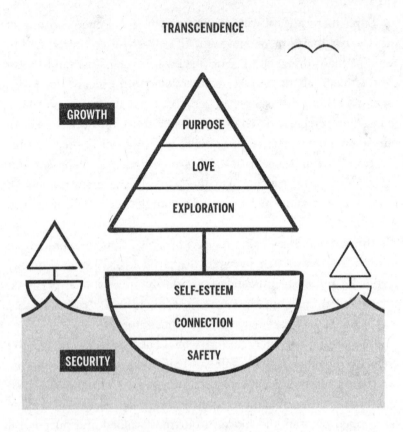

Given that, let's consider some honest truths about life itself, which can lead us toward the critical step that I call *life-acceptance*:

- You aren't alone in your suffering.

- Life is sometimes unfair.

- Life is ultimately unpredictable.

- You can't completely control your life.

- No one is coming to save you.

- You and only you are ultimately responsible for your reactions to the world.

Viewed together with the givens of human existence, we can see the common humanity of our needs, along with the common humanity of our circumstances.

So while the particulars in all of our lives are decidedly different, there is so much we share. I want to underscore that yet again because so much of today's messaging has focused on creating divisions among us. That sense of separation from others is fertile ground for growing a victim mindset.

LIFE IS WHAT YOU MAKE IT

People are always blaming their circumstances for being what they are. The people who get on in this world are the people who get up and look for the circumstances they want, and if they can't find them, make them.

—*George Bernard Shaw*

Life is what you make of it, at least to a larger extent than you may realize. You can resist this notion all you want—citing all the real injustices in the world that exist and all of the things in life that are holding you back. And while all that may very well be true, what I said is also true. It's a Both/And situation.

Most people wait for the world to react to them. We expect people to read our minds about we want, or we expect others to assess our emotions. We wait until we get approval before we bring our whole self to the table, or at least a more authentic version of ourselves. When I say life is what you make it, I mean we grossly underestimate the extent to which we can make magic happen. And by *magic* I mean create lives rich with meaning and satisfaction.

We have a lot more power to make magic in the world, instead of waiting for it to poof out of nowhere and conform to our every desire, goal, and dream. To paraphrase Gandhi, *you've got to bring the energy you want to see in the world!*

Yes, you can absolutely sit there and watch other people around you get after it, and you can certainly make a million excuses why they have what it takes and you don't because of what you've been through in your life. But again, while even some of that may very well be true, they certainly don't have what others have either! More importantly, they don't have what *you* have.

It's easy to disparage ourselves or our circumstances. Everyone can find someone else who is a little bit more talented, more good-looking, or more driven, or who started life with more opportunity. So what are you going to do about that? Are you going to fold your hands, or are you going to get in the game? I, for one, wanna see you get in this thing. Because the truth is we need you. We need your skills and your talents and your energy. After all, life is a shitshow, remember? If we're gonna make something better out of it, it's an all-hands-on-deck moment, and that includes you. It's time to take the wheel and captain your own damn ship!

One of the most world-changing, groundbreaking shifts in consciousness you could possibly make right now is to realize just how much life really is what you make it. I'm not saying that's easy. In fact, nothing in life that's truly worth having is easy. But it's possible, and it's worth it.

This book will use the latest tools of science to help you confront life with healthy vulnerability, bravery, wisdom, self-acceptance, life-acceptance, compassion, creativity, and healing. I assume these are things you want out of your life, and as you're about to see, to a very large extent, you can have them.

Let's find out how.

PART I

Don't Be a Victim

1

Don't Be a Victim to Your Past

The Past: Our cradle, not our prison; there is danger as well as appeal in its glamour. The past is for inspiration, not imitation, for continuation, not repetition.

—Israel Zangwill

I saw something nasty in the woodshed!" It's the tormented refrain uttered by Aunt Ada Doom in Stella Gibbons's comedic novel-turned-movie *Cold Comfort Farm*.[1] As the story goes, when she was a young girl, Ada encountered a disturbing sight. Sixty-nine years later, she still has not recovered. She lives as a recluse, shut up on the second floor of the family home, having her meals brought to her on a tray that's left outside her door. Whenever someone implores her to leave the room, she moans, "I saw something nasty in the woodshed!"

And it's not only Ada who suffers. When her spritely and determined young niece Flora Poste arrives at the farm to meet her kin, she asks one of the family what Cold Comfort Farm is like. "There's a curse on the place," she's told. The seeds won't grow, the soil is destitute, and the animals are barren. "All is turned to sourness and ruin!" When Flora asks why they don't just sell the farm and move on, she's told it's impossible for the family to leave because the farm is their lot in life—their cross to bear. And it's all because of what Ada saw.

Now, this is an obvious farce. Yet at the same time, all too often I see some version of this plot play out in real life. People have an experience—they suffer adversity, they have a difficult start in life, or they're confronted with challenges to their physical or mental health or performance—and that's where they stop. They fixate on what happened, or on the obstacles in their path, and all turns to sourness and ruin. They become attached to a belief that their life is over, or at least severely limited. In short, they become stuck.

Several decades ago, psychologist Martin Seligman conducted seminal research on something he called *learned helplessness*.[2] Starting with a series of studies on dogs who learned to stay imprisoned even when they were free to escape, he showed that adversity can cause us to give up hope that life can be different. When opportunity does arise, from this state we fail to capitalize on it, or even recognize that it's there.

Humanistic psychotherapist and Holocaust survivor Viktor Frankl, author of *Man's Search for Meaning*, describes how when Allied forces arrived to liberate prisoners from concentration camps, some rejoiced.[3] Others, however, stumbled numbly through the gates only to pause, then turn around and wander back into the camp. It had become impossible for them to contemplate another reality. I realize this is an extreme example, but I've included it here because it shows just how powerful learned helplessness can be.

While some of us may gravitate toward it more easily than others, research conducted over many years suggests that in humans (not dogs), helplessness is actually the *default* response.[4] What must be learned is *hopefulness*. Through the human capacities for consciousness, intention, and action, we can all decide to cultivate learned hopefulness.[5] This chapter is where we'll start!

LEARNING HOPEFULNESS

Learned hopefulness isn't just a made-up self-helpy feel-good phrase; it's backed by science. Our future expectations of life are based mostly on our prior experiences. When we cultivate experiences that provide us with more empowered messages about life and our abilities, that becomes what we expect out of life. In other words, much like a weather forecast, we can reprogram our expectations about what weather to expect from the world.[6] This concept is important, so let's look at it in a bit more detail.

In her book *7½ Lessons about the Brain*, neuroscientist Lisa Feldman Barrett describes how our brains function to create our experience of life. Most of us believe that the brain is like a reporter.[7] It takes in the information from our senses and uses that input to tell us what's going on in the world around us. But that's not how things really work. Let's look at an example to see what actually happens.

Say you're out hiking and you look out across the landscape and see a large lump way off in the distance. *It's a rock!* your brain reports. Then, however, the rock moves! Realizing its error, your brain starts to look for other possibilities, and it does this primarily by scanning your past experiences. (Or, more accurately, what it *thinks* your past experiences were. Memory is reliably unreliable.) Once while out hiking as a child you saw a bear. *It's a bear!* Your heart races. Then the bear shifts position and you realize it's not large enough to be a bear. Finally, you land on the correct answer. It's a hirsute hiker—a human with a rather impressive beard. As you get closer, you also see a red-and-white checked blanket. It's a human having a picnic!

So if the brain is a reporter, it's not a particularly good one. For one, it likes to turn in its stories before they're fact-checked. It's also not great about attribution. For instance, it can misinterpret body signals. Like, if your body feels a lack of energy, the brain might hastily announce, *We're hungry! Give us food!* In fact, that lack of energy is because of dehydration, and what you really need is water. Or, you might experience a rapid heart rate and sweaty palms. *We're afraid!* your thoughts declare. In reality, you're about to step onstage to deliver a presentation for which you're well prepared. The truth is that you're more excited than anxious.

What does all of this have to do with overcoming adversity and learning hopefulness? When our brain tells us, "Life will always be like this," it's not stating a fact, it's making a prediction. You see, instead of a reporter, your brain is actually a *prediction machine*.[8]

Let's say you grew up in a highly unstable and unpredictable environment, in which case your brain may be sculpted to forecast a life of instability. So you may overgeneralize ("The world is unsafe!") and be acutely attuned to cues of instability. Coupled with this, your brain might ignore all the good things happening around you, including important contextual information to tell you what's really going on.

Here's something that's really important to understand: Fear learning and fear unlearning happen in *separate parts of the brain*.[9] Fear is automatically learned, and fear must be actively unlearned. We have to *choose* a different way of living, and we can start by taking responsibility for the fact that unlearning fear—or any past patterns—can take a lot of inner work.

Unlearning fear— or any past patterns—can take a lot of inner work.

Now, many of us equate the notion of responsibility with saying it's our fault, but that's not what I mean. As Barrett astutely explains, "Sometimes we're responsible for things not because they're our fault, but because *we're the only ones who can change them*" [emphasis mine].[10]

When you take responsibility, it's not about saying that you're to blame for the fact that your mother wasn't a present parent, that you're neurodivergent, that you were assaulted, or that you have a temperament that's predisposed to experience stress more intensely (we'll talk about that in a moment). It's about saying, "This is the hand I've been dealt and I'm going to play it out. I'm going to make active, intentional choices about how I engage with life." Again, I don't want to make it sound like taking control of your life is a small or simple thing—it's not. Not by a long shot. What I'm saying is that the only person who can determine what you do with what happens to you *is you*.

The only person who can determine what you do with what happens to you *is you*.

Aunt Ada chose the passive route, demanding that her family dote on her and bend to her every whim. This protected her status as one who was wronged, but it also kept her from living a rich and full life. Then she made a different choice . . .

One day, young Flora knocks on the door and Ada finally bends to Flora's repeated pleas to engage with her. "I saw something nasty in the woodshed!" she says.

"What was it?" Flora asks.

There's a pause.

"I don't know. I was little," Ada replies. "Something terrible!"

"Are you sure?" Flora asks, prompting Ada to revisit her potentially faulty memory.

"'Course I'm sure!" Ada declares, but there's another pause. And then . . . "Or maybe the potting shed. Or the bicycle shed."

Aha! So maybe the story isn't the story after all. Maybe what she saw wasn't so horrible. Or maybe it was. The point is, this brief moment of questioning raises the possibility that this memory—whether faulty or not—doesn't have to have the hold on Ada that she has assumed it does. A belief that's been reinforced for sixty-nine years suddenly seems less certain. The question then becomes: *What other assumptions have I made that may not be true?*

Taking responsibility involves recognizing that our brains are just doing the best they can with the information they have. We can make a concerted effort to start to feed them different information by having more varied experiences. And we can become more critical of the negative things our brains tell us. We can start to second-guess the messages we get, not only about what's possible in life but about what we're thinking and feeling in any given moment.

If we feel sad, we don't have to jump to the conclusion that we're clinically depressed because life is just too hard. (Then tweet about it. #depressed #empath #trauma #life.) Of course people absolutely can and do experience depression, and of course we're facing massive challenges on a global scale. That's real. And of course, getting attention and sympathy from strangers on social media can offer a temporary dopamine hit that can momentarily distract us from our woes and anxiety. But in the exact moment when you feel sad, you can pull an Aunt Ada by making a different choice. You can opt to pause, put down your phone, and analyze the situation.

You can realize, "Well, my cat is sick and so I didn't get much sleep last night. Maybe I'm just really tired, and worried about Mr. Fluffy." Recognizing what's really going on in this particular moment, you can make an appointment with the vet and carve out time for a nap. (Yes, *I know*—not everyone has access to veterinary care because of geographic factors or their economic or transportation situation. And sometimes people don't have time for a nap because they have to work two or even three jobs to pay the bills. I do believe in meeting people where they are. At the same time, regardless of one's limitations or challenges, there's always room for at least some degree of reflection and reframing.)

Okay, so people sometimes weaponize responsibility. For instance, they use it politically, as a way of advocating for reduced spending on social programs. But advocating responsibility doesn't have to be politicized. This is not a political book, it's a *human* book. What I'm talking about is recognizing the very real role you can play in shaping your human experience of life. In being a more informed user of your own brain and not simply accepting everything it hands you, because a rather surprising amount of the time, it's actually wrong! Or at least, not totally right.

As research has shown, our level of happiness in life correlates strongly to our sense of responsibility and agency—specifically, to something called our *locus of control*. When we have an internal locus of control, we believe that even when life hands us a boatload of lemons, we still have the ability to make sweet lemonade.[11] When we have an external locus of control, we believe that factors beyond our grasp dictate our destiny. When we're in this headspace, we see the world in more negative terms, making it easier for our darker emotions to get the best of us. Not surprisingly, people with an internal locus of control tend to be much happier in life.

So how can we make the switch to this more agentic view of life? One actionable step we can take to turn down the volume on our emotions and see things more clearly is to learn to ask ourselves *what*, not *why*.

What, Not Why

Organizational psychologist Tasha Eurich studies the insights we have about ourselves, including why some of us possess high self-awareness while others struggle. She and her team found fifty of what she terms "self-awareness unicorns"—people who used to have low to moderate self-awareness but now are highly self-aware.[12] In analyzing transcripts of their conversations, the team discovered an interesting speech pattern: The participants often reported asking themselves "what" questions, but rarely described engaging with "why" questions.

One participant—a forty-two-year-old mother—explained, "If you ask *why*, [I think] you're putting yourself into a victim mentality. . . . When I feel anything other than peace, I say 'What's going on?'; 'What am I feeling?'; 'What is the dialogue inside my head?'; 'What's another way to see this situation?'; or 'What can I do to respond better?'"

See what's stamped all over those questions? Responsibility.

As Eurich observes, "*Why* questions can draw us to our limitations; *what* questions help us see our potential. *Why* questions stir up negative emotions; *what* questions keep us curious. *Why* questions trap us in our past; *what* questions help us create a better future."

Take the example of Mr. Fluffy and the sleepless night. If we're feeling sad and we ask ourselves why, our brain will be more than happy to offer all kinds of answers. "Why am I sad? What kind of question is that? The world is in ruins, that's why!" (And we reach for our phone.) Instead, asking yourself *what* you're feeling drills down to a more precise answer. "I'm feeling tired. I'm feeling depleted. I'm feeling worried about Mr. Fluffy." (Notice I didn't say, "I *am* tired." We want to name what we're feeling but not over-identify with our emotions. This little distancing trick helps to keep us from getting overwhelmed by what we're experiencing. We'll talk more about healthy ways to deal with emotions in Chapter 5.)

From these observations, we can construct a useful response. First, you can have some compassion for yourself—it's hard to have a sick pet, and it's hard when you lose sleep. Then you can take steps—call the vet and take a nap. The world isn't coming to an end, after all. (At least, not in this moment.)

Eurich does make the distinction that there are some cases where *why* is a helpful question, such as with business decisions or procedural issues. "Why didn't that product sell like I thought it would?" We need to examine how we arrived at those projections. "Why was I late to work again?" We need to examine our schedule, or the route we took. As Eurich summarizes it, *why* questions can help us understand issues *around us*, while *what* questions can help us understand issues *inside us*.

That brings to mind a related insight from another psychologist and Holocaust survivor, Edith Egar. As Egar has observed, *victimization* comes from the outside world, but *victimhood* comes from the inside.[13] She writes:

> We are all likely to be victimized in some way in the course of our lives. As some point we will suffer some kind of affliction or calamity or abuse, caused by circumstances or people or institutions over which we have little or no control. This is life. . . . No one can make you a victim but you. We become victims not because of what happens to us but when we choose to hold onto our victimization.[14]

Islamic poet and theologian Rumi once posed a powerful question: "Why do you stay in prison, when the door is so wide open?"[15] It's a valid question. And Egar's observation is similarly valid—that keeping yourself locked up is an inside job.

Still, I can hear the protests now. "But Scott, I've got *trauma!*"

Join the club, my friend. These days, the entire world is traumatized. For some of us, it seems to require little more than a sideways glance or an unreturned smile to create lasting damage to our psyche. Still, some people have experienced truly horrible things in their lives, and I'm not trying to discount that at all. It's just that today, the bar for what we describe as trauma is exceptionally low, and we're suffering tremendously as a result. So let's take a moment and address the enormous elephant in the room. Let's talk trauma . . .

THE TROUBLE WITH TRAUMA OBSESSION

Let's acknowledge two things right away. The first is that trauma is real. The second is that *we can heal from trauma!* (Here I duck and cover.) To many, that's an unwelcome truth. Some will fight tooth and nail to defend the idea that trauma is permanent. But I ask you: *Why?* (Okay, so that's a *why* question. You got me!)

It's true that trauma can leave indelible marks on us, but as research has consistently shown, adversity can also be a powerful lever for learning and development. Both of these can be true at the same time. We can be permanently affected by our experiences *and* use our challenges to become stronger.

I'm not saying that the road is easy. Edith Shiro, a clinical psychologist who has spent decades helping people not only survive severe trauma but grow as a result, makes a distinction between *recovering* from trauma (returning to the state you were in before you experienced trauma) and experiencing *post-traumatic growth* (having a life that's actually better than before). She writes:

> *Trauma is complicated. The road to posttraumatic growth is hard. It requires daily, conscious awareness of our intention to move beyond the traumatic event or situation, without dismissing or downplaying the difficulties we're going through. In order to do that, however, we need to know that transformation is possible; that it can't be rushed; and that there's a way to get there.*[16]

In saying we have a choice about how we react to the events in our lives, I'm definitely not trying to minimize the severity or impact that adversity can have on us. Even among those who've experienced post-traumatic growth, given the opportunity, most would opt to have the past reversed. Consider the words of Rabbi Harold Kushner in regard to the death of his son:

> *I am a more sensitive person, a more effective pastor, a more sympathetic counselor because of Aaron's life and death than I would ever have been without it. And I would give up all of those gains in a second if I could have my son back. If I could choose, I would forgo all of the spiritual growth and depth which has come my way because of our experiences. . . . But I cannot choose.*[17]

People's suffering is real; they deserve to have it acknowledged and they deserve to be supported in their healing journey. But instead, we often get stuck in our suffering. Then we're no longer the narrator in our story, or the hero—we're simply a victim.

Sadly, much of our current culture supports and even encourages this. Don't get me wrong, some of this is well-intentioned; after all, it's important to recognize and validate people's experiences. But somewhere in all of this we've crossed a line, assigning a special social status to those who've suffered, and that has started to backfire. We've begun to disempower the very people we're praising because in order to keep that status, they have to remain a victim, even adopting that label as part of their identity. To move on would mean moving out of this protected or celebrated class, thus losing valuable social capital.

In 2023, Nicole LePera—also known as "the holistic psychologist"—tweeted, "Culture doesn't celebrate trauma healing because it means we would wake up. It means we would no longer sleep walk through life accepting dysfunction as 'normal.'"[18] While our culture may not celebrate healing, in recent years, it sure does seem obsessed with trauma. According to *Vox*, the year before LePera's tweet, a search using the Listen Notes podcast search engine returned 5,500 podcasts with *trauma* in the title.[19] By far, the most podcast pitches I get are for authors who just published a book on how to overcome trauma.

Turning greater attention to the reality of trauma and the multifaceted impacts that traumatic experiences can have on us is, in many ways, a good thing. Developing a greater understanding of ourselves and how we react to the world around us and the things we've experienced is a key element of growth. (That's one of the ways that interventions such as talk therapy can provide a big benefit.) For too long, our culture ignored the potential long-term impacts of adversity. But at the same time, like a driver who yanks the steering wheel to avoid one crash but then causes a different one, we seem to have overcorrected.

Today, it seems like absolutely everything comes down to trauma, and we talk about it ad nauseam. (And that's one of the ways that talk therapy can be less helpful—if we're simply using it to rehash our experiences or assign blame with no intention of moving on.) As podcaster and author Tim Ferriss—who recently opened up about his own history of sexual abuse—bemoans, it's become disturbingly common to "trauma vomit" on someone within ten minutes of meeting them, sharing all the ways the world has wronged you.[20]

If your adverse experiences don't somehow feel that they merit the *trauma* label, have no fear. Now, there's "tiny trauma," where, as psychologist Meg Arroll writes, "you don't know what's wrong, but nothing feels quite right."[21] What's next—traumas so small that we don't even notice them? *Nanotraumas*, perhaps?

Frankly, I think we're selling humans short. As my friend and colleague George Bonanno has reported, we're actually pretty damn resilient.[22] That doesn't mean that everything just bounces off us, but overall, we have a remarkable ability to recover from even the most difficult experiences. Yes, some people do suffer a full derailment after a spouse dies, for instance, but most are eventually able to get back on track after such a tragedy.[23]

Now, I know how all of that sounds, and people of a certain belief system are probably applauding, ready to clap me on the back and give me an "Atta boy! The problem isn't trauma, it's that everyone is so damn fragile these days!" But please, hold your applause and your chest bumps because that's not exactly what I'm saying.

What I am saying is that in all of our mostly well-intentioned efforts to name real challenges and help people get real support, we're inadvertently (and sometimes even intentionally) catching people in a trap that can be very hard to get out of. By overemphasizing trauma and attributing absolutely every normal challenge we might experience in life to it, we've gone down an adversity rabbit hole, and it's just not helping us.

Check out this excerpt from an article by Shannon Palus in *Slate* titled "Why TikTok Is So Obsessed with Labeling Everything as a Trauma Response":

> In current TikTok parlance, almost any behavior can be a trauma response. Struggling to make small decisions? Possible trauma response. Overpreparing, overanalyzing, overachieving? All possible trauma responses. Scrolling on social media to the point where you wonder if you have a problem with scrolling? Trauma response. Getting defensive and lashing out in fights with your significant other? Trauma response. Being a perfectionist? You guessed it, also a possible trauma response.[24]

Yes, any of these *could* be a trauma response. That is true. But in order for "trauma response" to mean anything at all, it can't mean everything. Unfortunately, as with so many other topics on the interwebs, in our quest to compress a potentially very complex set of physiological and emotional responses into material short and snappy enough to share via a tweet or a twenty-second video, we've dramatically oversimplified things. And there's big money in trauma right now. Loads of folks who aren't nearly qualified enough to be speaking on such complex topics are raking in followers and moolah by convincing people that absolutely everything that's wrong in their life is due to trauma. More often than not, they also happen to be offering a (usually expensive) solution. Sometimes, though, the solution is simply coddling.

I know that's a charged word, but when someone tells someone else, "Man, what happened to you was wrong, and you would be totally justified to do nothing but sit on your bed and cry for the rest of your entire life," well, I don't know what else to call it. I mean, is that not the most disempowering thing you've ever read? If that guy didn't feel terrible about himself before, he sure does now! And not only that, he probably also believes there's no chance for him to ever get past it. And frankly, that kind of bullshit just pisses me off, and I want better for him! Now, I know this might sound like some kind of overboard caricature, but sadly it's not. It's a paraphrase of an actual post that I saw online *from a therapist.* (I've changed the exact wording to protect his identity.) This is where we've gotten, folks, and it's why I've felt the need to speak up. If you've experienced trauma, this is not what you need to hear.

Yes, you can opt to sit in your room for the rest of your life like Aunt Ada Doom, but that's a choice. And I question the motivation of anyone who encourages you to make that choice in the name of "compassion."

I'm also not trying to single out Dr. Arroll, who I'm sure is very well-intentioned in writing about "tiny traumas." That concept may have some utility for people trying to cope with the everyday annoyances of life. It is true that developing our *psychological immune system* can help us be more aware, accepting, and action-oriented about life. But calling them "tiny traumas" can give the impression that absolutely every slight or insult sparks a full-blown trauma response, and that's just not accurate.

You know, these days, when I encounter the word *trauma* (as I do about every thirty seconds, especially on Instagram), I can't help but hear the memorable words of Inigo Montoya, a character from the movie *The Princess Bride*: "You keep using that word. I do not think it means what you think it means."[25]

Some of what's happening here is that we've tasked one word with far too much work. We're making *trauma* do the heavy lifting of describing every single type of negative or adverse event a human being might experience. And that's extremely disempowering. As new research shows, our propensity to see trauma lurking around every corner and to self-diagnose with mental health problems has the effect of "pathologizing everyday life."[26] Many of us now view ourselves as hopelessly traumatized, which we interpret as damaged beyond all repair. Thank goodness that's not actually the case.

A More Empowered Approach to Trauma

Today's trauma-discussion landscape is chock-full of extremes. On one side, we have people claiming that absolutely every insult causes lasting trauma that can't be healed or resolved. On the other side are those who say that trauma is something only experienced by war veterans and survivors of sexual assault, but even if you do have "legitimate" trauma, you need to press on and get over it, already.

Let me be clear: Resolving trauma is not like deciding that you're not going to wear one pair of shoes anymore, and you're going to put on a different pair instead. It isn't something that's done instantly or easily, especially when one has suffered significant trauma. In her memoir, *What My Bones Know: A Memoir of Healing from Complex Trauma*, author Stephanie Foo recounts her experiences of horrifying abuse at the hands of her parents. She delves deeply into the incidents, along with her struggle to identify how trauma patterns play out in her current life and relationships. At the same time, her memoir tracks her courageous healing journey, where she struggles to not only understand what happened to her and grow from it but also recognize and take responsibility for her present behavior. Without a doubt, as Foo shows with healthy vulnerability and eloquence, trauma is complex. To some extent, as Foo notes, she will always be dealing with the legacy of trauma. And at the same time, she is doing her best to break out of the victim box and live a life that is richer and fuller not only in spite of her trauma but in some ways because of it.

Make no mistake: Trauma can make real, lasting changes to the brain and the rest of the nervous system.[27] It can significantly alter how we perceive the world and our sense of agency.[28] *But this can also change.* The reality is that, as we do with so many complex topics, we've completely oversimplified the discussion. So let's try to add a little nuance back in. For starters, let's consider the word *trauma*. What any of us means when we even say it can be vastly different.

And as we'll see later, some researchers and clinicians have begun to use more descriptive (and less charged) terms, such as *stored survival stress* (more on that term in a second).[29] This can help us understand some of the mechanisms through which the body (including the brain) can experience and be altered by adversity.

Still, if you ask ten clinicians or researchers what trauma is, you're likely to get ten different definitions, some of which vary quite broadly. Some scientists reserve the term for the serious long-term manifestations that characterize post-traumatic stress disorder (PTSD). Others, including many clinicians, will offer a tautology, telling you that trauma is anything that has a traumatic impact on us. Yet as fuzzy as that may sound, it's true. To a large extent, trauma is in the eye (or rather, the brain-body) of the beholder.

Why is that the case? For one, human development involves incredibly complex interactions between a person's unique genetics and their unique environment. While extreme experiences can alter the brain, preexisting personality traits and brain wiring can have a substantial effect on how. The upshot is that no two people will experience the same adverse event in exactly the same way. That's why George Bonanno uses the term *potentially traumatic experiences*.[30] Any universal declarations about what's traumatic or not are bound to be false.

Personally, my definition of trauma is relatively broad: It's anything that substantially violates our expectations of the world and causes a major shift in our worldview and perception of safety.[31]

Trauma is a tremendously rich and detailed topic, and it's not in the purview of this book to explore various theories about how trauma (or survival stress) can affect us. But let's carve out a few concepts that I think are important to understand when it comes to developing an empowered relationship with life, including working with trauma. That includes acknowledging a potentially disempowering narrative that's out there. . . . Okay, here we go.

Sadly, I see many attempts to help people with trauma that—as well-intentioned as they may be—can sometimes backfire. Take the incredible popularity of a book called *The Body Keeps the Score*, by psychiatrist Bessel van der Kolk.[32] As journalist Danielle Carr put it in her cover story "Trauma: America's Favorite Self-Diagnosis" in *New York* magazine:[33]

> *In his ascent, van der Kolk has done for trauma what Carl Sagan did for the galaxy. Today, the prevalent trauma concept is fundamentally van der Kolkian: trauma as a state of the body, rather than a way of interpreting the past. This means that getting the patient unstuck from the past requires working with the body and teaching it to unbrace itself from a chronic "fight or flight" mode.*

Without a doubt, over the course of his long career van der Kolk has made significant and meaningful contributions to the world of trauma research. Also, it is undeniable that his writings have helped many people suffering with trauma feel more empowered to change their lives. At the same time, his ideas have run amok in our society and often go way beyond what van der Kolk ever intended.[34] What's more, other researchers are taking a closer look and pointing out some of the errors of the research presented in the book.[35]

Take the idea that trauma constitutes a special type of *memory* that is stored in the body and that the traumatized person often can't access until years later at best. Using the word "memory" in this way can be a barrier to understanding the mechanisms or systems at work. It strikes me that the concept of *stored survival stress* might be more useful here. As Barrett, Bonanno, and others are quick to point out, narrative memory by its strictest definition is a function of the brain.[36] So saying or implying that the body "remembers" trauma can be misleading if we're trying to understand the mechanisms through which adverse experiences can affect us over the long term.

Traumatic experiences can certainly affect the body in lasting ways, but those effects aren't really memories as we typically think of them, and even saying it's a special kind of memory can be confusing. Storing integrated memories of events is something only the brain can manage. And memories can last forever. What happens to the body in response to trauma is better described as survival stress, and this can potentially be integrated later as we learn to reregulate our nervous systems and relax stress-induced tensions. That can certainly be a long and involved process depending on how much stress you're storing, but it's possible. And to be fair, van der Kolk himself has said that change is possible, provided we change our relationship with our body. That's a much more hopeful prospect than forever being saddled with the lingering effects of trauma, or thinking that every negative reaction or uncomfortable emotion you experience in your life is a result of your unconscious "trauma response." This is unfortunately what I see a lot on social media. I even saw one ad on Instagram that said "Procrastination is not laziness. It's a trauma response." Come on!*

Look: In the psychodynamic sense, we can describe our unconscious as perceptual memories and emotions that we don't understand linguistically. We can't capture them in a way that we can put words to them. This is true. We know that emotions have bodily components, which helps to explain why relieving body-based stress can be a helpful element of trauma healing.

But while the phrase *the body keeps the score* is catchy, it's potentially misleading and disempowering. When we keep repeating it, people can erroneously conclude that (1) trauma is permanently stuck in the body and there's nothing we can do about it; (2) only therapies that focus on the body will be effective; and/or (3) every little physical pain and emotional pain we experience likely stems from a past trauma.

The brain and the body are vastly intertwined.[37] As an editorial in the prestigious journal *Nature* put it, "A host of disorders once thought to have nothing to do with the brain are, in fact, tightly coupled to nervous-system activity."

Of course, this works both ways: The body and the brain have a complex system of feedback loops. Yes, the (rest of the) body impacts

---

* I mean, procrastination might not be laziness, it could just be avoidance. But not all avoidance behaviors are a trauma response! https://www.instagram.com/p/CuL0Qxqui06/.

the brain, but the brain and human consciousness can also have a dramatic impact on the (rest of the) body, as well.

That's why I favor approaches that target the whole system. For instance, I'm a big fan of the book *101 Trauma-Informed Interventions: Activities, Exercises and Assignments to Move the Client and Therapy Forward* by Linda Curran. Curran's book includes helpful exercises for you to connect with your body and become more aware of your emotions and how they're affecting you.[38]

Critically, while Curran incorporates a bottom-up experiential approach, she also employs a top-down approach, initiating change at the cognitively conscious level. She includes exercises to change your self-talk, set proper boundaries, use imagery, and apply psychodrama techniques to heal and move forward with your life. I'm not saying that top-down exercises can fully heal all the effects of trauma. The key here is to recognize that by changing the mind, and the narratives we tell ourselves, we can initiate at least some changes in the body, as well.

Now let's circle back to language and consider how our overuse of the word *trauma* influences how we process our experiences.

Shift Your Language, Shift Your Perception

This poor word, *trauma*—we've saddled it with so much, it must be absolutely exhausted! After all, every insult these days is trauma. In addition to the other points I'm making in this chapter and throughout this book, I submit that one of the things we're actually suffering from is a limited vocabulary. And I mean suffering quite literally.

In many ways, how we interpret circumstances relies at least in part on the language we have—or don't—to characterize them. If the only term we have to describe the challenges we're facing is *trauma*, then every adverse event becomes *traumatic*.

Words matter because they bring with them an entire array of beliefs. If you're a college student and you struggled in a certain class, that easily can be an isolated experience. But if you were *traumatized* by how hard the class was for you, that indicates a deep and lasting impact that may have rewired your brain and shifted your entire perception of life. And by employing that language, you may actually shift your perceptions to believe it. See the problem here?

Of course trauma is real, but it would benefit us to have a broader language we can invoke when describing challenging experiences. This is linked to the concept of *emotional granularity*, where we're able to describe our feeling states with nuanced terms that more accurately characterize what we're experiencing. We're not just *sad*; we're *disengaged, lethargic, disenchanted, worn out*, and so on. Interestingly, research shows that people with more emotional granularity—who can differentiate more specifically what they're feeling and label their experiences with more precise language—tend to be less reactive to negative circumstances and have greater psychological resilience.[39] If we can learn to connect with and describe our experiences beyond this one big word, it can actually help us relate to what's happening in more subtle and meaningful ways.

But if you're disappointed that you can no longer blame everything bad that happens to you on trauma, rest assured that you can still blame your parents. But perhaps in a different way than you might think.

IT'S YOUR PARENTS' FAULT!
THE ROLE OF GENES AND ATTACHMENT

When I say you can saddle your parents with all of your woes, it doesn't all come down to how they raised you but rather a combination of how your parents raised you and the genes they gave you. Research shows that everything from how we react to adversity to our general disposition and outlook on life is due to a combination of nature *and* nurture.

Yet these days, if we're struggling in any way, we're often encouraged to believe that everything that's "wrong" or difficult in our lives is due to external factors. Trauma is one of them, and attachment is another. (Or maybe you have attachment trauma!) If you're not familiar with attachment, it essentially boils down to the bonds we formed—or didn't form—with our caregivers. But as with trauma, there's a whole lot we get wrong about attachment.

The Truth about Attachment

Attachment theory as we often interpret it holds that if our primary caregivers didn't provide us with an adequate and consistent sense of safety and security, we're essentially destined for a life of unsatisfying relationships. Yes, it's reasonable to attribute some of our adult outcomes to the quality of our early childhood attachment. But many see attachment and its potential impact on our developing nervous system as a panacea. Can't get your work done on time? It's because Mom wasn't around!

Early childhood relationships do matter, *a lot*. They can shape us and our outlook on life—and yes, mold our nervous systems—in critical ways. At the same time, research now shows that those effects aren't as significant or lasting as we've been led to believe. Plus, a variety of life events—from starting new relationships to changing jobs—are associated with enduring changes in adult attachment styles.[40] Also, even if you historically have had anxious attachment and constantly worry that your partner's one day going to declare that they've found someone else and move on, attachment patterns can change with the support of a sensitive partner who is considerate of your attachment triggers.[41]

Given enough exposure to healthy relationships and some other work on our part, it's possible to shift our childhood attachment behaviors and develop healthier attachment patterns as an adult. So, even if Mom's inability to be fully present for you has left a long-term mark, like a bad tattoo, with some effort and some discomfort, it *can* be removed. And yes, it may leave a scar, but the point is that you don't have to walk around your entire life with a full-color image of the Tasmanian Devil emblazoned on your ankle. Thank goodness!

Also, there's more that impacts your attachment style than just your experiences. Enter: the forbidden, taboo, and dirty g-word!

Reprogramming Your Genes

In the predominant trauma narrative that is so popular in our culture right now, trauma is thought of as primarily the result of nurture. It's not you. The world messed you up. It's all the fault of the "toxic culture" you live in.[42]

But that's not the whole story. Truth is, who we are and how we approach life is the result of a complex mix of inborn and environmental influences. A lot of popular discussions about trauma, including van der Kolk's writings as well as physician Gabor Maté's writings, ignore or downplay the contribution of *preexisting temperamental differences*. These differences come partly from our genetics and help to color our world and interpretations of the events in our lives.

This includes our attachment style! That's right—the latest science shows that your attachment style doesn't entirely come down to environmental factors but also includes your genetic makeup.[43] While social psychologist and leading researcher on attachment R. Chris Fraley and his colleagues found that life events can lead to enduring changes in adult attachment styles, they still found considerable individual differences in the extent to which people changed. These differences are rooted at least in part in genetic proclivities.[44]

As Fraley told me in a correspondence, current views of attachment—based on research including twins studies—are more "multi-deterministic." Study results indicate that our inborn temperament can have an important influence on our attachment style. For one, some genetic predispositions can influence how external factors impact us. For instance, Fraley and his colleagues found that the ways people construed events (positive vs. negative) were related to the extent to which their attachment styles changed. *Some of us may be more disposed to feel hopeless in the face of challenging events.*

This colors how we interact with life, determining whether we view the world through rose-colored glasses or a perennial smog.[45] As another example, "sensory processing sensitivity" is a real trait (one we'll discuss in greater detail in Chapter 7). Some people are born with a proclivity toward higher sensitivity, and so they might be more apt to develop insecure attachment, to take slights more seriously, or to have more trouble bouncing back from difficult experiences. To Gabor Maté's credit, he does recognize the impact of sensitivity genes on behavior, even though he downplays the impact of other genes and his primary focus is on trauma as the most important causal force.

It's the same with sensitivity's close cousin, neuroticism. Now, as with narcissism, neuroticism is a personality trait that exists on a continuum. I prefer to use the term "people who score high in neuroticism" rather than labeling people as "neurotic," which feels like a fixed label. However, in the interest of sparing you the mouthful of extra words, I will simply use "neuroticism" and trust that from this point on, you won't get too hung up on the label and will be able to see what's underneath the label. As I mentioned previously, neuroticism is a dimension of personality that relates to emotional instability, negativity, rumination, and anxiety.

With this lovely trait, our minds are more apt to feed us constant anxious concerns and worries, and we're more likely to pay a *lot* of attention to them. Now neuroticism, like sensitivity or any other trait, is neither positive nor negative. If someone has extremely low neuroticism and a perennial "Don't worry, be happy!" attitude, they could fail to anticipate negative events at all, and that can pose its own challenges. ("Should I double-check if I packed this parachute properly? Nah—it'll be fine!")

I could view my high neuroticism as a disadvantage that will always hold me back, but that would be a choice. Instead, I choose to see it as something I can learn to deal with. I recognize that it can present very real challenges (Hi, lifetime of generalized anxiety!), and so I have worked to identify and engage with tools to help me (many of which you'll read about in this book). When I struggle in spite of these tools, I lean on generous doses of self-compassion and absurdist humor . . . *especially* the absurdist humor.

Plus, I also try to harness the *benefits* of neuroticism. After all, it's precisely because I'm so hyperattentive that I'm so engaged with my work, and that I attend to my relationships so thoroughly. Plus, I'd be the first to notice danger and get the hell out of a bad situation. See ya, guys! But if I start to go overboard, I engage my tools.

If that sounds like a lot of work, it is. But it gets easier over time because some of it becomes habituated. Right now, there's a lot of habitual behavior at work in your life. Much of it you're probably not aware of because you've been doing it for so long. Some of it's probably heavily linked to your personality traits—which all develop as the result of a lifetime mixture of your nature interacting with your nurture.

But wait! Doesn't the idea that our genes play a huge role in our outlook and behavior support a victim mindset? Actually, no! That's a common misconception of how genes work. I actually find it much more empowering to know that my genes play a substantial role in who I can become than to see myself as mindlessly influenced completely by environmental circumstances.[46] Who wants to live in a completely environmentally determined world? That sounds horrible. I'll take some inner agency and self-expression, thank you very much!

But here's the thing: Genes are not deterministic. Genes are all about our vulnerabilities and our potential. Genetic information merely provides instructions for building proteins, which then organize themselves into an organism. It's emergent self-organization based on only some very limited instructions—nothing like a blueprint. Genes influence our proclivities, but they don't program definite outcomes. That's up to us, because with awareness, attention, and active engagement, we can change the expression of our genes.[47] Early life stressors do create constraints on development, but the brain leaves itself open to the possibility of future revisions. As Martin Teicher and his colleagues explain, "Brain development is directed by genes but sculpted by experiences."[48]

As with healing trauma, it's not as simple as flipping a switch. For one, it requires real effort. But also, the genetics I'm talking about—mainly genes that contribute to our temperament—aren't on or off. They're more like dials. I can't turn off my neuroticism completely, but I can dial it down from an 11 to hopefully a 2 or 3 most days. The same is true for you and your traits.

Now, I don't want to dismiss the impact of our environment.

To be sure, dysfunctional systems—from families to larger societal structures—have a very real impact on us. I'm not trying to say that agency overcomes all external influences. Yet all too often, we engage in a false belief that our past experiences, our environment, or our genes necessarily dictate the entirety of who are and what's possible in our lives. The truth is, we have a lot of control over our outcomes, or at least a lot more than you may think.

YOUR PAST WILL NEVER CHANGE—BUT *YOU* CAN!

Regardless of our experiences or our genetic makeup, we all have the ability to learn the cognitive and somatic tools to withstand and overcome adversity. Additionally, our mindset and our capacity to deal with challenges are not predetermined—they can be learned. If some part of you didn't already believe or at least suspect that, you wouldn't be reading this book!

You arrived here with certain genetic instructions—hazy instructions at best—and some of those instructions were implemented more readily into reality by what you've experienced in your life. But now it's time to step up to the control board, take a good, honest look at what you're working with, and start making some choices and some real changes. To write a new story.

The existential psychiatrist Irvin Yalom describes one of his patients, a strong and resourceful woman who was CEO of a major industrial company. As a child, she suffered vicious and continual verbal abuse from her father. In one session she described a daydream she had where she was seeing a therapist who had the technology to cause total memory erasure in a patient. In her daydream she was asked by the therapist if she would like to do a total erasure of all memory of her father's existence. While this sounded great at first, she told Yalom that it was a tough call. "Why a tough call?" Yalom asked her. She responded:

> *Well, at first, it seems a no-brainer: my father was a monster and terrified me and my sibs throughout childhood. But, in the end, I*

decided to leave my memory alone and have none of it erased. De-
spite the wretched abuse I suffered, I have succeeded in life beyond
my furthest dreams. Somewhere, somehow, I have developed a
lot of resilience and resourcefulness. Was it despite my father? Or
because of him?

Yalom notes that this fantasy was a first step in a major shift toward not only forgiving her father but also coming to terms with the
inalterability of the past. He writes, "She was shaken by my comment
that sooner or later she had to give up the hope for a better past."[49]

To orient ourselves in the direction of growth, just like this patient, we need to ultimately accept what has been and turn toward
the future. Not by ignoring our past but by processing it in a meaningful fashion and using it as the seeds to become the person we wish
to become, sometimes even changing our own trauma narrative.

That's exactly what Aunt Ada Doom did. With some help from
young Flora, she realized that there was a whole world out there she
was missing out on. She accepted that she couldn't unsee whatever it
was she saw in the woodshed, or the potting shed, or wherever it was,
and realized that while she sat confined to her upstairs room dwelling on it, life was passing her by. So she got up, combed her hair, put
on her fancy clothes, and flew off to Paris.

Moving on doesn't mean that what happened and what you experienced doesn't matter. *Of course it does.* And it always will.

It means that you're no longer going to allow past experiences to
control how you experience your life right here, right now.

Moving on also doesn't mean that you're accepting blame. It
means that you're accepting responsibility.

It means you're deciding that you're going to slide on over into
the driver's seat and take it from here. Yes, crappy experiences can
change your brain. But you know what else can change your brain—
in the way you want it to be changed? *You.*

2

Don't Be a Victim to Your Emotions

One ought to hold on to one's heart; for if one lets it go, one soon loses control of the head too.

—*Friedrich Nietzsche*

I used to be afraid of flying. Not just a little afraid—we're talking terrified. I was also afraid of public speaking. And again, not just mildly apprehensive, but monumentally scared. Then I published *Ungifted*, the book I had wanted to write my entire life. It was my call to expand our ideas of human intelligence and my attempt to help those neurodiverse children who are left behind by our limited views on what categorizes someone as smart and capable. Fortunately, the book was well received, and I started getting speaking invitations left and right, and few of them were local. Meaning they required flying. Lots and lots of flying. I was delighted and nauseated, all at once. I'd poured so much into this book, and yet its success meant that suddenly my worst fears were coupled with my biggest dreams. Which would win?

I decided that the opportunity to get my message out there was too great. I'd need to do whatever it took to get over my fears, or at least figure out some strategies to stop them from stopping me. When it came to flying, I went to my doctor and got a prescription for anti-anxiety medicine. Then, before each of my talks, I would engage in long meditation rituals to help me acknowledge my fear and move forward anyway. Little by little, my fear of flying diminished, and I even started to enjoy public speaking. Once my anxiety faded into the background, I was able to connect with other things I was feeling; I could express my humor and the genuine joy I feel about life. And, most importantly, I could share my message. None of that is to say that the journey has been easy, or that my struggles are over, but facing the tough task of tackling my fears has been so worth it.

As is the case for most of us, my fear and anxiety didn't just come out of nowhere. I grew up with an overly protective mother. Bless her (she meant well), but I was taught to fear *everything*, including fear itself! My mother embedded in me the message that life is a dangerous business and extreme caution is warranted at all times. Case in point: By my senior year in high school, my mom still insisted on driving me to the bus stop, which was just down the street!

This might conjure for you the notion that I must have grown up in a neighborhood so rough that it could have doubled as a live set for *The Wire*. But no, we're talking suburbs here, people. Tree-lined streets and little kids riding their bikes. To be fair, my mother wanted everything to be easy on me. She wanted to eliminate any potential threat I might face, so she was well-intentioned. But what I've since come to realize is that eliminating all potential threats also means eliminating all potential for growth. So even if you didn't grow up with an overprotective parent, if you struggle to face difficult emotions like fear, then you, too, are limiting your own growth.

"BAD" FEELINGS MAKE FOR A BETTER LIFE

Have you ever heard the expression that someone is pulling a high-wire act? It means they're walking a very thin line where one misstep could prove catastrophic. Well, one man who has actually walked a tightrope has some interesting insights on fear. Philippe Petit is a high-wire artist who came to fame through daring acts such as walking a tightrope across Notre Dame Cathedral in Paris, the Sydney Harbour Bridge in Australia, and NYC's former Twin Towers (all unauthorized). When asked how he deals with fear, Petit says he re-ally doesn't feel afraid when he's on the wire. "I know my limits, I know myself, I know my wire," he says.[1] In his view, fear is caused by a lack of knowledge.

Though Petit doesn't fret over daring feats, he gets quite anxious about spiders (something I can definitely relate to). If he wanted to conquer this fear one day, he says his plan would be to get to know our arachnid friends a bit better by reading books and watching vid-eos to educate himself about them. The point is that if there's some-thing fear is stopping us from doing, we should embrace that thing. We should enmesh ourselves in it until we understand it better. As the French say, "Le connaître c'est l'aimer," or, "To know is to love." But instead, most of the time we opt to try to protect ourselves, and that supposed safety comes at a high cost. As Petit so eloquently puts it (as only a Frenchman can), "We should not allow fear to fade the song of our soul."

When I faced my own anxiety around flying and speaking, that's exactly what I did—I turned toward my fear. I exposed myself to air travel and to public speaking over and over again until eventually neither was especially scary. And in my quest I developed the cour-age and self-confidence to deal with the fear that remained. Plus, the rewards I experienced—getting to discuss work that was incredibly meaningful to me and sharing in the fellowship and good vibes of the folks who came to hear me speak—gave me the positive feedback I needed to soldier on.

We're often taught that uncomfortable emotions such as fear are to be avoided. Though all of our emotions are natural (after all, the fact that we're able to experience them categorizes them as such), we tend to label some as good, and others as bad. In her research, psy-chologist Susan David found that one-third of us either judge ourselves for having "bad" emotions (see also: sadness, anger, grief, and so on) or actively try to push aside these feelings.[2] The truth is that emotions are simply signposts signaling that something important is going on internally, or that something matters to us. No more, no less.

As Susan told me, we need to stop pathologizing normal emotions simply because they don't feel great.[3] Harvard Medical School's David Rosmarin has similar concerns. As he observed in his *Wall Street Journal* essay titled "Screening for Anxiety Will Only Make Us More Anxious," we're becoming too quick to label normal life challenges as something requiring a diagnosis. He wrote, "All of us experience anxiety, and it's awful—but it is not a disease."[4]

Of course we don't want to feel disappointed. Of course we want uncomfortable feelings to go away. But are those realistic goals? Again, doing hard things is how we grow. And hard things typically come with hard feelings. Plus, even if we try to keep our head down and hide from difficult experiences, they will find us. That's a guarantee. If you ever care about anyone or anything, you will experience pain. As psychiatrist Colin Murray Parkes wrote in his book on bereavement, "The pain of grief is just as much a part of life as the joy of love; it is, perhaps, the price we pay for love, the cost of commitment."[5]

Similarly, Susan David, an expert on the psychology of emotions, describes the attempt to avoid uncomfortable emotions as having "dead people's goals."[6] She says that if we want to live richly and experience a full, meaningful life, we must experience discomfort.

Doing hard things is how we grow.

Psychiatrist Mark Epstein has said, "Grief and love are connected. If we push the mourning, the grief, the sadness away, we are also pushing the love away. By doing so, we are creating a much more constrained way of living."[7] To the extent that we can open our hearts to ourselves and what we are feeling, we encounter a more complete aliveness—tender, vibrant, precious—that has been, for many of us, long hidden from expression.

Humans evolved a long list of psychological fears: fear of failure, fear of social rejection, fear of losing control, fear of losing emotional contact, fear of losing reputation.[8] Many thousands of years ago, when we were living on the savanna, our finely tuned fear response helped us survive. But now it can be a source of suffering. Yet rather than find constructive ways to confront our uncomfortable emotions, as Philippe Petit suggested, our instinct is often to try to avoid any experiences that spark discomfort. We bubble-wrap ourselves, and as a result, we just become more and more sensitive. We increasingly close ourselves off to experiences, to relationships, to conversations that challenge us, so instead of growing, we begin to wither. But like the beautiful bougainvillea—a tough tropical vine that can flower even under the harshest conditions—we, too, can learn to thrive whatever the weather.

Yet too often, we let our feelings direct us. We either avoid every potential trigger of uncomfortable emotions, or we let our mood dictate our actions. You wake up in the morning and don't feel like going to the gym, so you don't go to the gym. You are hungry and don't feel like sticking to your diet, so you down some chips. You feel anxious to approach that attractive person, so you turn around and walk home instead.

But here's a little secret that can change your life forever (as it did mine): You can feel something negative—you can feel demotivated or defeated or depressed—and *still act in the service of your longer-term goals.* You don't have to let your emotions govern your actions. (After all, who's in charge here—you or your feelings?) And you certainly don't have to avoid every circumstance that might prompt you to feel uncomfortable or challenged.

> You don't have to let your emotions govern your actions.

How Trigger Warnings Can Hold Us Back

From radio and television programming to college lectures, much of the content we consume these days is prefaced by a trigger warning. Trigger warnings are essentially caution signs: They alert us to potentially upsetting content that could provoke a negative emotional response. Initially, these warnings were meant to aid individuals with PTSD and more general trauma by helping them prepare for or avoid distressing content.[9] While this original intent is certainly commendable, more recently the use of trigger warnings has spread into schools, classrooms, art exhibits, movies, and nearly every aspect of our lives. Many college professors now include trigger warnings in their syllabi. In fact, a survey found that half of professors employ trigger warnings in their classrooms, and some universities even *require* the use of trigger warnings.[10]

Regrettably, the use of trigger warnings has now expanded to warn virtually everyone when any content whatsoever might cause discomfort. The term "being triggered," once a clinical descriptor of a specific nervous system arousal, is now casually used to describe feeling upset or uncomfortable. This overuse has blurred the terminology, leaving those with PTSD who really do experience being triggered without language to describe their experiences. In our rush to claim victim status over absolutely everything, we've trampled the very people we were originally trying to help.

Trigger warnings are intended to safeguard individuals from distress. However, the constant barrage of warnings also communicates a subtle message: Discomfort is bad, even harmful. It implies that people aren't equipped to handle their emotional responses, that they should dodge discomfort at all costs. In effect, it brands people as victims of their emotions.

The repercussions of this are wide-reaching. Individuals start to wall themselves off, and they attempt to silence others who hold differing viewpoints. A survey of more than thirty-seven thousand students across 159 U.S. college and university campuses revealed a startling fact: More than two-thirds at least partially agreed with the notion that it's acceptable to drown out on-campus speakers with opposing views, making it impossible for their ideas to be heard.[11]

In 2017, in an incident that would go on to be mirrored at institutions of higher education across the country, students at Middlebury College shouted down Charles Murray, author of *The Bell Curve*, with the justification that his views are "racist, sexist, and anti-gay."[12] Now, I don't fully align with Murray's interpretation of his data regarding IQ and society, but I wouldn't mind engaging in a dialogue with him. Respectful discourse is essential to societal progress. On my podcast, I host individuals I don't always agree with, as understanding and considering diverse viewpoints is critical. Even if we never find common ground on certain topics, I can at least learn why the other person believes what they do. Plus, people are rarely wrong about absolutely everything. There's usually something we can connect on. ("Hey, you like absurdist humor? So do I!") An ability to work together in spite of our differences and a willingness to broaden our own perspectives are essential to meeting the challenges that we face in the world today.

It's no coincidence that we find ourselves in the midst of what has been referred to as a "loneliness pandemic."* In a survey of eighteen- to twenty-five-year-olds, 61 percent reported intense feelings of loneliness.[13] Interestingly, this group is among the most vocal advocates for trigger warnings and also their most frequent recipients. When we distance ourselves from anything that prompts discomfort, we risk isolating ourselves from a vast number of people.

The trend of dismissing or shouting down everyone who doesn't see the world exactly as we do, to essentially vote them out like we're on a massive game of *Survivor*, drastically reduces our circle of connection. We are isolating ourselves when we most need each other. Maintaining relationships with people we don't always agree with requires patience, humility, and compassion, yet the payoff is profound. It not only widens our circle of connection but also exposes us to diverse ideas, which is essential for personal growth.

Imagine if Abraham Lincoln had done the Civil War–era version of canceling Frederick Douglass because he didn't want to be challenged to think differently. At one point Douglass expressed that though he and Lincoln disagreed, he always felt that the president truly listened to him. Indeed, the great orator and abolitionist did eventually succeed in helping to change Lincoln's mind about several policies. Lincoln's open-mindedness allowed him to seek out diverse viewpoints among his political peers, and he consistently revisited his own beliefs.[14] Of course Lincoln had his faults—as we all do—but narrow-mindedness was not among them. We need to have more

---

* Although it's important to acknowledge that some people, like Steven Pinker, argue it's not technically a "pandemic."

faith in our ability to be exposed to different ideas and opinions, including those that upset us.

Indeed, the ability to anticipate a response can enhance our capacity to manage stress.[15] Yet expecting a specific reaction can amplify our response. It's like preparing for a car crash when you see it coming in the rearview mirror—the very act of bracing for impact can lead to more severe injuries. In many situations, relaxing (while wearing your seat belt, of course) allows the impact's energy to pass through you.

Research shows that people warned about graphic violence in a suspenseful film clip experienced more distress than those informed about the violent content being cut.[16] Also, detailing all potential adverse effects of a medication to patients can increase side effects due to an expectation-driven "nocebo effect."[17] Paul Bloom, in his book *How Pleasure Works*, argues that pleasure heavily depends on expectations.[18] The same principle applies to emotional pain.

Trigger warnings can lead people to more intrusive thoughts after exposure to certain content.[19] It's like being told not to think about a pink elephant—you end up thinking about nothing else! Although trigger warnings don't instruct you to avoid the content, those who choose to do so may inadvertently think more about it, or even imagine it to be worse than it is.

An increasing number of scientific studies now show that trigger warnings may not work as intended and can even backfire.[20] One study by Benjamin Bellet and his colleagues found that trigger warnings could unintentionally undermine resilience.[21] They discovered that people who received trigger warnings before reading literary passages reported greater anxiety when reading potentially distressing passages, but *only if they believed that words can cause harm*. This aligns with the idea that exposure to any language we disagree with is akin to being a victim of violence.

In an op-ed in the *New York Times*, Lisa Feldman Barrett discusses whether words can constitute violence, as we're so fond of saying these days.[22] She argues that while abusive speech can trigger a similar physiological response to physical violence, merely offensive speech doesn't harm our bodies or brains. She writes, "Offensiveness is not bad for your body and brain. Your nervous system evolved to withstand periodic bouts of stress, such as fleeing from a tiger, taking a punch or encountering an odious idea in a university lecture." She continues, "When you're forced to engage a position you strongly disagree with, you learn something about the other perspective as well as your own. The process feels unpleasant, but it's a good kind of stress—temporary and not harmful to your body—and you reap the longer-term benefits of learning."

Confronting uncomfortable situations can be beneficial. Avoiding such situations can make us weaker and less capable of handling adversity. And again, we cannot form meaningful relationships if we only surround ourselves with like-minded individuals. Instead, we can challenge our own aversions to discomfort and open up our minds a little. Or even a lot. Le connaître c'est l'aimer.

Life's challenges and feelings of distress aren't actually obstacles to well-being. Instead, it's our focus on escaping uncomfortable experiences—whether it's tackling public speaking, listening to the viewpoints of those we disagree with, or having a difficult conversation with a loved one—that limits us from engaging with our deepest values and self-actualizing. When we avoid negative feelings, we become more attached to them. Our focus shifts to everything we want to avoid, consuming our thoughts and energy.

> **When we avoid negative feelings, we become more attached to them.**

There's a parable about two monks who encounter an injured woman along the road leading into town. In spite of their order's prohibition against mingling with the opposite sex, one monk lends the woman assistance, picking her up and carrying her into town. After delivering her to her home, the monks continue onward. About an hour later, the second monk, who has been fuming, turns to the first monk. "Are we not going to talk about what happened back there? I can't believe you *touched* that woman!" The first monk nods and smiles. "The difference between us, my friend, is that I let go of that woman an hour ago, and you are still carrying her."

Similarly, we can learn to just let it go, to let the upset and the discomfort pass through us. As author and sociologist Martha Beck describes it:

> *What happens when we're willing to feel bad is that, sure enough, we often feel bad—but without the stress of futile avoidance. Emotional discomfort, when accepted, rises, crests, and falls in a series of waves. Each wave washes parts of us away and deposits treasures we never imagined.*[23]

But *how* do we do that? How do we soften our grip on challenging feelings and let those waves crash over us? We can start by getting out a map and understanding where it is we're trying to go.

FLOWING WITH YOUR FEELINGS: CULTIVATING PSYCHOLOGICAL FLEXIBILITY

As Susan David observes in her riveting TED Talk, "How we deal with our emotions drives every aspect of our lives."[24] Fixating on what we think shouldn't be shrinks our world. Too often, our strategies to cope with life's challenges, though they may provide momentary relief, take us further away from the life we really want. Instead, we can become expansive. We can see difficult emotions as opportunities to engage with life and the people in it more richly. Instead of fixating, we can become more flexible. Dare I suggest we can even start to embrace life rather than avoid it.

Embrace Life

Lori Deschene, an author and the founder of the website Tiny Buddha, is no stranger to avoidance. She writes:

> *For most of my life I was a fugitive from my feelings. . . . From a very young age, I felt overwhelmed by pain. As a pre-teen, I ate my feelings. As a teen, I starved them away. In college, I drank and*

smoked them numb. And in my twenties, I felt and cried my eyes red and raw. I sobbed. I wailed. I shook and convulsed. And I wished I'd never chosen to feel them, but rather kept pushing them down, pretending everything was fine. Except when I did that, they didn't just go away—they compounded on top each other and built up until eventually I exploded, with no idea why I felt so bad.[25]

While friends wondered if something larger and darker was at play, Deschene's struggle had a relatively simple source—avoidance. It wasn't any one or even a collection of experiences, themselves, that were causing her suffering. It was the fact that she'd never allowed herself to experience and process her feelings about them. "I'd never dealt with my feelings from events large and small, and eventually they dealt with me. As unpleasant as it may sound," she writes, "I needed to learn how to feel bad." She needed to cultivate the ability to handle uncomfortable feelings with self-compassion.

So, how are you doing with processing *your* uncomfortable feelings? You guessed it! It's time for a psychological scale. Go ahead and take a moment to reflect honestly on how much you agree with the following statements:[26]

- My painful experiences and memories make it difficult for me to live a life that I would value.

- I'm afraid of my feelings.

- I worry about not being able to control my worries and feelings.

- My painful memories prevent me from having a fulfilling life.

- Emotions cause problems in my life.

- It seems like most people are handling their lives better than I am.

- Worries get in the way of my success.

These items measure something psychologists call "experiential avoidance." Researchers have found that higher levels of experiential avoidance are associated with a staggering number of negative outcomes in life, including depression, anxiety, stress, substance abuse, negative body image, disordered eating, pain catastrophizing, thought suppression, job burnout, and work absenteeism.[27] That's quite a laundry list!

As I mentioned a moment ago, and as Lori Deschene experienced, attempts to avoid uncomfortable experiences and feelings can actually have the opposite effect and increase their hold on you. First, avoidance increases salience, or the amount of relevance something has to us. (It's that old pink elephant again. Don't think about him!) So we should acknowledge what pops up for us. But, acknowledging is different from dwelling. And while we don't want to avoid negative thoughts and feelings entirely, at a certain point it might be entirely okay and even beneficial to go ahead and give them the Heisman.

You know how we've been taught that it's always terrible to try to suppress negative thoughts? Well, maybe not so much. At least in some circumstances, exercising the ability to block gloomy or distressing thoughts could actually *help* our mental health.[28] In the wake of COVID-19, when many around the world understandably catapulted into a fear spiral, researchers at the University of Cambridge were curious about whether there could actually be a benefit to suppressing some of our negative thoughts. Could engaging with *inhibitory control*, as psychologists call it, actually be useful? To find out, they enrolled 120 participants from sixteen countries and had them list out scenarios that they could envision occurring during the following two years—some things they hoped would happen, some that were neutral, and some they were afraid would occur. Then they took the participants through an exercise designed to train them to suppress their thoughts.

Immediately after the training, participants reported that the events they'd blocked were less vivid in their minds—and the same was still true when the researchers checked in with them three months later. Not only that, but suppressing thoughts resulted in an

increase in feelings of positive mental health and a decrease in negative mental health, *especially among the participants who had PTSD!*

Now, further research is needed to more fully explore these results, and it's safe to say we don't want to suppress everything unpleasant we feel. Suppression can be a helpful tool, but it's one you'll
want to employ both thoughtfully and sparingly. And to be clear,
suppression is not the same as avoidance. With the former, you're
simply choosing not to let disruptive thoughts be at the center of
your focus. You're still aware of them, but at least for a time, you're
nudging them to the periphery, telling them, "Take a seat over there,
please." With avoidance, you're sticking your fingers in your ears
saying, "La-la-la, you don't exist!" and that contributes to negative
outcomes.

When we avoid our feelings altogether, by extension we narrow
the range of behaviors we undertake. That's because we start to steer
clear of anything that might "trigger" these feared experiences or
feelings. It's like when one dude tries to express platonic love for another dude. "I love you, man!" he declares. But instead of coming in
for the proffered hug, his avoidant friend steps back and instead offers an awkward fist bump. He doesn't want to have to go there—to
climb up into his emotional attic and unlock that foot locker of
feelings he's been conditioned to suppress (after all, what else
might come out?), so he avoids experiences
that threaten to take him there. As a result,
he misses out on opportunities for life-
enriching love and connection.

When we avoid our feelings altogether, by extension we narrow the range of behaviors we undertake.

When we exercise experiential avoidance, our distant goals and dreams take a
back seat to our more immediate impulse to
avoid fear and discomfort. Over time, we be-
gin to lose contact with what we really want out of life, and instead
continue to focus on avoiding psychological pain. Psychologists call
this *promotion versus prevention*.[29] When we're motivated by promotion, we focus on opportunities to grow and advance, while in pre-

vention mode, we're more concerned with staying safe. Just like we don't want to categorize emotions as good or bad, neither motivation is better than the other. But when we focus too much on protecting ourselves, we're less likely to try new things, and that narrows our experience of life.

Address Your Distress

Instead, let's think about distress differently. What if you could develop a "do it anyway" mentality, where distress may be present, but it doesn't prevent you from taking meaningful action, like engaging with others? Or, what if reducing distress was only a goal if it helped you pursue other meaningful goals? For instance, I needed to reduce my distress over flying and public speaking in order to accomplish meaningful goals in my life. I still don't love flying, but I do it anyway, with my anxiety riding shotgun beside me. I don't love the feeling of anxiety (and it often hogs the armrest), but the payoffs of doing it anyway are worth it. This is part of *psychological flexibility*: when we can assess a situation and determine the best steps to take to achieve a life-enhancing result. The process doesn't necessarily feel good, but the outcome contributes to our overall well-being and sense of vitality in life.

Develop a "do it anyway" mentality.

Research shows that increases in psychological flexibility are linked to improvements in mental health.[30] Psychological flexibility is also connected to self-compassion, distress tolerance during valued goal pursuit, job performance, job satisfaction, psychological health, and higher levels of life satisfaction.[31] It's also associated with reduced pain and depressed mood in patients with chronic pain.[32] And it's connected to a wider range of daily emotion regulation strategies, effort, joy, and meaning.[33]

Psychological flexibility is a close cousin to what Susan David calls "emotional agility." And there are three key insights that David says can help us develop this superpower.

Three Truths about Emotions

Just as a soccer player needs to be agile so they can respond to the shifting dynamics on the field, to manage *our* field of play, we want to develop emotional agility. As Susan David wrote in her book *Emotional Agility*, people who have high levels of emotional agility "demonstrate flexibility in dealing with our fast-changing, complex world. They are able to tolerate higher levels of stress and endure setbacks while remaining engaged, open, and receptive. They understand that life isn't always easy, but they continue to act according to their most cherished values and long-term goals."[34]

The thing is, when we're rigid, we become fragile. So those shifts in life's circumstances feel like they could break us. But when we're limber and loose like a Cirque du Soleil acrobat, we can respond to those inevitable ebbs and flows with relative ease. Agile or fragile? The choice is yours.

Of course, few of us are naturals when it comes to emotional agility. Instead, it's something most of us need to cultivate. I also want to note that if you really have been badly burned by life, opening yourself up to feel your feelings can be truly daunting. I get it—that's a real and valid thing. So be patient with yourself. Take your time and if you need to, go slow. Just remember that all forward motion, no matter how plodding the pace, is progress.

Susan says that to develop emotional agility, we can start by recognizing the following three truths about our emotional lives:[35]

1. *Emotions are transient.* Emotions come and go, emerging and then disappearing just like those waves Martha Beck described. If we get stuck in an emotion, that's because we're the ones holding on to it. Instead, we can learn to relax in the face of discomfort, kind of like breathing through the pain of getting a tattoo. You acknowledge the feeling but don't amplify it. The more practiced we become with experiencing difficult emotions, the more we recognize that all emotions pass—even happiness! But

while frustration or irritation might have just pulled up to the station, don't worry, it will head out again, and joy may be on the very next train.

2. *Your emotions don't define you.* When's the last time you said or thought, "I'm angry!" (Maybe it was just a minute ago, reading what I wrote about trigger warnings.) But consider that language. The reality is that there is nothing about an instance of feeling a particular emotion that defines you. You are not angry, you are *experiencing* anger. Emotions are part of us but they are not all of us. But it sure is easy to forget that when you are "hooked" on an emotion, as David describes it.[36] When you're hooked on a feelin' and have a lot of cognitive fusion with your emotions, it's easy to adopt this idea that a feeling can define you.

   We're hooked when we blame our thoughts for our actions, when we act in counterproductive ways based on old, outgrown ideas, or when we get so fixated on being right that we don't try things that might get us out of our comfort zone. When we take our emotions too seriously, our feelings start to paint the boundaries of our lives, drawing out safe spaces and no-fly zones. Instead, treat your feelings like the mischievous toddlers they are and gently and lovingly remind them who the boss is around here. They are welcome, but they don't get to run the show.

3. *Emotions are data, not directives.* Our feelings are beautiful. Again, just like those toddlers they are, they need to be honored and seen. When they're acting up, they don't need to be locked up but understood. But feelings aren't fact. Toddlers are wonderful, but they have a limited worldview. They see things through one lens, and their truth is not *the* truth. Love them and listen to them, but don't let them make your decisions for you.

(Otherwise, you'll end up watching *Thomas & Friends* all day and eating marshmallows for dinner.) Emotions give us information, but they don't show the whole picture.

So attend to your emotions, but don't coddle them. Otherwise, your emotions can keep you stuck.

We also can learn to critically examine what that data is telling us. As Lisa Feldman Barrett explains, emotions don't arrive fully formed in our brains, they're constructed *by us* based on signals from our body. Essentially, your brain starts shouting out guesses like your body's playing charades. For instance, let's say your heart rate speeds up. Your brain notices this and shouts *Fear!* Maybe your jaw tightens slightly, to which your brain shouts *Anger!* But as Barrett points out, these are just guesses, and we shouldn't assume they're right. In fact, in some cases we can actually learn to direct our emotions by re-educating our brains about what certain body signals mean. "You can train yourself to experience your heart pounding in your chest as determination," she says.[37] That has its uses, like if you're Simone Biles stepping up to the balance beam at the Olympics, or you're in a sit-down with your boss, preparing to ask for a raise.

Feelings aren't fact. Attend to your emotions, but don't coddle them.

Instead of automatically indulging every emotion that pops up, get curious about it. Start by asking yourself: *Am I depleted, physically? Am I underslept? Have I been eating junk or drinking alcohol or lots of caffeine? Am I dehydrated?* Believe it or not, when we're physically depleted, it can pop up in our brain as frustration, anger, loneliness, and on. So, tend to those things first, *then* see how you're doing.

The investigation doesn't stop there, though. Let's say you feel lonely. That feels bad, but could it potentially have an upside, as well? To find out, try asking yourself: *What need or value is being signaled by my loneliness?* Health psychologist Kelly McGonigal says that in her view, loneliness has a massive benefit, which is that it motivates us to seek connection.[38] But if we get stuck on the feeling and fixate on how much we dislike the experience of loneliness, we don't reach out, and so we don't resolve our loneliness. We don't do the very thing it's trying to get us to do.

Artist Timothy Goodman has struggled with the intensity of his feelings but has learned that the power of his emotions actually signals his passion for life. As he writes, "I used to curse at myself and anyone who hurt me. Now I know it's my biggest blessing, to actually really care and fight for something."[39] Goodman also channels his feelings into his art, including penning a graphic novel titled *I Always Think It's Forever*, about a devastating experience of heartbreak. In it he reflects on the insights he gained from his pain, and how his life is richer because of the overall experience.

> **The goal here is to move toward what we truly value in life.**

The goal here is to move toward what we truly value in life. That's also the core aim of something called acceptance and commitment therapy (ACT): to help people have more psychological flexibility so that they can live a life that aligns with their values and longer-term goals.[40]

ACT-ing in Your Best Interests

Psychologist Steven Hayes, who helped pioneer the ACT approach, holds that psychological flexibility allows us to have a greater sense of control and enables us to find multiple alternatives and solutions to difficult life situations.[41] Psychological flexibility is most important in situations that are challenging and provoke distress. For instance, let's say you receive an email from your accountant informing you that he just received a corrected form from one of your clients and as a result, you will actually owe more money on your taxes than you thought. How do you respond?

I think some choice expletives are appropriate, but I mean after that? Do you close your computer and pretend you didn't see the message? Do you go into shutdown mode? Do you become furious with your accountant? Or do you take a deep breath and shift into solution mode? Perhaps you look for areas where you can adjust expenses to cover the additional sum? Or you ask your accountant to run the numbers just to be sure, or to double-check that you're taking all the deductions you're eligible for. Notice that in none of these scenarios does the news feel good, but in the former you're avoiding it, while in the latter, you're accepting and dealing with it.

According to Hayes, psychological flexibility involves engaging "self-regulatory strategies," where we direct our thoughts and behavior in ways that are appropriate to the situation. ACT offers six such strategies.[42]

Experiential Acceptance

Ah, is there anything more Buddhist than mindful acceptance? Seriously, though, this was a key part of Lori Deschene's work to feel all of her feels, not just the positive ones. This strategy involves (you guessed it!) *accepting* your own internal experiences so that you can engage in a behavior you value. For instance, if you're experiencing anxiety, instead of trying to ignore or diminish it, you simply let it exist alongside you. Okay, yes, I said "simply." The concept is basic, but it can take practice to execute.

Buddhist monk and teacher Mingyur Rinpoche shares that for much of his childhood, he struggled with anxious feelings.[43] "I tried so many ways to deal with my anxiety: running, playing, escaping into the nearby caves to hide. But nothing worked. In fact, I learned that aversion only makes anxiety bigger, stronger, and more solid." When he began to study as a monk, things got even worse. (Yes, even monks experience anxiety!) "Sometimes doing traditional ritual practices with drums and the long, loud horns," he says, "my throat would tighten, I couldn't breathe, I'd get dizzy. I would have to leave in the middle of the prayers." He writes:

> I decided to really let go of wanting to block, get rid of, or fight it. I would finally learn how to live with it, and to use it as support for my meditation and awareness. . . . What began to happen was that

the panic was suspended in awareness. On the surface level was panic, but beneath it was awareness, holding it.

His anxiety didn't disappear, but when he stopped resisting it, it stopped affecting him as much.

Similarly, people experiencing physical discomfort are given tools to help them disengage with their *struggle* with the pain. Such an approach is not an end in itself, but it does allow you to continue to pursue your goals in spite of negative or challenging emotions or sensations.

Defusion

Just like rendering a bomb useless, defusion keeps us from being able to detonate the thoughts that feel so threatening. The act involves not trying to change your thoughts themselves but shifting the way you relate to or interact with them. It's the old "Don't believe everything you think" idea. You don't have to let your thoughts run the show. Instead, imagine that you're a parent at a playground, sitting there observing as your thoughts go nuts. There they are swinging on the jungle gym. Now they're over there flying down the slides. Our thoughts become observed events, and just like you wouldn't let your kid be in charge, you don't have to let your thoughts dictate your behavior.

You don't have to control your environment or your experiences. And you can witness your unpleasant or uncomfortable thoughts without trying to change them. Instead, you can view them with curiosity. "Huh, that's interesting. I wonder where that came from?" As a quote attributed to psychiatrist and Holocaust survivor Viktor Frankl notes, "Between stimulus and response there is a space. In that space is our power to choose our response. In our response lies our growth and freedom."[44] While it's most likely that the humanistic psychotherapist Rollo May deserves the credit for this quote, the concept holds: By taking this observer perspective, you're helping to expand that gap—to give yourself more space to contemplate your choices.

Ongoing Nonjudgmental Contact with the Present Moment

That's a seriously catchy title, eh? Seriously, though, when we practice ongoing nonjudgmental contact with the present moment, we allow ourselves to be fully aware of our internal experience without labeling it. Whatever we're feeling right now isn't positive or negative, it just is. "I feel useless and ineffective. This moment feels challenging. I am experiencing loneliness." Okay. So be it. That doesn't mean you *are* useless and ineffective, by the way, you're simply acknowledging that you *feel* that way.[45] One of the reasons this is useful is that by not judging your thoughts, you release their power. When we judge, just like when we avoid, we attach. Instead, we want to be more like Teflon so our thoughts can keep on moving.

Self without Identification

Conceptualized Self, meet Observing Self. Remember the parent at the playground who watched their thoughts running around? That was your Observing Self. When you practice nonidentification, you hold an awareness of your Observing Self and you try to let go of your Conceptualized Self, the latter being the self you conjure when you think things like "I am boring," or "I am unlovable." What you realize in this process is that you can release your Conceptualized Self and still have a self to come home to. Releasing yourself from these ideas doesn't mean you'll just disappear. You can just let your experiences flow and observe them as they happen without investing in them. If Observing Self catches Conceptualized Self saying "I am angry!" it can offer a gentle reframe: "I'm noticing that I'm *feeling* angry."

Values

Values are like our compass; they help us navigate what direction we want to go in life and help us identify the behavior that will get us there. When we're enmeshed in experiential avoidance, we're more likely to engage in behaviors that are not consistent with our values. Let's say you value your relationship with your partner, but you're afraid of intimacy, so you avoid it. Even though you care for your partner, you repeatedly ignore their bids for connection, which causes a disconnect in the relationship. If you're willing to let your values direct your behavior, even if you still find intimacy to be uncomfortable—at least for now—you will opt to connect with your partner anyway.[46]

Committed Action

Typically, it takes time and repetition to change our outlook and our behavior over the long term. Choosing to connect with your partner once doesn't mean it will be easy or automatic to do so again the next time; it's a choice you'll have to make again, and probably again. Eventually, however, you'll reach your goal of behaving in alignment with your values.

Now, none of these self-regulatory strategies are ends in and of themselves, but they will help you develop psychological flexibility. Each of these approaches can be helpful for dealing with difficult feelings, but they still might feel a little too theoretical to put into action. So let's look at some more specific techniques to manage and even channel challenging feelings.

FEELING THE FEELS: TECHNIQUES FOR HANDLING DIFFICULT EMOTIONS

Several of the most helpful methods for dealing with challenging feelings involve softening their urgency or their hold on us, or changing our perspective. Here are a few of my favorites. (And when I say "favorites," I mean the ones that I not only think are most helpful for others but are ones I use myself. Because again, we all have trouble being with our feelings sometimes.)

Create Distance

Have you ever had that experience where you've said a word, then repeated it, then said it a dozen more times and each time, it sounds more and more ridiculous? Like, how does this even make sense? Seriously, just say "pistachio" about ten times. It's just a bunch of weird mouth sounds! Well, Buddhist meditation teacher Sharon Salzberg (who is also a dear personal friend) has an approach to our undesirable feelings that is somewhat similar. Here's my riff on it.

First, isolate the thought you're having. Let's set the bar low and simply say, "I'm uncomfortable." So, say that out loud. Now say it again. Practice lengthening the vowels and otherwise experimenting with how you utter it, kind of like a DJ playing with sounds. Notice how it's losing its original shape, and how as it transforms, it becomes harder to hold on to as a concrete thought. The more you repeat it, the more meaningless it becomes. That's not to imply that your feelings are worthless; this is simply a technique to help you create distance from them—to defuse them so you can tone down your reactivity and interact with them more productively. Or, forget the agenda and simply observe them.

Notice the gentleness and even playfulness of this technique. As Sharon Salzberg notes, "We move from constriction to expansion not by demanding that a painful emotion just simply disappear, or by straining to change its nature, but by surrounding it with spaciousness—a spaciousness infused with kindness."[47]

Make It RAIN

(Yes, I am particularly proud of this subtitle.) Most mindfulness meditation practices are designed to help us relate differently to pain. The RAIN model is one such practice. It was first developed by Michele McDonald and popularized by psychologist and meditation instructor Tara Brach:[48]

R is for Recognize: Notice the predominant emotion in your emotional landscape.

A is for Allow: Allow the experience of the emotion without trying to resist or change it.

I is for Investigate: With care and curiosity, explore the emotion. Notice how it feels in your body and whether there are any specific thoughts connected to it.

N is for Nurture: Offer yourself compassion. Whatever you are feeling is part of being human. Hold a feeling of kindness toward yourself and recognize that you are simply having a human experience.

Here we get into the space of acknowledging our feelings, including those that can make us feel like, well, a monster.

Your Beautiful Monsters

Lady Gaga isn't the only one who has beautiful monsters. Tibetan teacher Tsoknyi Rinpoche, author of *Open Heart, Open Mind: Awakening the Power of Essence Love*, shares a way of connecting to ourselves called the handshake practice.[49] He invites us to shake hands with what he calls "our beautiful monsters." A beautiful monster is a challenging emotional pattern that makes our lives and relationships more difficult. Maybe we tend to overreact when we sense criticism. We often feel ashamed and irritated by these patterns and so we resist and react to them; sometimes we hate them. Beautiful monsters may seem ugly at first, but when we heal one, it becomes beautiful.

How do we melt the ice? The warmth of our kindness toward our beautiful monsters, in the form of nonjudging, allows the softening. It's a lot like how in the face of Belle's kindness, the beast in *Beauty and the Beast* showed his own true nature. How do we face our own beautiful monsters with friendliness rather than fear?

As Tsoknyi Rinpoche says, "To actually transform, we need to make friends with our emotions."[50] The handshake practice creates a bridge between our awareness and our feelings.

Whatever feeling is there, we just feel it. When a thought arises, become aware of it and just relax into it. We don't need to make up any stories about the thoughts or feelings we experience; we simply watch them as if they're written on a billboard, and we accept them. Tsoknyi Rinpoche writes, "Come into your body. Don't look for special things, just be with what's there. No need to impress anyone, or impress me. Just be honest with yourself, be with yourself, with whatever is there. Be kind to your phenomena. Every feeling is price-less."[51]

Once you're able to just be with your beautiful monsters, they may start to relax and open up. Something magical and unexpected happens when we stop trying to fix them or make them go away. The raw emotions, the stuckness, the numbness, are not as scary as they seemed.

This practice helps you to develop a healthy relationship between your mind and your feelings. Beautiful monsters carry their own wisdom. As Tsoknyi Rinpoche explains, "Once we make friends with our beautiful monsters, then we are no longer afraid of ourselves."

Broaden Your Zone

One way to manage our reactivity or the intensity with which we respond to distressing emotions is to modulate our *window of tolerance*. This is the term that psychiatrist Dan Siegel uses to describe the zone of nervous system arousal where we can interact with our emotions thoughtfully instead of letting them take over. For people who've experienced significant trauma, that zone may be relatively small, at least at first—meaning they can't tolerate a high intensity of emotion without their nervous system shifting into survival mode. When our window is small, it doesn't take much to set us off-kilter. Suddenly, we might feel agitated, overwhelmed, fuzzy, confused, numb, or tired; these are some signs that we've gone into hypoarousal or hyperarousal. In other words, we're disconnecting in some way from the present moment, by either dropping out or amping up. This isn't intentional, but we can do some intentional work to widen our window so that we can deal with distressing emotions more effectively.

For instance, when you're starting to feel overwhelmed, stop, take a breath, and ground yourself. Orient yourself to your surroundings. Notice the sensations in your body—of your chest rising and falling with your breath, of your feet as they touch the floor, or your body as it rests in the chair. Another way to connect with your senses is to notice any smells in the air. Or look around you and notice everything you see that's the color green. Once you feel your body start to balance and regulate, you can slowly and gently revisit the emotion or the situation that prompted it.

Notice that these methods aren't about suppressing or avoiding your feelings but managing your level of arousal. Over time (and depending on your experiences, it could be a long time, but that's okay), your window will get bigger and you'll have a greater capacity to be with difficult feelings.

Experience Bothness

Mixed feelings can be among the most confusing and difficult to process. On one hand, you're delighted to start your new job, but at the exact same time you really miss your former co-workers. Both are true, but that conflict often confounds us and so we try to suppress some of our feelings in favor of the relative simplicity of a single sensation. Yet when we do this, we limit the truth of our experiences. The reality is, we can do as Susan David says and "learn to walk with fear in one hand and courage in the other. You can be brave and afraid at the same time."[52]

Susan David's language of bothness is helpful here. It's a recognition of the fact that just as more than one thing can be true at once, we can also feel conflicting feelings simultaneously, and neither is good or bad, and neither is more right or appropriate to feel than the other. They simply are. You can be happy for your friend that she's marrying someone she loves, and you can also feel sadness that you've not yet found that person. The capacity to have multiple emotional experiences at once is a beautiful aspect of the complexity of being human. As Timothy Goodman describes in *I Always Think It's Forever*, "It's a double-edged sword; that loneliness can feel yucky, but a lot of times it's when I'm the most creative, it's when I feel the most alive."[53]

Developing our bothness muscle helps us engage with life more richly and authentically. As Susan David writes, "Too often, we think that the world is a series of either/or decisions. Be bold. Choose both."[54]

Gain Some Perspective

Often we're challenged by the intensity of our emotions because we're too close to them. We're fused with them. It's like that old comedy gag when someone's got something stuck to their back and another person points it out to them. They then turn themselves literally in circles straining to see it, but they can't. One way we can view our emotions more clearly—so that we can identify those values or needs they're signaling—is to create distance from them. One method is what Susan David calls the "empty chair technique."[55]

So let's say you're feeling stuck in life. Maybe you're struggling to decide whether you should stay living where you are or move to a new city, and you just can't get clear. Imagine you're in a room where there are two chairs (you can even act this out if it's helpful by setting up two actual chairs). You are in one chair and the other is reserved for someone you know who you feel is especially wise or insightful. Maybe it's your mother, or an old boss, or your high school track coach. Imagine that person taking the seat facing you, and then you tell them about the issue you're struggling with. How would they advise you? As David says, it's funny how quickly we often come up with a response: "Oh, well they'd say I should . . ." We immediately know what a wise other would tell us, but we have trouble accessing that very same information from our own perspective.

There are many more techniques out there, and I encourage you to explore these and, to the extent it serves you, try others as well. And yet being able to simply *be* with uncomfortable emotions is not the end in itself. Ultimately, our goal is to not let our fears prevent us from living the life we want to live. We often act as though the only reason to regulate emotions is to obtain a particular emotional state. However, people may pursue a particular emotional state in service of a larger goal.

For example, an athlete may actually choose to upregulate feelings of anger or an uncomfortable desire to seek revenge in order to enhance motivation and arousal prior to competition. (Think of all the chest thumping that can happen in a locker room before a big game.) In this situation, the athlete's primary goal is not to feel particular emotions but to harness whatever emotions she believes are necessary to achieve her goal.

Extreme skier Kristen Ulmer says that in the first part of her career, she tried to suppress her fear, but that led to physical and mental burnout and even PTSD. So she switched gears and decided that instead of running from her fear, she'd try to get closer to it to understand it. As she now says, "Your relationship with fear is the most important relationship of your life because it's the relationship you have with your core self." She's learned to embrace her fear as fuel, turning it from something to conquer into a welcome companion that energizes her efforts.[56] It's similar to how Timothy Goodman uses his difficult feelings to power his creativity.

The term for what Ulmer and Goodman are doing is *harnessing*, or using distress instrumentally to stay focused, motivated, and energized while pursuing important life aims.[57] And you don't have to be an ultra-athlete to do it. For instance, if you're feeling anxious over a job interview, instead of trying to ignore the anxiety, you can simply accept it. Or, better yet, use it to help you focus. Zoom in. What are you anxious about? Maybe you feel unprepared. Great! Have a friend help you run through some possible interview questions. That won't

necessarily resolve your anxiety, but that's fine. Some amount of jit-
ters can actually help you stay focused during the interview. After
all, if you're too laid-back, you might not dial in fully and perform at
your best.

There are all kinds of creative ways we can use tough emotions to
our advantage—I challenge you to find some more!

THE BIGGEST EMOTIONAL SKILL OF ALL

So now you have a variety of concepts, frameworks, and exercises
that can help you be more psychologically flexible and emotionally
agile. And yet I've left one skill out, and it's probably the most important one of all.

When we feel uncomfortable or we're challenged by our emotions, the deepest reason often boils down to some aspect of a loss of
control. We just want things to go our way, to be predictable, and to
follow an if-then set of rules whereby we can be guaranteed a specific
outcome. Well, that ain't gonna happen. It's just not life. There will
never, ever be a point when everything is 100 percent predictable,
and to fight against that fact is a losing battle. Therefore, I believe that
the most important emotional skill of all, or perhaps the core skill, is
being able to accept the inevitable uncertainty of life.

Anxiety is one of our biggest struggles, and it often arises because we seek certainty, but certainty doesn't exist. As British philosopher Alan Watts put it, "There is a contradiction in wanting to be
perfectly secure in a universe whose very nature is momentariness
and fluidity."[58] To struggle against that fact is to create our own suffering.

I believe this excerpt from a beautiful poem from Buddhist nun
Pema Chödrön says it all:

> When there's a big disappointment,
> we don't know if that's the end of the story.
> It may just be the beginning of a great adventure.
> Life is like that . . .[59]

So leave space for the not knowing. Welcome it, even, because the very fact of an uncertain future means that your story is still being written.

The key with challenging emotions is to recognize exactly that—that they are difficult to deal with, not just for you but for all of us. Otherwise, they wouldn't be called challenging! The point is, if you're struggling, you're not alone, so try to exercise some compassion and patience with yourself. Just hang in there and keep moving forward, one baby step at a time—with patience and self-compassion—because the rewards of expanding your emotional capacity are enormous.

3

Don't Be a Victim to Your Cognitive Distortions

Don't stumble over something behind you.

—*Seneca the Younger*

will talk to Eddie *tomorrow*." I would say this to myself every single day. Eddie was a ten-year-old girl. I was a ten-year-old boy. In summer camp. I was smitten with Eddie. I would see her by the pool and start to walk over to her, and with palms and face sweating, feeling like my heart would beat out of its chest, at the last moment I'd jump awkwardly into the pool, making it look like I was clearly *not* walking over to talk to her.

When the last day of summer camp arrived, I knew it was my last chance. As I was playing tetherball by myself, I saw Eddie and her friends walking out of the mess hall. This was my moment. *You can do this, Scott!*

I look at her, trying to seem cool. Just as she's about to pass me, I blurt out, "I love you, Eddie!" with all of the heart and soul my ten-year-old self can muster. There's half a beat in which time stands still, then Eddie and her friends burst into uncontrollable laughter. Still snickering, they walk away, leaving me alone and traumatized. (And yes, *trauma* is definitely the proper word for what I experienced in this situation.)

For the next few months I couldn't stop crying. I felt mortified, rejected, and humiliated. Understandably, my parents wondered what the hell had happened at that summer camp. I was too ashamed to tell them about it. To this day, especially when the Roxette song lyrics "It must have been love, but it's over now" come on the radio, I remember the day like it was yesterday.

That's a sad story, but the truth is, almost every young boy has his own version of the Eddie experience. For most guys, they eventually learn that this is a normal part of putting yourself out there (maybe not the laughter part, but some kind of rejection). The fact is, not everyone is going to love you back. As a man, you learn that courtship is more than just blurting out "I love you!" to someone you've never actually met. It's a delicate dance that evolves over time and often starts with a simple "Hello."

Most men whose advances are rejected move on and understand that hearing "no" is a normal part of the courtship process. While most men have been low-key traumatized by approaching someone they're interested in and being turned down, it doesn't prevent them from talking to an attractive human ever again.

That's *most* guys. Then there are "incels" (short for *involuntarily celibate*), who seem to never have gotten this particular memo. Incels provide a striking example of people who embody a victim mindset because they dwell on past rejection to the point of pathology. Incels form an online subculture of men who forge a sense of identity around their perceived inability to form sexual or romantic relationships.[1] Incels provide a quintessential illustration of what happens when a victim mindset is taken to extremes. Research shows that self-identified incels show much higher scores on all four elements of a *tendency for interpersonal victimhood* compared to non-self-identified incel men, specifically:

- *Incessant need for recognition* (such as making people acknowledge that they were right to take the "black pill" truth about what women really want in a mate)

- *Moral elitism* (such as sneering about the mate preferences of women, which they see as superficial and promiscuous)

- *Lack of empathy* (such as believing that since no one else cares about their suffering, they don't need to care about the suffering of others)

- *Frequent rumination about victimization* (such as extremely heightened sensitivity to rejection and obsessing over perceived instances of being slighted)[2]

Granted, incels serve as a radical example. Yet at the same time, I believe it's important to note just how far astray cognitive distortions can lead us. Thankfully, most men never reach incel status. Still, men who've faced repeated rejection may internalize distorted thinking that lands somewhere along this continuum, such as a belief that they are unappealing or even unlovable.

The reality is that we all (not just brokenhearted men) struggle with cognitive biases, many of which can fuel a victim mindset. If we're going to become more empowered, we need to recognize and confront these biases so we can develop a more accurate perception of both ourselves and the world around us. Let's start with one of our most common foils—confirmation bias.

CONFIRMATION BIAS

Throughout our evolution, humans have developed ways of navigating the world to make it easier to make decisions when we are inundated with information. *Confirmation bias* is one such shortcut, defined as the tendency to notice, remember, and value information that supports our beliefs and disregard and devalue evidence that conflicts with our beliefs. The problem is, our beliefs themselves are often fraught with cognitive distortions or irrational patterns in our thinking.

We often then rely on faulty beliefs to make judgments about the world, others, and ourselves.[3] Consider this example from the world of sports, illustrating how our beliefs about the world influence our attitudes and our actions. It's the 2016 Olympic trials in track and field, and Brenda Martinez is in the finals of the 800-meter run—she's not just in the race, she's winning it.[4] Then, just as she takes the final turn, Martinez is tripped from behind by runner Alysia Montaño. By the time Martinez recovers, it's too late—she is out of podium contention. Now, consider how each of these athletes responded to the incident.

In the aftermath of the race, Montaño denied tripping Martinez, saying Martinez jumped out of her lane, yet the replay showed that Montaño was clearly at fault. Because of some truly unfortunate and unfair circumstances (having lost two medals because of other athletes' doping), Montaño actually came into the race with a victim mindset squarely in place. In an interview after the Olympic trials, Montaño said, "My entire professional career has been a farce, basically." Instead of acknowledging the incident (and, dare I suggest, apologizing), she denied it, then highlighted her own past misfortunes.

How did Martinez, the *actual* victim in the incident, respond? As she later told writer Brad Stulberg, "I just quickly let go of what happened . . . and got back to my routine—to focusing on all the little things I could do that would give me the best chance of running well later in the week."[5] Separately, she told a reporter, "There has been so many times in my life when I felt sorry for myself and that got me nowhere, so why waste your time doing that?"[6] Incidentally, Martinez went on to qualify for the Olympic team in the 1,500 meters.

Brenda Martinez corrected her past thinking errors and went on to create a different future for herself, and we can each do the same. (Well, maybe not the part about securing a spot on the Olympic team, but you know what I mean.) Part of it involves taking our negative automatic thoughts less seriously and questioning our widespread beliefs about life. When you do this, you free yourself from some of your own angst, frustration, shame, and neuroticism.

Piece of cake, right? Don't worry—it's totally doable. Let's start by taking a look at some of the most common cognitive distortions associated with a victim mindset.

THE COGNITIVE BIASES OF A VICTIM MINDSET

Most of us want to see ourselves as good, moral people. So when we face adverse situations, we tend to view them in a way that situates ourselves as the good (or at least not-so-bad) guy. For instance, as psychologist Rahav Gabay and her colleagues demonstrated, perpetrators often downplay the negative impact of their actions, while victims tend to do the opposite, playing up the extent to which they were affected, or painting the perpetrator's actions as senseless or immoral.[7] Whether we see ourselves as the doer or the done-to also has a big influence on how we process and remember what happened.

Gabay and her team identified four cognitive distortions that are most prevalent when we cast ourselves as the victim:[8]

Interpretation bias: There are two types of interpretation bias, the first of which involves the perceived offensiveness of a social situation. People more likely to show interpersonal victimhood tended to view both less-severe trespasses (such as someone not offering assistance) *and* more severe ones (such as someone questioning their integrity) as more severe.

The second type of interpretation bias involves anticipating slights in ambiguous situations. For instance, the researchers found that victims were more likely to assume that a new manager *whom they'd not yet met* would be less willing to assist them.

Attribution of hurtful behavior: The researchers found that the self-perceived victims were more likely to assume negative intent on the part of an offender. Also, they were likely to feel more negative emotions, which lasted for a longer period of time after the event was over.

This is consistent with findings showing that people are more hurt by a trespass if they view the offense as intentional.[9] People with a tendency for interpersonal victimhood may experience offenses more intensely because they attribute more malicious intent to the offender than those who score lower in a tendency for interpersonal victimhood.

Memory bias: Gabay and her colleagues also found that those scoring high in a tendency for interpersonal victimhood had a greater *negative memory bias*. That is, they recalled more words representing offensive behaviors and feelings of hurt (*betrayal, anger, disappointment*) and also brought to mind negative emotions more easily. These findings align with prior studies showing that rumination facilitates increased negative recall of events and recognition in different psychological situations.[10]

Forgiveness: Finally, the researchers found that those with a high tendency for interpersonal victimhood were less likely to forgive and were more likely to express a desire for revenge. Plus, they were more likely to act on that desire and engage in vengeful behavior. The researchers speculate that the victims felt a need for some kind of recognition of what happened to them. Importantly, this was mediated by perspective taking.

All of these cognitive biases have been found to exist at the collective level as well, as I'll discuss in Chapter 10.

To this list of biases, we can add these other common cognitive distortions that are highly relevant to the victim mindset.[11] I'll include examples that keep with the theme of the fear of rejection (a common fear not just for men!):*

---

* These examples were adapted from the examples I used in my book *Transcend: The New Science of Self-Actualization.*

- *Black-and-white thinking:* Viewing everything in extreme terms. *("If I get rejected by this person, I'm a total loser in life.")*

- *Catastrophizing:* Believing that the worst will happen. *("If I approach this person, I am 100 percent going to get rejected harshly and everyone will see and I will feel totally humiliated and the video of this happening will appear on Instagram somewhere and my mom will see it and . . .")*

- *False sense of helplessness:* Believing we have less power to reach an outcome than we really do. *("There's no point in approaching them anyway; I'll probably just come across as creepy.")*

- *Minimizing:* Undervaluing positive events. *("They seem interested in me, but they were probably just being nice and will ghost me later.")*

- *Personalizing:* Attributing the outcome of a situation as solely the result of one's actions or behaviors. *("They said they have a partner; they just made that up that because they're not interested in me.")*

- *Shoulding:* Thinking the way we wanted things to turn out is how they *ought* to have turned out. The legendary psychotherapist Albert Ellis called this "musturbation."[12] *("They really should have liked me, it seemed so meant to be.")*

- *Entitlement:* Expecting a particular outcome based on our status or behavior. *("I deserve for them to like me because I'm such a nice person.")*

- *Jumping to conclusions:* Feeling certain of the meaning of a situation despite little evidence to support that conclusion. *("They haven't texted me back in two days; they're avoiding me!")*

- *Overgeneralizing:* Drawing conclusions or settling on a global belief based on a single situation. *("Since I was rejected by them, I might as well never approach anyone else I'm inter-ested in ever again because I am obviously unlovable.")*

- **Mind reading:** Assuming others know what you're thinking or vice versa, despite not communicating directly. *("They should know that I'm interested in them romantically; I shouldn't have to say it.")*

- **Emotional reasoning:** Reasoning that what we feel is true, without evidence. *("I feel jealous when I see my new partner talking to other people. They must be cheating on me, or why else would I feel this way?")*

- **Discounting the positive:** Rejecting positive experiences by insisting they "don't count." Feeling that nothing is ever good enough. *("Sure, I got their number, but I'm sure they won't respond to my texts.")*

- **Outsourcing happiness:** Making external factors the ulti-mate arbiter of your happiness. *("I can't be happy in life unless I'm attractive to as many people as possible.")*

I can already hear the rebuttal from some people: "Yeah, okay, this is all well and good, but is it really catastrophizing if the worst-case scenario is true? I mean, I *do* get rejected immediately every time I talk to someone I find attractive."

I hear you. But here's the thing: With that attitude, how are you ever going to learn, grow, and improve? Relatedly, there's an implicit assumption here that you just can't handle being rejected; that it's such a terrible, horrible experience with absolutely no value. Let's say the worst-case scenario *does* happen. Are you going to be mindful and productive about it, or fall apart and give up forever?

And seriously, I want to encourage you to really, deeply question your beliefs about "the way life is." Any time we find ourselves think-ing in these terms, it should be a red flag that we're likely making at least a few sweeping generalizations that wouldn't hold up under a closer, more thoughtful analysis.

Even ideas that seem obvious are often wrong. For instance, there's a common meme that people who grow up around violence necessarily see the world as unsafe. While there is a correlation, it's far from perfect. Also, the reverse is not always true—being "privileged" doesn't mean you'll necessarily see the world through rose-colored glasses. Researchers at the University of Pennsylvania led by Nicholas Kerry and Jer Clifton examined people's beliefs about the world across multiple dimensions.[13] They fully expected that those of us who grow up with socioeconomic advantages and in relatively safe neighborhoods would have correspondingly positive worldviews, but, not so. As Kerry told *Penn Today*, having positive beliefs about the world is actually a poor predictor of privilege.[14]

Clifton explained that prior research has shown that "people who see the world as just tend to work harder, presumably because they expect good things to come from it. They tend to act nicer. They tend to be more successful, partly because they work harder and were nicer, and partly because seeing the world as just is a good ad hoc justification of the success you have."[15] But this attitude that the world is a just place? It doesn't magically appear as a result of growing up safe and financially secure. As the science shows, people from significantly disadvantaged backgrounds can have positive worldviews as well, and those beliefs can become a self-fulfilling prophecy.

One man in particular serves as a stellar example of making his positive presumptions about life into his reality. Talking to Arnold Schwarzenegger, you might think he had an easy path to becoming a top international body builder, blockbuster action hero, and governor of America's most populous state. He just set his mind to each thing, then set about accomplishing his goals. But while that formula may be simple, his path wasn't easy. Schwarzenegger didn't grow up in an idyllic home with supportive parents, but instead with an alcoholic, authoritarian father who physically abused Arnold and his brother and forced them to compete with one another to win his approval.[16]

The difference between the two Schwarzenegger brothers, as Arnold recounts, is that his older brother internalized the abuse.

"We were opposites," Arnold told the *Hollywood Reporter*. "[My brother] was more fragile. He got the same treatment and became an alcoholic and died drunk driving. What tore him down built me up. It goes back to Nietzsche: What doesn't kill you makes you stronger."[17]

If, from that quote, you get the impression that Arnold is just one of those pumped-up muscle heads who admonishes "girly men,"[18] think again. As Schwarzenegger said in his Netflix documentary, when he got into acting, he realized that he'd forcibly suppressed all of his feelings about his childhood. And though that worked to get him out of Austria and all the way to America, in order to be both a believable actor and a fully functioning human, he had to learn to acknowledge his feelings, including processing what he'd experienced.

But Schwarzenegger still refused to claim victim status. While he acknowledges the terrible abuse he and his brother experienced, he also puts it into context. His father had served in World War II on the losing side, having been brainwashed and lied to by the Nazis. Like so many men Arnold grew up around, his father was devastated by that experience, creating a country of men who were shells of their former selves. While that certainly doesn't justify abuse, that insight enables Schwarzenegger to exercise compassion toward his father and see him as a complex person (as we all are). In fact, Arnold also had many good times with his father and has applied some of his father's wisdom to his own life.

There's one particular piece of advice that Arnold has especially taken to heart: Don't be distracted by how you feel about life in any particular moment. The solution for all of it is to *be useful*.[19] "You can feel shitty, you can feel happy—the world is not going to change, so let's get going," Schwarzenegger says.[20] "You know, some people take seminars about this stuff—how do you feel better about yourself? But I always tell people, stay busy. *Be useful*." In other words, don't overthink! And one remedy for overthinking is to start seeing the world more accurately.

By now you're saying, "But how, Scott?

Don't be distracted by how you feel about life in any particular moment.

How do I learn to see the world as it is?" The good news is that there's a wonderful approach that can help us all do just that.

THINK, ACT, BE

Clinical psychologist Seth Gillihan developed a unique approach to a therapeutic modality called cognitive behavioral therapy (CBT) that integrates mindfulness.[21] He calls it "Think Act Be," and I think it's an especially effective method for identifying our biases and shifting our thinking patterns so we can see reality as it really is.* Here's how it breaks down . . .

Think

In the prior section we went through some of the most common cognitive distortions among humans. Now pick out some of the cognitive distortions that you find yourself falling subject to regularly. Ask yourself:

- When do you typically fall into these patterns?

- How do these patterns impact your sense of self-worth and sense of competence?

- How do they affect the way you view others?

- How might you prevent yourself from falling into some of these patterns in the future?

Now, let's run through the various cognitive distortions and see if you can recall a specific example of when you experienced each (understanding that there may be some that don't apply). I encourage

---

* I also discussed Seth Gillihan and CBT in my book *Transcend: The New Science of Self-Actualization*. This material is adapted from that book.

you to write down each response, noting what trap you fell into. Then ask yourself the critical questions for each distortion:

- *Black-and-white thinking:* What might the gray area be here? (*"If I get rejected by this person, might there be some alternative explanation other than 'I'm a total loser'?"*)

- *Catastrophizing:* How likely is it that this worst-case scenario will happen? What evidence do you have? Do you have a sense of agency here to improve the potential outcome? (*"If I do happen to get rejected, what can I do to ensure that I maintain my dignity and self-respect?"*)

- *False sense of hopelessness:* What could come of taking a risk here, even if the odds of success are low? (*"They may downright reject me, but what if they don't? What do I have to lose?"*)

- *Minimizing:* What could you have done to contribute to the situation? (*"What might they have liked or what might have appealed to them about me?"*)

- *Personalizing:* What could others have done to contribute to the situation? (*"They very well might have liked me, but they already have a partner. Sometimes it's just not the right timing."*)

- *Shoulding:* Is this thought rational? (*"What about the situation led me to think we 'should' be together?"*)

- *Entitlement:* Is this thought rational? (*"Does my being a nice person automatically mean that they should be attracted to me romantically? Why do I deserve this particular person in this particular instance, without them even getting a chance to get to know me? Or could there be other factors at play?"*)

- *Jumping to conclusions:* Could there be other explanations for this situation? (*"They haven't texted me back in two days;*

other than avoiding me, could they be busy? Without reception? Working?")

- **Overgeneralizing:** Is this a fair global assessment? *("Am I universally unlovable, or is there another explanation for why this did not work out?")*

- **Mind reading:** Were you clear in communicating your feelings? Are you missing critical information? *("Did I adequately express my feelings to them? How could I have been clearer in getting my message across?")*

- **Emotional reasoning:** Do your feelings accurately reflect the facts of the situation? *("Do I have factual evidence to support my feelings of jealousy? Is it possible that I am wrong here?")*

- **Discounting the positive:** Did something good happen that you're diminishing? *("Hey, I got their number, and we had a really nice exchange. I don't know if we'll end up going on a date, but that's a good start!")*

- **Outsourcing happiness:** How can you rely on your inner self for happiness in this moment? *("What do I love about myself, and how can I use my own strengths to get me through this moment?")*

This exercise was retrospective, but how might you notice when you're falling into a distortion in real time, and how can you avoid some of these patterns in the future? Be a scientist! Keep track of the evidence for and against your negative core beliefs during the course of your day. Then analyze the data. How strong is the case for your belief, really?

In time, you can build new core beliefs that are more conducive to growth. When you zero in on a concept that might be faulty (again, look for those red-flag assumptions about life), see if you can identify a more realistic belief. As Gillihan notes, "Don't worry if you have a hard time feeling like your alternative belief is true. Negative core beliefs can be persistent, and modifying them takes time and repetition."[22]

Act

Thinking about your cognitive distortions isn't all there is to it, though. Sometimes it's important to just *act*. We can get so stuck in our own heads that we avoid activities that we actually really want to engage in. According to Gillihan, there are two main reasons why we avoid activities:

1. An immediate sense of relief from dodging what we think will be difficult.

2. Not experiencing the reward from engaging in the activity, thereby further diminishing our motivation for it.

Behavioral activation allows us to break the avoidance cycle and activate alternative behaviors. Behavioral activations connect you to the things that really bring you alive—accepting that things may go wrong (yes, your worst fears may really come true) but moving forward anyway. It's a simple and highly effective way to reengage with life. The approach involves a systematic plan for building rewarding activities into your daily life. These activities help to make your days more satisfying and enjoyable, shifting your actual experience of life.

The key to behavioral activation is to lead with action. (Remember Arnold's father's advice!) There is a human tendency to wait to do the thing we want until we feel good enough, we feel motivated, we're fully prepared, yada yada. However, it's far more effective to gradually start doing the activities that bring you closer to your goals even if you don't feel like it. You heard me right: *Lead with action and let the interest in the activities follow.* Change the script! I mean, has the old script of avoidance really been working for you? Eventually, enjoyment will follow, helping the behavior become automatic. Trust me—I

The key to behavioral activation is to lead with action.

now not only go to the gym regularly, I actually look forward to it! (And—true story—sometimes I run into Arnold Schwarzenegger at Gold's Gym in Venice and I take selfies with him!)

Gillihan offers the following behavioral activation strategies[23] (which are actually quite similar to the approach Arnold takes to achieving his goals):[24]

- *Build a game plan around your goals.* The goals you set will guide the activities you choose and your activities will move you toward your goals.

- *Work progressively toward goals.* The success we find in the easier initial steps lays the foundation for more difficult— and rewarding—activities.

- *Think holistically.* The areas of our life don't just exist in isolation. As you think about activities that will help you move toward your goals, think three-dimensionally. For example, could tending to your domestic responsibilities affect your relationships? Could eating better make you a more productive worker? Progress in different areas of your life is likely to be mutually reinforcing.

Behavioral activation is one of the best-supported treatments for depression, in part because it's so simple. And yet that simplicity doesn't make it easy. There will be times when we don't complete our plans. When that happens, the number one thing to remember is to be compassionate with yourself. Remember that you're human and that this work is *hard*.

Additionally, Gillihan offers some behavioral activation strategies for working through roadblocks:

- Make sure tasks are rewarding.

- Break down big tasks.

- Plan activities for specific times so they're more easily done and repeatable.

- Make yourself accountable.

- Focus on completing one task at a time.

- Address distorted or disruptive thoughts that get in the way of doing your planned tasks, such as thoughts that minimize the feeling of accomplishment you get from completing a task or reducing the rewards you get from it.

- Track your activities.

Now on to the final phase of the process—Be!

Be

If you spend enough time observing your mind, you'll notice that it frequently focuses on things other than what's happening in the moment. Our mind is often busy ruminating about the past or planning for the future. "Thus our well-being is often affected by things that have little to do with the moment in which we find ourselves," as Gillihan notes.

Something else you'll notice about your mind is that it loves evaluating things in black-and-white terms, as either "good" or "bad." Remember that our brain is a prediction machine. If something doesn't meet our expectations, it's bad, and if it lines up with what we expect, it's good (even if the expectation is negative).

These tendencies of the mind are part of what makes us human. However, they can lead us to needless suffering and prevent us from really seeing—and experiencing—what is right in front of us. We often spend so much time resisting things in the moment that we don't like and that we can't even control—such as bad weather—that we miss out on fully experiencing all the aspects of the moment that may bring us joy or even teach us an important lesson.

According to Gillihan, the antidote to this is *mindful awareness*, of which there are two main aspects: presence and acceptance. Presence involves really showing up to the moment, intentionally cultivating a connection with your experience. It's opening your awareness to the full spectrum of the moment and intentionally observing aspects of your experience that you might ordinarily miss. Presence allows you to discover the richness of your reality, which often has the effect of dampening rumination about the past or fearing the future.

Acceptance involves really showing up to the moment no matter what is happening. Of course, we have preferences and expectations about how we *want* things to be. But that's not actually *being*. Accepting involves holding your preferences lightly, and not immediately assuming that just because the reality you're facing doesn't meet your expectations or desires, that doesn't mean it's bad. It just is.

The benefits of mindful awareness are vast (although sometimes oversold by marketers). They include greater awareness of your thoughts and feelings, better control of your emotions, an ability to give less weight to your thoughts, and decreased habitual reactivity to things in your environment that you don't like or that don't meet your expectations.

Mindful awareness can also help you become aware when you are overidentifying with your beliefs about your victimhood. You are allowed to have passing thoughts about being a victim without believing them. Yes, that's right: I just gave you permission to have a victim identity. *But hold it lightly!* In fact, the best antidote to a victim mindset is having presence and acceptance with others. The moment we witness the good in others and become motivated to bring it out of them, our preoccupations with our victim identity are forgotten, even just for a moment.

Another important benefit of mindful awareness is that it allows you a greater connection with yourself. When you're more connected with you and the reality around you, you can learn to trust yourself, trust your experiences as real and valid, and bring yourself into greater alignment. Ultimately, mindful awareness allows you to *come home.* As the legendary meditation expert Jon Kabat-Zinn points out, "Wherever you go, there you are."[25]

BRING IT ALL TOGETHER WITH MINDFUL ACTION

There are many misconceptions about mindfulness. While many people equate it with meditation, they aren't the same thing. *Mindfulness isn't just for the cushion or done with a meditation instructor.** You can cultivate mindfulness in every aspect of your life, throughout your entire day and in every interaction.

Another major misconception about mindfulness is that it's weak or passive—that it never involves you taking a stand or going after your goals. This couldn't be further from the truth. For one, letting go is often immensely difficult and involves inner strength. Releasing prior habits and self-narratives takes real determination.

Mindfulness doesn't have to be a passive awareness—it can be deeply integrated with taking action and with taking control of your life. We can go after what we want with presence and acceptance. We can be intensely mindful as we are setting goals or making plans for the future, or even while we're actually moving in the direction of our goals. Mindful action is possible.

The reality is that we spend *a lot* of energy fighting against what is, and resistance creates *a lot* of stress. Acceptance actually helps us feel **Mindful action is possible.** better, even if we don't love what's happening. While acceptance may not mean getting rid of all the things in your environment you don't like, it can help you move forward in a way that allows you to respond more appropriately to reality as it's unfolding, and ultimately be more effective in reaching your goals. Seeing reality as it is and not denying it can often be a catalyst for great positive change for ourselves and for the world.

---

* It should also be noted that research shows that meditation can sometimes be harmful and can even make existing mental health problems worse. It's important for people to be aware of the potential adverse effects of engaging in a meditation practice without proper guidance and support. See https://theconversation.com/meditation-can-be-harmful-and-can-even-make-mental-health-problems-worse-230435.

Finally, there's a misconception that mindful awareness means that you live in your head. In reality, mindful awareness allows you to stop overthinking your life! Rather than drowning in our ongoing stream of thoughts, we connect with our experiences and let go of the stories we tell ourselves, which are a major cause of our suffering.

Here are six principles you can apply to harness more mindful action in your everyday life, according to Gillihan:[26]

1. Focus your attention on your sensory experiences (sights, sounds, and so on) as well as your thoughts, feelings, and bodily sensations.

2. Be open to what is happening in the moment, allowing your experience to be as it is rather than resisting.

3. Bring a "beginner's mind" to the activity, as though it's the first time you've ever done or witnessed it. Let go of preconceived expectations of how it will be.

4. Allow the experience to take as long as it takes, rather than trying to rush through it to the next thing.

5. Notice the urge to grab on to aspects of the experience you like and push away the parts you don't.

6. Allow thoughts to come and go, recognizing that they are just thoughts. Practice neither getting lost in the thoughts nor resisting them but simply letting them flow.

When we are mindful of our many cognitive distortions, and we take mindful action toward our goals in life, we can reclaim a sense of agency and feel a greater sense of hope toward the future. We can do as my friend and colleague Steven Hayes advises: "Get out of your head and into your life."[27]

4

Don't Be a Victim
to Your Self-Esteem

No one can make you feel inferior without your consent.

—Eleanor Roosevelt

There's a popular fable that goes something like this: Once upon a time there was a small town, and in that small town was an old man. Every day, this old man would go to the local park, where he'd plop down on the bench and cross his arms, and the complaining would begin. It was too hot. It was too cold. The bench was too hard. There were too many pigeons. There were too many children. The grass was too long. You get the picture.

Not surprisingly, people would avoid the old man. They'd take a different path, or if they had to pass by him, they'd pretend to be talking on their phone. But one day, something happened. The old man was actually *smiling*. Word traveled fast and people flocked to the park to take surreptitious glimpses at the senior. Finally, one courageous soul took a seat next to him, turned to the man, and said, "Sir, can I ask you a question?"

"Certainly!" He beamed.

"Well, it's just that every other day that I've seen you, you've sat on this bench complaining. Now, suddenly, you're smiling. What happened?"

The man nodded. "Well, it's like this," he said. "For years I sat here brooding about all the reasons I wasn't happy. Then, last night as I was going to bed, I reached the end of my rope. 'I give up!' I shouted. 'I'm done! I'm not going to fixate on happiness anymore!' And this morning when I woke up, something incredible happened. I noticed the birds singing the most joyful songs. I felt the warmth of the sun as its beautiful beams tumbled across my bed. It was like the whole world had changed. And now, *I feel happy!*"

So okay—teaching parables tend to simplify some pretty complex concepts, and they don't always hold up under scrutiny. But the main takeaway here is solid: that happiness, itself, is a false target. Instead, it's the thing that happens when we're living a life that's full of meaning and we're deeply present. The same is true with love and connection. When we focus on the lack of love in our lives, we can become the type of person who actually drives others away, or we're so busy self-obsessing that we overlook opportunities to connect.

Generally speaking, the people who experience the most love and connection are those who are the least concerned with how much love others are giving them. They simply give without expectation of reciprocity, and one way or another, love finds its way back to them.[1]

Self-esteem is similar. Often we target self-esteem, wondering, "How, *oh how*, can I get others to accept me so that I can feel better about myself and get the very best partner and friends and job and house and car and *all the things*?" And yet despite our best efforts, self-esteem can feel elusive. (Or in some cases, our self-esteem is based on an inaccurate self-assessment. More on that in a minute.)

If you check out the self-help section of the bookstore, you're sure to find any number of books that will happily tell you that you are awesome, you are a badass, you are great, you are perfect and whole just the way you are. Reading these books may give you a temporary rush of pride and glee. That is, until you realize a few things.

First, if you feel a connection with their message, it may simply be because they are really good at doing something marketers call "identifying your pain points." Second, you really aren't perfect just the way you are, and chances are that you damn well know it. After all, isn't that why you're combing the virtual shelves for titles aimed at self-improvement? And isn't that why you're reading this book, because you want to improve your self and your life?

Look: Our faults and our foibles are not evidence of our failure or inadequacy but of our humanity. So it's normal and admirable to want to improve, but simply trying to enhance your self-esteem isn't what's going to get you there.

The massive number of pop psych books and psychological articles devoted to self-esteem are often laced with common assumptions:

1. People are motivated to increase their self-esteem.

2. Increasing self-esteem is a great goal in itself.

3. High self-esteem is always more desirable than low self-esteem.

4. Raising low self-esteem will necessarily improve happiness, relationships, and success.[2]

In this chapter I'll challenge all of these assumptions and offer you a more nuanced way to think about self-esteem, along with a healthier and more sustainable way to connect with it.

WHAT IS SELF-ESTEEM?

So, what does it even mean to have high self-esteem? Broadly speaking, self-esteem is about how you evaluate yourself, but it contains many aspects. For instance, here are five items that appear on the well-studied Rosenberg Self-Esteem Scale:[3]

• On the whole, I am satisfied with myself.

• I feel that I have a number of good qualities.

• I am able to do things as well as most other people.

- I feel that I'm a person of worth, at least on an equal plane with others.

- I take a positive attitude toward myself.

Whether your answers to these questions hover in the realm of "No way!" or "Heck, yeah!" or somewhere in between, that gives you a general sense of your present level of self-esteem.

Self-esteem is correlated with many important life outcomes. For instance, people who score higher on this scale tend to report more satisfying relationships, better job performance, better academic performance, and higher life satisfaction. People who score lower are more likely to experience depression and anxiety and tend to feel a lack of control over their lives. The message is clear—to unlock all the good stuff, simply increase your self-esteem!

Not so fast.

In the so-called self-esteem movement of the 1980s and 1990s, educators, parents, and even lawmakers viewed high self-esteem as a means to guarantee everything from better grades and better employee performance and productivity to lower crime rates and even less littering. And yet it backfired. *Badly.* That's perhaps because the movement wasn't really a self-esteem movement but more like a narcissism movement. People largely assumed that the way to boost others' self-esteem was through extreme amounts of praise. If you put in little effort or your efforts were off the mark, no matter! You were still heralded as the best thing since sliced bread. (And, by the way, what's really so special about sliced bread? That's a pretty low bar, if you ask me.) As research has shown, offering overabundant and indiscriminate accolades in childhood can lead to the development of grandiose narcissism.[4]

Another problem with the movement was that it was predicated on the assumption that self-esteem is the cause of positive life outcomes, but that doesn't tell the whole story. Current psychological research suggests that high self-esteem can also be thought of as the *result* of positive outcomes.[5] In other words, having high self-esteem could help us perform well at our job, but we also could have high self-esteem *because* we're performing well, which makes us feel good about ourselves and our abilities. It can be a self-reinforcing cycle (and the reverse can be true, as well, when we underperform).

There's little evidence that common interventions aimed at raising self-esteem are actually successful. Quite the opposite, in fact. Research suggests that attempts to enhance self-esteem have been linked to not only increases in narcissism but also inflated and unrealistic self-views, prejudice, and even bullying behavior.[6] When it comes to students, for instance, helping them feel worthy and competent and assisting them in actually developing their skills and abilities would be more effective at improving both their classroom outcomes *and* their self-esteem.

Since we touched on narcissism, let's take a minute to dispel some myths about the relationship between narcissism and self-esteem.

NARCISSISM: NOT JUST INSANELY HIGH SELF-ESTEEM

It's a common belief that narcissism is just a form of super-inflated self-esteem, but the two are actually quite different. The latest research supports the perspective that narcissism differs rather significantly from self-esteem in terms of how it originates, along with its consequences and outcomes.* For one, the two tend to be mirror images of one another: When we look at self-views in adolescence, it's a time when self-esteem is often at its lowest, but narcissism is at its highest.

Also, while narcissism tends to develop in part from parental overvaluation ("My little Atticus is the best kid ever and is going to change the world!"), high self-esteem tends to be an outgrowth of parental *warmth*. That means that instead of viewing your child as better than other kids, you treat them with genuine fondness and affection, and demonstrate that they matter and are worthy of love. (More on the role of parenting in self-esteem in a moment.)

---

* See here for a review of the research: Kaufman, S. B. (2024, February 20). Narcissism and self-esteem are very different. *Scientific American.* https://www.scientificamerican.com/blog /beautiful-minds/narcissism-and-self-esteem-are-very-different/.

In terms of outcomes, those scoring high in grandiose narcissism tend to demonstrate a sense of superiority to others and experience an excessive need for acclaim, while those with high self-esteem have a general sense of satisfaction with themselves, but without the superiority. Or, in the words of psychologist Carl Rogers, they have a sense that "I'm not perfect, but I'm enough."

As mentioned throughout this book, there are different forms of narcissism. The admiration the grandiose narcissist seeks—and often demands—is an attempt to stave off feelings of inferiority that would send them into vulnerable narcissist mode. Let's now take a deeper look at vulnerable narcissism.

VULNERABLE NARCISSISM
AS A SELF-PROTECTIVE STRATEGY

In a paper published in 2018 with my colleagues Brandon Weiss, Josh Miller, and W. Keith Campbell, we took a personality perspective on narcissism, taking it out of the clinical realm (meaning either you're diagnosed with clinical narcissism or you're not). Instead, we viewed it as a variable aspect of personality that we all differ on throughout our days. With that, we also took the clinical judgment out of it, considering it to be just another source of personality variation like extraversion, openness to experience, and conscientiousness. Taking this approach, I was *blown away* by what we found.[7]

For one, we found that people who scored higher on our scale of vulnerable narcissism scored significantly lower on *every single measure* of well-being we examined. I'm talking lower self-acceptance, lower life satisfaction, lower levels of authentic living, a reduced sense of autonomy, a reduced sense of mastery over one's environment, a reduced sense of personal growth, fewer positive relationships, and a reduced sense of purpose in life.

On the darker side, those scoring higher in vulnerable narcissism were more likely to feel a pervasive sense of shame in life and to avoid negative experiences (particularly experiences that may bring a feeling of anxiety); they were more likely to feel like an impostor and to feel a greater sense of alienation from their self; they experienced a weaker sense of self and were more likely to be influenced by external factors. Vulnerable narcissism was also related to a whole host of protective strategies that may insulate the vulnerable self from being hurt but ultimately stunt growth.

These were some of the statements we found most strongly correlated with vulnerable narcissism:

- "I get more satisfaction from my fantasies than from my real life."

- "I am sure I get a raw deal from life."

- "I work more things out in my daydreams than in my real life."

- "People tend to mistreat me."

- "No matter how much I complain, I never get a satisfactory response."

- "I get physically ill when things aren't going well for me."

- "Doctors never really understand what is wrong with me."

- "After I fight for my rights, I tend to apologize for my assertiveness."

- "I get openly aggressive when I feel hurt."

- "I often act impulsively when something is bothering me."

- "Sometimes I think I'm an angel and other times I think I'm a devil."

- "I'm (not) able to keep a problem out of my mind until I have time to deal with it."

If we look beneath the label *vulnerable narcissism*, we see that these are all strategies to protect the vulnerable self. People high in vulnerable narcissism tend to fear the pain of being rejected and the shame of displaying their fragility. They can become incredibly sensitive to the fact that they are not living up to their dreams, which brings them even further shame. As a result, they may engage maladaptive defense mechanisms to cope. Interestingly, it's these more hostile self-protective defense mechanisms that are particularly linked to frequently playing the victim card and having biased perceptions of people's perceived transgressions.[8]

Since our initial study, my colleagues and I have published additional papers showing similar patterns and further linking vulnerable narcissism to fear, anxiety, and depression.[9] The depression that vulnerable narcissists experience is deeply rooted in self-criticism and feelings of emptiness, uselessness, and incompetence.[10] As much as they may posture about their deservedness, inside they often feel the opposite. Afraid of letting people down and ashamed of needing others, they may self-isolate or avoid meaningful social relationships.[11] In the words of comedian Greg Giraldo, "I feel like I'm 'the piece of shit at the center of the universe.'"[12] (Sadly, Giraldo died in 2010 of an accidental overdose of prescription drugs.)

As psychologist Radosław Rogoza and his colleagues put it, "They shield their secret fragile core from their own conscious awareness and also prevent others from discovering it."[13] They often deal with their shame by engaging in grandiose fantasies of prevailing over others and winning admiration, but at the same time they frequently withdraw from social situations and challenges that might trigger feelings of shame, rejection, or envy.[14] This cycle can further exacerbate feelings of anxiety and depression. They are often fully unaware of their own deep feelings and motivations, which can make it especially difficult for them to break the cycle.

How does this come to be? Vulnerable narcissism has been linked to a history of real traumatic experiences, including emotional, verbal, physical, and sexual abuse.[15] It is often a compensation for experiences of shame and humiliation.[16] Unfortunately, such early life experiences can cause us to perceive our social value and capacities in ways that are inaccurate.[17]

Ironically, acting on these extremely miscalibrated beliefs can bring about the very outcomes we fear the most. To be sure, there is also a substantial genetic contribution to the development of vulnerable narcissism, but the point for now is that there are often very real and very powerful reasons that these beliefs and behaviors develop.

The same is true for those who do not score particularly high in vulnerable narcissism but who score high on the trait of neuroticism. While vulnerable narcissism is strongly correlated with the personality trait of neuroticism,[18] it's still possible to score high in anxiety and pervasive rumination in everyday life *without* the entitlement and hostility. Even so, these folks may have experienced challenges and adversity that have significantly impacted their anxious worldview, along with their own sense of self-worth and competence. It's all understandable.

Perhaps at some point those protective and insulating mechanisms were helpful. But if you break your leg, at some point you've got to take the cast off and start doing what you need to do to really heal. You've got to go to the mental and emotional (and perhaps somatic) version of physical therapy, so that instead of relating to life from a place of perceived weakness, you can learn to relate to it from a place of strength. And to develop that strength, we need to develop the ability to hear the truth about ourselves.

If someone scores high in vulnerable narcissism, it's likely that they actually experience an *uncertain* self-esteem—which means they're highly dependent on the acceptance and validation of others—and use narcissistic strategies to insulate themselves from feelings of low self-worth and competence. This is preventing them from discovering and accepting their full depths.

When it comes to improving our self-esteem (as opposed to our vanity), I think of it like taking a vitamin supplement. If you're severely deficient in a sense of self-worth or you constantly feel incompetent in reaching your goals, there are real consequences for health outcomes, and you would benefit from boosting your self-view. For one, low self-esteem (or more accurately, an uncertain self-esteem) is a major risk factor for depression.[19] It also becomes difficult to function as a human being in the world, meaning you will tend to second-guess things and blame the world for your problems.

On the other hand, if you already have a healthy level of self-esteem, fixating on getting more of it (rather than actually developing more competence or higher-quality relationships) can come with consequences—just like overloading on certain vitamins or minerals. We'll examine some of those consequences—along with how to actually foster healthy self-esteem—throughout this chapter. First, let's start somewhere counterintuitive: considering the *benefits* of low self-esteem.

To clarify, generally it's better to have a more positive evaluation of yourself than to go around lacking in self-respect and self-confidence. Having chronically uncertain and unstable self-esteem not only feels bad, but as I mentioned it's also associated with a host of negative outcomes. However, even those among us with the highest self-esteem will feel less enthused about ourselves from time to time, and that's not necessarily a bad thing.

THE BENEFITS OF FEELING BAD ABOUT YOURSELF

As it turns out, it's useful to have at least one person in your life who will lovingly tell you if you're being a jerk—that the reason your relationships don't work out is that you play games and you're unreliable. Or that you didn't get that promotion because you've been showing up hungover and taking afternoon naps in the supply closet. And if you don't have those folks in your life, there's always the internet. The popular "Am I the Asshole?" page on Reddit invites people to post about an event and receive a ruling from the community.[20] Or, there's Robert Sutton's "Are You a Certified Asshole?" test.[21]

I'm not seriously suggesting you lean on these sites for meaningful support, but it can be reassuring to note that for most of us, at least some of the time, *we really are the asshole*. It's useful to know when that's the case because it enables us to course correct—except that often, our relationship with shame prevents us from doing that.

Understanding Shame

Much of the modern rhetoric around shame is that shame is bad, and if we learn how to rid ourselves of shame, our lives will be better. Yet this gives shame short shrift. In the research community, so-called *attributional theories* around shame hold that we feel this emotion when we attribute a negative outcome to ourselves rather than a specific act or circumstance. Yet, that doesn't explain *why* we feel shame, especially when we have nothing to feel ashamed about. So is shame a useless feeling just like the appendix is a useless organ? Oh, except that now we know that the appendix actually seems to support the immune system.[22] So let's see if shame might serve a useful purpose, as well.

A group of researchers led by Theresa Robertson and Daniel Sznycer set out to discover just that.[23] In one study, the scientists had a group of subjects imagine that they worked at a bar waiting tables. The scenario went like this: It's the custom of the staff to pool their tips, so all of you on the shift put all of your tips in a communal box and split them at the end of the night. At some point, you realize that you need change, so you put a fifty-dollar bill in the box and take out the equivalent in smaller bills.

Then some participants were led to believe that there was a possibility that two co-workers saw them remove the small bills, but not put in the fifty. In other scenarios, it was a definite that they were seen and likely they would be believed to be stealing. It turns out that the more likely participants were to believe that their co-workers saw them, the more likely they were to experience feelings of shame, *even though they did nothing wrong.*

In a second study, participants were either kicked out of a group game or not, supposedly based on their level of contribution. In actuality, whether or not they were excluded was random. Those who'd been kicked out tended to feel shame, whether or not they'd been good teammates. But among those who were lousy teammates but allowed to continue? No shame.

These studies strongly suggest that the real trigger of shame is not about what we did or didn't do, but the prospect of failing in others' estimation. The researchers write, "The innocent can feel shame if they simply know or suspect that others view them negatively. This is because it is primarily others' beliefs—and not the facts of the matter—that determine a person's reputation and value to others." And reputation matters.

Human brains are commonly geared to be sensitive to social cues—to notice whether we seem to be out of favor with others, or whether we have a secure place in "the group" (whatever that group is). If we're excluded, we could be cut off from essential resources and that could jeopardize our (and even our family's) well-being. In ye olden days, that could have meant being kicked outside the village walls and left to fend for ourselves during the long winter. In modern times, a negative assessment could get us kicked out of the neighborhood moms' group or ejected from the pub quiz team, and we could experience a kind of social death.

Sometimes we feel shame because we acted like a jerk, and we need to save our social standing by apologizing. At other times, we did nothing wrong, but we're worried that someone else will assess us negatively and we'll lose our social standing anyway. In this theory (which if you want to geek out about it is called the *information threat theory*), that's why a person who is not culpable, such as a victim of violence, may feel shame.[24] They could be concerned that if others are aware of what happened, their social status could decline.

As social psychologist Mark Leary shared with me in an email exchange, "One of the biggest surprises of my research career has been how many negative emotions can stem from perceived or potential relational devaluation, including hurt feelings, social anxiety, embarrassment, anger, guilt, shame, fear, sadness, and dread. It shows that natural selection clearly favored things that helped us detect rejection and motivated us not to try not to lower our relational value in other people's eyes."[25]

It's worth pausing on this idea for an extra beat, as it seems to me that this could help to explain some of the value of sharing our stories. When we bring our shame-inducing experiences into the light—

whether or not we were innocent or responsible—with receptive others who then embrace us, it shores up our social standing. And not just our shame stories, but potentially any experience that we believe could cast us in a negative light with others. When we're reassured that we will not be out-grouped (at least not by everyone), we can release or at least greatly decrease our feelings of distress. This is likely one of the great values of programs such as Alcoholics Anonymous, which promise acceptance, warts and all. So, instead of letting shame make us feel isolated, we can actually use it as a lever to propel us toward a greater sense of connection and community.

The Social Protection System

Anyone who always feels good about themself no matter how other people respond is ignoring important feedback at their own risk. They're possibly deluded and are likely to behave in ways that hurt others and themselves. Evolutionary psychologists Lee Kirkpatrick and Bruce Ellis argue that the function of self-esteem is not to maintain high self-esteem.[26] Instead, they believe that the self-esteem system is a feature, not a bug. The information it's giving us, with all its praise and pain, can help protect us. It can even motivate us to be better humans across a variety of important evolutionarily evolved domains of interpersonal relationships. So instead of having a goal of experiencing high self-esteem all the time, maybe we should seek to have *healthy* self-esteem, and to do that, we should tune in to—not ignore—our social protection system.

The need for belonging—to feel accepted, respected, and valued by other people—is a deep-seated primal need.[27] But what is the need to belong, really? When we say we want to belong, rarely are we talking about a relationship with a close friend, family member, or partner. I mean, have you ever heard anyone say "I belong to my mother"? That sounds a bit strange and perhaps unhealthily possessive. As Albert Einstein once said, "I have never belonged wholeheartedly to a country, a state, nor to a circle of friends, nor even to my own family."

Instead, we tend to mean that we want to feel included in a group,

whether it's a sports team, work group, club, religion, or political organization. If we dig deeper, we see that underlying this desire is really the wish to have high social value.* We want to feel as though we
matter, or at least possess some qualities that are valued by others.

According to Mark Leary's "sociometer theory," we have evolved
a *social protection system* that continuously tracks our perceived social
value.[28] We monitor the reactions of others, looking for cues indicating disinterest, disapproval, avoidance, or outright rejection—any signal that we're not being accepted as a member of the group.[29] To be
clear, there are multiple types of social value. For instance, psychologists have distinguished between "relational social value" and "instrumental social value"—either our value to others as a friend or a
member of a family or social group, or our usefulness to society, re-
spectively. And they have different impacts on us. When we perceive
high relational value, we're more likely to like ourselves, and when
we perceive high instrumental value, we're more likely to see ourselves as competent.

Just how exquisitely sensitive is the social protection system?
Consider a series of experiments conducted by Mark Leary and his
colleagues.[30] Using four different approaches, they found the same
basic result: The relationship between perceived acceptance and self-
esteem was nonlinear. The social protection system was most sensitive to ambiguity, or being unsure of what others think of us. Also,
most people interpreted neutral reactions as negative. For instance,
when told that someone didn't care one way or the other whether
they showed up to an event, they interpreted that as rejection rather
than ambivalence. The researchers found that the curve flattened
when people received clear positive or negative feedback.

Psychologist Erica Boothby, who studies our perceptions about

---

* Mark Leary suggests that the thing that really matters here is *perceived* relational value, not
necessarily acceptance and rejection. Research shows that self-esteem is highest when people
are told they are the best member of a group and lowest when they are told they are the worst
member, *regardless of whether they are included or excluded in the group.* People seem to be far
more concerned about having low relational value than they are simply being excluded or left
out. Leary's research suggests that being included randomly in a group or, worse, being included in a group because of one's low value (e.g., to reach a quota) does little to satisfy people's
desire to belong. See Leary, M. R. (2019). The need to belong, the sociometer, and the pursuit
of relational value: Unfinished business. *Self and Identity, 20,* 126–143.

what others think of us, says that many of us actually underestimate how much other people like us.[31] In an interview on the *Hidden Brain* podcast, Boothby recalled a time when a friend introduced her to another woman that she thought Boothby would get along with. Boothby met the potential new friend for coffee and had a great time, but then she didn't hear from her. Immediately she began to second-guess herself. Maybe the "date" hadn't actually gone that well. As it turned out, Boothby and the other woman both had a great time, but each was so concerned about hearing from the other first that neither reached out. Then, when they didn't hear anything, both assumed that the other didn't like them.

It's common to react this way, but Leary and his colleagues found that those who scored low in self-esteem were *particularly* sensitive to signs of interpersonal rejection. So much so that for them, neutrality was as bad as extreme hatred! This brings to mind a particularly neurotic bunch of people: stand-up comedians. Imagine Rodney Dangerfield trying desperately to get a laugh from an audience that has their hands folded and a neutral expression on their faces. They are not outright booing, but neither are they cheering him on. This uncertainty tends to drive stand-up comedians absolutely bonkers. In the classic words of Dangerfield, "I get no respect." In fact, he once said in an interview, "I got no respect the day I was born!"[32]

On psychological surveys (which presumably did not include Rodney Dangerfield), people rarely report having *zero* social value.[33] Most people score either high in self-esteem or somewhere in the middle, suggesting that people who have traditionally been characterized as having "low self-esteem" probably really have a highly *uncertain* self-esteem that is highly dependent on validation from others. People with uncertain self-esteem respond strongly to perceived slights and can even become addicted to validation.

ADDICTED TO SELF-ESTEEM

Your phone pings and you reach for it to find that you've got notifications on Meta and X (or whatever they are called now). You tap on them to find that the post you shared this morning has already garnered a bunch of likes and shares. Jackpot! You feel the familiar thrill, that special mix of excitement and satisfaction, wash over you. Does this make you weak-minded or a narcissist? Not at all. The intoxicating effect of having our esteem bolstered by others is totally human. It's normal to feel pumped when you receive praise. However, it's possible to become addicted (in the actual sense of the word) to esteem provided by others, and also to become preoccupied with avoiding any negative feedback that could cause hurt feelings. When your decisions are focused mostly or entirely on maintaining your self-esteem, that's an indication that something has gone wrong.[34]

In her online essay "High on Compliments: What It Feels Like to Be Addicted to Validation," Zara Barrie describes her young-adult self as neither a brain nor a misfit.[35] Instead, she was the worst thing you could be (at least in her eyes): mediocre. "When you're deemed not particularly *good* or particularly *bad*, you're loudly ignored. . . . I wasn't being validated, therefore, I didn't exist." Her solution? To start doing absolutely everything she could to gain approval from others. Barrie describes the rush she felt at gaining her peers' attention, and from there she was hooked. Most of us engage in some amount of validation-seeking (especially if we hang out on social media, which often encourages and rewards this behavior), but Barrie adopted it as a lifestyle. From that point on, her decisions were guided less by any kind of internal compass and more by what would garner approval.

Research shows that developmentally, a secure and supportive home life tends to set us up for healthy self-esteem later, yet any of us can become addicted to self-esteem—pursuing ever greater doses of validation from others to keep the high going. In line with what Barrie describes, social psychologists Roy Baumeister and Kathleen Vohs argue that narcissism is an addiction to the feeling of self-esteem, not unlike other, more familiar addictions (such as to cocaine or gambling) in which appetites are indulged to destructive extremes.[36]

When things are going well and people feel like royalty in the social status hierarchy, the rush of pride and excitement floods in.

However, over time, it's harder and harder to experience that high. That's when people seek even greater glories, looking for reassurance of their superiority, and this can lead to grandiose narcissism. But their sense of self is a house of cards, and when it falls, they can experience episodes of withdrawal, shame, or depression. That's when vulnerable narcissism can flood in, causing a preoccupation with social validation and acceptance. Their social protection system sounds the alarm, causing them to feel extremely vulnerable. But rather than recognize that perhaps it's time for a little self-awareness, once the deep despair and feelings of unworthiness subside, the craving for that buzz of inflated self-esteem comes roaring back and the cycle begins again. So we could draw a distinction that for those who score high in grandiose narcissism—or more precisely, those in the grandiose phase—the addiction is to praise, while for those in the vulnerable phase, it's to social acceptance.

For Barrie's part, she had a reckoning when, during the process of a breakup, a partner told her, "You know what, Zara, no amount of compliments in the world will ever be enough for you." To her credit, she took the words to heart. "It was true," she writes. "Even an everlasting stream of compliments couldn't fill the empty pit of my addiction. I had sorely mistaken validation for self-esteem."

Again, whether or not we become a praise or acceptance addict versus someone with healthy self-esteem can be influenced, at least in part, by early childhood experiences. In his seminal book *The Six Pillars of Self-Esteem*, Nathaniel Branden describes the importance of "psychological visibility"—feeling seen and understood—for a child's healthy development of self-esteem.[37] If a child comes home from school obviously upset and says, "Susie didn't want to play with me at recess," how a caregiver responds can make a significant impact. If they acknowledge the child's experience by saying something like "That must have been tough," the child feels seen and acknowledged. But if the caregiver says something like "Well, that's life!" or "Why do you care about Susie, anyway? She's kind of a brat," that can lead to the child feeling invisible, like their experience or how they felt about it didn't matter. Or, consider a child who enjoys taking leading roles—like, they love to play school, and they're always the teacher. One day a parent tells them to "Stop being so bossy!" Suddenly, they may feel ashamed and as if they should suppress their behavior.

As Branden notes, "When we convey love, appreciation, empathy, acceptance, respect, we make a child visible. When we convey indifference, scorn, condemnation, ridicule, we drive the child's self into the lonely underground of invisibility." This can cause us to develop a social protection system that is hypervigilant to signs of acceptance and rejection. There are many benefits of feeling a sense that we matter to others, including higher well-being, life satisfaction, purpose, meaning, and social connectedness.[38] However, it's possible to become too preoccupied with the feeling of mattering and lose sight of the importance of also *giving back to the world*.[39] Branden writes:

> *If we are to love effectively—whether the object is our child, our mate, or a friend—the ability to provide the experience of visibility is essential. This presupposes the ability to see. And this presupposes the exercise of consciousness. And in giving this to our child—visibility, consciousness—we model a practice that he or she may learn to emulate.*

Let's zoom in on the preoccupation with social acceptance for a moment. Psychologist Gordon Flett and his colleagues have studied individuals who chronically feel as though they're not being seen, heard, or valued by others.[40] They created a scale to measure this trait and called it the "anti-mattering" scale. To be clear, here we're not talking about the Stephen Hawking type of anti-matter, but rather the social experience. Their scale was inspired by Paul Dirac, who originated the modern theory of anti-matter. Throughout his own childhood and adolescence, Dirac was subjected to his father's mistreatment and lack of warmth in ways that would foster his own feelings of not mattering.[41] Here are the items on the anti-mattering scale:

Anti-Mattering Scale

1. How much do you feel like you don't matter?

2. How often have you been treated in a way that makes you feel like you are insignificant?

3. To what extent have you been made to feel like you are invisible?

4. How much do you feel like you will never matter to certain people?

5. How often have you been made to feel by someone that they don't care what you think or what you have to say?

University students with high anti-mattering scores tended to report that they liked themselves less and felt a lower sense of general competence in their lives.[42] Plus, anti-mattering was linked to a "validation seeking orientation" centered on the need to prove oneself to others.

In a follow-up study, psychologist Flett and his team administered measures of narcissism along with their anti-mattering scale. While there was a significant correlation between anti-mattering and narcissistic grandiosity, the researchers found an even stronger connection between anti-mattering and our old friend vulnerable narcissism. They also found a significant association between anti-mattering and *entitlement rage*, or "intense anger, aggression, or passive-aggression when a narcissist experiences a setback or disappointment that shatters his (or her) illusions of grandiosity, entitlement, and superiority, and triggers inner inadequacy, shame, and vulnerability."[43]

Again, from the addiction perspective, it seems that while those scoring high in grandiose narcissism are primarily addicted to the rush of admiration and acclaim for their greatness, those scoring high in vulnerable narcissism are more preoccupied with feelings of not mattering. They tend to avoid negative feedback about themselves, believing that they're too fragile to handle it. Either way, the research suggests that when we obsessively fear others' assessments, it has a drastic effect on our mental health, well-being, and happiness.

Do You Have FOPO?

It's perfectly normal to care about other people's opinions, but fearing them can actually stunt our growth and development. My friend the sports psychologist Michael Gervais coined the term FOPO, for *fear of people's opinions*.[44] According to Gervais, "FOPO is an *anticipatory* mechanism that involves psychological, physiological, and physical activation to avoiding rejection and fostering interpersonal connection." FOPO is a "preemptive process" that is characterized by hypervigilant social readiness, relentless checking and scanning in search of approval, and an overvaluing of what others might be thinking. FOPO is the social protection system in overdrive.

FOPO is exhausting! We're so busy second-guessing ourselves and obsessively scanning for cues as to what we think others are thinking about us that we fail to be truly present. Our relationships can suffer as a result, sadly creating a self-fulfilling prophecy.

Gervais describes the "FOPO loop." Check out the main components of the cycle and see if they resonate.

THE FOPO LOOP

Anticipation Phase: You become preoccupied with the likelihood of acceptance or rejection. Like a war games computer on steroids, you run endless simulations in your mind, playing out scenarios and predicting how the other person will feel about you in each case. This differs from simply being a thoughtful communicator in that the focus is on anticipating acceptance or rejection, not fostering a healthy intimate connection with another person.*

---

* As Gervais notes, the "persistent rumination of FOPO pulls resources away from being able to sustain deep focus on the task at hand (required for growth and improvement), inhibits our ability to take in new information and ideas, and creates a tax on human energy, which in return necessitates even greater recovery."

Checking Phase: This phase occurs during a social interaction, when you continuously scan for real-time cues of acceptance or rejection. These cues could include tone of voice, body language, and other nonverbal cues. According to Gervais, such a focus on cues increases the chance that you'll miss important aspects of the interaction, limiting possibilities for deeper engagement and connection. "Attention is a zero-sum game," he notes. "The time you spend checking in is time diverted away from the actual experience." (For examples, see the incessant scanning behavior of every lead character in every episode of *Sex and the City*.)

Responding Phase: In this last phase, we evaluate our status. "Am I good? Do I feel accepted, seen, and respected?" According to Gervais, if the answer is yes, the FOPO cycle ends (that is, until the next interaction). If the answer is no or "I'm not sure," you're likely to respond by taking any number of actions to fit in, such as contorting your own beliefs and values (sacrificing your authentic expression on the altar of approval), conforming to the perceived social norms of the group, or initiating conflict. Or you may have a healthier response, such as turning inward to gauge your reaction based on your own values and standards. In this way, you can actually use FOPO as a cue that you need to invest in more self-discovery, build psychological skills, and focus more on who *you* want to be, versus who you think *they* want you to be.

Gervais notes that a common "on-ramp" to FOPO is a poor sense of self, which can prompt us to look outward for validation. Another is having a "performance-based identity," where your sense of self is defined by your performance as judged by external standards. But what about the *off-ramps* to FOPO? And how do we not just let go of FOPO but stop chasing self-esteem altogether and focus instead on what will truly improve our lives (and, ironically, ultimately our self-esteem)?

The good news is that while it can be challenging to shift away from obsessive external validation and stabilize your self-esteem, it is possible, and the benefits are boundless.

STOP PLAYING THE VALIDATION GAME: DEVELOP A DEEPER SENSE OF SELF

When Zara Barrie realized that her ex was right—that no amount of compliments or reassurances could satisfy her need for validation—she started her rehabilitation by examining what would make her proud of herself. For years, she'd taken on pursuits merely because of their potential for praise. Instead, she asked herself what *she* genuinely wanted to do. As she describes it, "I started to write, and act and help my friends sort through their problems. I discovered my love for design and my untapped talent for helping others. I started to understand that while it feels undeniably good to be recognized for what I invest my energy into, that can't be the lone reason I do it." She says that compliments are icing on the cake, but "the cake is good by itself, too."

That's the good news: When we invest in cultivating and nurturing our own deep sense of worth, we get to have our cake and eat it, too. Sometimes there's frosting, sometimes not. But either way, *cake*! And one of the ways we can deal with that lack of icing is by developing our tolerance for being disliked, which enables us to function in the absence of others' approval.

Have the Courage to Be Disliked

So here's something interesting: Nothing in the sociometer theory suggests that we have to actually *respond* to our emotions. Of course, we want to experience acceptance and belonging, but we don't want to be beholden to those motivations, as deep as they are. Sometimes, we want to be able to tell our overactive monitoring system to *Chill out, already!*

Consider eating as an analogy. We have systems that motivate us to eat, especially when food is present, but we often consciously decide to ignore those urges, knowing that we'll be better off in the long run (unless the food that's present is sour cream and onion potato chips, because seriously, who can say no to all of that crunchy, salty goodness?). The same is true of the systems that motivate the desire for acceptance and belonging. Both systems are also biased to overrespond. This might have been an evolutionary advantage seven million years ago, when we never knew when we might find food again. But today, relatively speaking, most of us have easy access to food, so the challenge is to control what we eat. Socially, the majority of us can experience dozens of interactions every day that really don't matter (at least in terms of our survival), so we have to control our urge to be valued and liked by *everyone*.

Understanding that we're sensitive to social threats doesn't mean we should try to forever live in someone else's comfort zone so that our meter never buzzes. That's not only incredibly restrictive, it's essentially impossible. Instead, we can say to ourselves, "Okay, I'm going to go against the group and that's not going to feel good, but it's worth it because this action is in line with my values." Or you could go all out and do what artist Pilvi Takala does and actually seek out awkward experiences.[45] Like the time Takala dressed up as Snow White and went to Disneyland, knowing that, ironically, it's verboten to show up there looking like a double for a Disney princess. As anticipated, she had an uncomfortable encounter with the security guard, who asked her to leave—uncomfortable for the guard, that is. Takala was unfazed. As she describes it, her work is designed to "stress test the conventions and codes that govern our daily interactions."

You don't have to go to those lengths, but you could dip your toe in the pool by exposing yourself to some form of lower-level awkwardness. For instance, when you go to the family reunion and your aunt Bernice asks how you like her infamous ambrosia, you could be honest and say that it's not your cup of tea.

Indeed, the hallmark of a self-actualizing person may be the ability to strive for a purpose that will make you unpopular with lots of people in your environment, particularly if that environment is unhealthy, hostile, or dangerous.[46] As the humanistic philosopher Erich Fromm noted, to be sane in an insane society is itself a marker of insanity![47]

In the book *The Courage to Be Disliked*, Ichiro Kishimi and Fumitake Koga draw directly on the writings of psychoanalyst Alfred Adler to argue that the greatest freedom in life comes when you have the courage to move forward with your goals without fearing what others think.[48] One character in the book (the "philosopher") argues that even if a person doesn't think well of you, that is their issue (or "life task"), which you must not attempt to control or change. Now, this doesn't mean you set out to be disliked, but you don't intensely fear it either. And there's also the possibility that others will simply disagree with you but not cast you out. That is, if you're hanging with other self-actualizing folks.

Think of it this way: The more you say what you truly believe and take a stand against things you don't like, the more you are actualizing *yourself*. The fact that you're disliked by some is a sign that you're willing to risk social disapproval if it means you're being you. As the philosopher in the book asks, "When one is tied to the desire for recognition, the interpersonal relationship cards will always stay in the hands of other people. Does one entrust the cards of life to another person, or hold on to them oneself?"

Another caveat here: When people disapprove of your actions, it's not a bad thing to institute a gut check and consider what their issues are. As my colleague Mark Leary told me, the trick is to find the sweet spot—to care when it matters but not care when it doesn't, and to be comfortable with the gray area of uncertainty. (Or at least not too uncomfortable.) And it's okay to lean more toward overcaring than undercaring. If we're imbalanced, that's the direction we want to go. Yet the more you can practice being comfortable with being disliked or not agreed with, or at least learn to tolerate it, the more you can learn to trust yourself. You can train yourself to keep moving forward so that others' opinions won't present an obstacle to your growth.

ESCAPE THE CONTINGENCY TRAP

While most of us care about what other people think more than is healthy or beneficial, we all differ in terms of where we're most sensitive to feedback. Fashion models may be exceptionally sensitive to feedback about their physical attractiveness, whereas statistical modelers may be much more attuned to feedback from academic reviewers. There are so many ways we can be accepted or rejected in society. From an evolutionary perspective, it wouldn't make sense that we would only garner our self-esteem from one domain of life.

Jennifer Crocker and her colleagues have been studying "contingencies of self-worth"—domains in which people believe they need to be seen as competent in order to have value as a person.[49] They've found that there are a variety of areas in which people invest their self-esteem, including appearance, others' approval, outperforming others, academic achievement, family support, virtue, and religious faith or God's love.

Expanding the picture, Geoff MacDonald and his colleagues found that having high self-esteem involves more than simply believing that you possess positive characteristics.[50] In most domains they studied, the highest self-esteem was reported by individuals who not only viewed themselves positively in the domain but also believed that the domain had important ramifications for winning others' approval or avoiding disapproval. In other words, "I'm a good-looking son of a bitch, and that matters!" In another context, more value could be placed on intelligence or academic achievement. Like, no matter how symmetrical your features or perfect your teeth, that's probably not going to get you hired as an astrophysicist (unless Louis Vuitton opens a space lab).

Interestingly, the strongest effects on average were found for competence/achievement, attractiveness, and wealth, and the weakest effect was for sociability. When an individual comes across as extraordinarily competent, attractive, or wealthy, they are likely to garner more attention and acclaim, whereas society just expects all its members to be reasonably sociable as a basic element of interacting with each other. In a classic scene from the movie *When Harry Met Sally*, the main character Harry Burns sets his friend Jess up on a blind date with his friend Sally.[51] Harry describes Sally by saying she has a "good personality." Jess stops in his tracks and turns to Harry. "When someone's not that attractive," he exclaims, "they're always described as having a good personality!" Harry counters, saying someone could have a good personality and be attractive or not. "So which one is she?" Jess presses.

"Attractive!" Harry responds.

"But not beautiful, right?" Jess retorts.

Going back to our addiction model of self-esteem, this may explain why people who score high in grandiose narcissism are addicted to "*#winning!*" and displaying signs of grandiose wealth and social status, and aren't as concerned with appearing as nice, sociable people. The rewards for the self-esteem system are greater in domains where acclaim and praise are given out to people in much larger doses.

And what about when that praise is withdrawn, or you're no longer in the spotlight? Whether you score high in narcissism or not, deriving your sense of self from external validation can make it much more difficult to adjust when life changes track. To be clear, there's nothing wrong with dedicating yourself to a passion; just beware how heavily you rely on it for your self-esteem.

While it's sensible to listen to the feedback of others (especially from people you value), the late psychologist Michael Kernis found that people who have what he described as *fragile self-esteem* tend to have a whole host of issues.[52] For one, they tend to have a *hostile attributional bias*—they assume that any ambiguous or even slightly negative social interactions have malicious intent. This bias makes it difficult for people with fragile self-esteem to form and sustain healthy relationships. This group is also likely to engage in maladaptive strategies for emotional regulation, being more emotionally volatile and less open to understanding the impact of their emotional reactions on others.

Another challenge of having your self-esteem be too contingent on external validation is that it can lead to lower effort and even a victim mindset. For instance, students who base their self-esteem on their academic accomplishments typically have self-validation goals, viewing homework as a way to demonstrate their intelligence. Because failure threatens their self-esteem, if they do fail, they're more likely to make excuses or blame others.*

Look, it's perfectly normal to feel a momentary sense of *I'm a loser!* when you fail at something. But there's no logical reason you should generalize a setback in one area to an evaluation of your entire being. I mean yes, getting a divorce, getting fired from your job, or not passing a driver's exam may be hard and may temporarily lower your evaluation of yourself. But remember: *This is only one domain of life.* It's not a universal proclamation.

Additionally, all success is built on failure. Having a path where everything is smooth sailing doesn't mean you're amazing, it simply means you've never been challenged. When you do meet real obstacles or adversity—because no one gets through life without it— you'll be more likely to crumble if your sense of value and worth is predicated on ease. It's similar with approval. If you've only ever gone with the group, it can get harder to stand your ground when the group eventually takes actions or adopts beliefs with which you don't agree.

So how can you get out of the contingency trap? One solution may be to replace self-validation goals with learning goals.

Shift Your Goals

In their book *The Passion Paradox: A Guide to Going All In, Finding Success, and Discovering the Benefits of an Unbalanced Life,* authors Brad

---

* Other research shows that the pursuit of self-esteem in an attempt to prove that one is a success can be very costly—including costs to learning, costs to autonomy, costs to relationships, costs to mental health, and costs to physical health. See Crocker, J., & Park, L. E. (2004). The costly pursuit of self-esteem. *Psychological Bulletin, 130,* 392–414.

Stulberg and Steve Magness praise the value of learning goals and having a *mastery mindset*.[53] "Individuals on the path of mastery are driven from within," they write. "Their primary motivation isn't external measures of success or fear, and it's certainly not satisfying others or conforming to a certain peer group or social norms." Instead, they're motivated by an internal desire to improve. There's no award that mastery confers (though you may happen to be recognized along the way)—we're simply seeking to do something as well as we can. Think about it: An athlete who's seeking external validation is only as good as their last victory, but one who seeks mastery can win every single day, simply by getting a bit better than the day before.

Another healthy alternative is to adopt goals that are good for you *and others*. Instead of focusing on winning at something in order to get a personal self-esteem boost, focus on how success in your goals will help others or make the world a better place.

Helping people identify where they've invested in their self-esteem and how this investment may be creating costs to their relationships, learning, feelings of autonomy, and ability to accomplish their goals is a crucial step in making this motivation shift.

Self-Check: Where Does Your Self-Esteem Come From?

If you're not sure the extent to which your sense of self comes more from external validation or an internal sense of self-worth, consider these questions:

- When do I feel good about myself? What makes my sense of self-worth increase?

- When do I feel bad about myself? What makes my sense of self-worth drop?

- How much does my sense of self-esteem change? Does it fluctuate often or is it relatively stable?

- Do I have a sense that at my core, I am worthy of love and belonging? Or do I look to others to indicate to me whether I'm worthy?

- What aspects of my identity make me appealing to others?

- What aspects of my identity make me appealing to myself?

Again, it's unreasonable to think we're not supposed to care how anyone else sees us, and it's not healthy. And it's normal for our self-esteem to fluctuate somewhat depending on our circumstances. But at our core, we want to have a sense that we're worthy of love and belonging, and that we matter.

It's also important to recognize that it may not always be necessary to immediately get out of the contingency trap. When you're feeling low self-esteem, it's worth reflecting on whether there is important information that people are telling you that can help you grow. If you're feeling low self-esteem because you're not receiving the validation you want from others, maybe reflect on what skills you could improve—not solely because you want to please others but because it could make you a better person and lead to genuine improvements in your life.

Consider the Value of the Feedback You Receive

A while back, I came across a great reframe courtesy of Mel Robbins. Instead of asking ourselves, "Why is this happening to me?," which is a question rooted in a victim mindset, we can ask ourselves, "Why the f*ck am I allowing this in my life?"[54] The latter invokes our personal agency, and we can apply that approach to how we assign value to the feedback we receive, sorting out what we'll accept and what we won't.

For starters, it's essential to recognize that the sociometer doesn't seem to care where our relational value comes from. For instance, you might receive tremendous approval from your group for racist behavior if your group is a bunch of white nationalists. That's obviously not a good thing. So we need to apply some sense of our own morality, ethics, and logic about when the group is giving us useful feedback and when they're perpetuating maladaptive (or just plain shitty) behavior.

As Mark Leary told me, it's also okay to derive some of our sense of worth from other people's feedback. "People should probably feel good about themselves when they behave in desirable ways that increase their relational value—by being kind and helpful, being successful at important pursuits, improving other people's quality of life (through work, entertainment, being funny), and so on. But they probably shouldn't feel good about themselves if they're accepted or validated for being a bully, gang member, or drug dealer."[55]

So it can be a valuable exercise to get clear about whose opinions matter and whose hold less value to you. Sometimes it's worth reflecting: Do I even *care* what this person thinks? I know you're getting hung up on whether someone likes you, but *do you even like them*? I know people who are so desperate for validation that they'll say or do anything to receive approval from certain people even if they really don't like or respect them.

When you receive some form of feedback from others, whether positive or negative, run it through your *feedback filter*. Practice parsing out the value of that feedback so you can make a conscious choice about how you let it affect you, or what action you take (or not) as a result. Here's an example. Let's say you have a problem being on time for dates, appointments, meetings—pretty much everything. You receive feedback about this through a variety of channels. A friend is annoyed when you slide into the movie theater twenty minutes after the show starts. When you rush in thirty minutes late, the doctor's office tells you that you've forfeited your appointment. And your boss brings your tardiness up on your performance review. Now, you could choose to ignore all of this, or you could recognize two things. First, your behavior is negatively impacting your life. Second, it's also negatively impacting others. So you decide to change it.

Fast-forward two months and you're doing amazing with your

new commitment to being on time. Plus, you're getting lots of positive feedback on your promptness, consistency, and general nonflakiness. Then a friend asks you to be their plus-one at a wedding the following weekend. You want to say yes, but you've got another commitment that morning, and you're not sure you can get back and be ready on time, so you decline. Now your friend is annoyed with you because they really wanted you to come. What do you do with *that* feedback? Do you take the action that will garner her approval, but violate your vow to manage your schedule effectively and not overpromise? This might be a case where your commitment to yourself is worth overriding the signal you're getting from your sociometer.

Inherent in the feedback filter is determining what we value about ourselves. If you'd have gone along with your friend, you might have procured her validation, but your self-esteem would have suffered. At least, it would if you valued promptness and loyalty over others' approval. Still, it doesn't feel great when our choices meet with others' ire. That's one reason self-compassion is an essential practice for cultivating and maintaining healthy self-esteem.

Be Kind to Yourself

In her book *Fierce Self-Compassion*, psychologist Kristin Neff argues that many of the tactics we use to bolster self-esteem can have a downside—such as raising ourselves up by putting down others; judging our own worthiness by arbitrary standards that we set for ourselves, which leads to distorted self-perceptions; and displaying prejudice and even violence toward people who threaten our ego.

Neff argues that there's another, more effective way of positively relating to ourselves that doesn't involve self-evaluations, social comparisons, or judgments: *self-compassion*. Her research, spanning many years, has demonstrated that self-compassion offers most of the benefits of high self-esteem, with fewer downsides.[56] Whereas self-esteem is a positive evaluation of self-worth, according to Neff, "self-compassion is a way of relating to the ever-changing experience of who we are with kindness and acceptance—especially when we fail or feel inadequate."[57] She says that self-compassion has three main components:

1. *Self-kindness versus self-judgment:* The tendency to be caring and understanding with oneself rather than being harshly critical or judgmental.

2. *A sense of common humanity versus isolation:* The recognition that all humans are imperfect, fail, and make mistakes.

3. *Mindfulness versus overidentification:* Being aware of one's present-moment experience in a clear and balanced manner so that you neither ignore nor ruminate on disliked aspects of yourself or your life.

To be clear: Self-compassion isn't about letting ourselves off the hook. In fact, research shows that when we demonstrate genuine caring for ourselves, we're actually *more* motivated to change. According to Neff, because self-compassionate people aren't cruel to themselves when they face a setback, they're more able to admit mistakes, modify unproductive behaviors, take on new challenges, and take responsibility for their behavior. They're also motivated to learn and grow for intrinsic reasons, not because they're desperate for approval.

Research also shows that self-compassion is associated with health-promoting behaviors such as reduced smoking, healthy diet and exercise, seeking medical care, increased physical activity, safe sex, and less bedtime procrastination.[58] And it's linked with more noncontingent and stable feelings of self-worth over time, while also offering stronger protection against social comparisons, public self-consciousness, self-rumination, anger, and closed-mindedness.[59]

In his seminal book *Toward a Psychology of Being*, humanistic psychologist Abraham Maslow argues that emotional maturity entails fostering nonjudgmental, forgiving, loving acceptance of oneself and others.[60] As Neff notes, "Self-compassion epitomizes this way of being." The self-compassionate way of being is there for us even through the inevitable hardships of life, and especially when we feel as though we don't matter or are not accepted by others. Neff observes that self-compassion allows us to be fully human:

> We give up trying to be perfect or lead an ideal life, and instead focus on caring for ourselves in every situation. I may have just missed my deadline or said something foolish or made a poor decision, and my self-esteem may have taken a big hit, but if I'm kind and understanding toward myself in those moments, I've succeeded. When we can accept ourselves as we are, giving ourselves support and love, then we've achieved our goal. It's a box that can always be checked, no matter what.

The Center for Mindful Self-Compassion offers a variety of exercises and meditations to help you engage in self-directed kindness.* This includes programs to help people develop self-compassion in conjunction with mindfulness. While this training can be extremely helpful, you can also just keep it simple. Research has shown that "informal practices such as putting one's hand on one's heart and speaking kindly to oneself in times of struggle were just as impactful in learning self-compassion as formal meditation practice."[61]

When we've learned to employ self-compassion, we feel more secure and able to evaluate ourselves more honestly. And that's exactly the vantage point we need to get real with ourselves about our impostorism.

Stop Being an Impostor

Once, over dinner, I was chatting with an author and journalist who was so frustrated that he hadn't won the Nobel Prize yet. He felt that his books have made a such an impact on science that he deserves the prize. (Far be it for me to point out that he had no scientific training

---

* Visit http://www.centerformsc.org for self-compassion resources.

whatsoever and didn't have a degree in a science field.) Yet at one point in the conversation, his tone softened, and he said, "But I'm going to be honest with you, Scott—I often feel like such an impostor." It took everything in me not to respond *That's because you are!*

These days, we hear a lot about the *impostor phenomenon*, which is characterized by the belief that though others may see you as competent, secretly you experience feelings of inadequacy. (You may be familiar with the colloquial term *impostor syndrome*. I use *impostor phenomenon* and *impostorism* here because these are the scientific terms. Clinically speaking, impostorism is not a syndrome.) People often describe feeling like a fraud and fearing they'll be found out.[62]

Make no mistake, impostor phenomenon is a real experience, and it's quite common (especially when we're starting out in a new job or have a run of good luck in which things go remarkably well for reasons that seem to have little to do with us). Even the much-revered Michelle Obama has described feelings of impostorism.[63] Rory McElwee and Tricia Yurak looked at the phenomenology of the impostor phenomenon and found that these types of feelings resonate with virtually everyone. Negative emotions are a common reaction when we genuinely feel that our abilities are being overestimated.[64] However, some people report a *chronic* sense of impostorism, and research on that has revealed some surprising findings.

Read through the following statements and see how much you agree with them (they're adapted from the Clance Impostor Phenomenon Scale):

- I'm afraid that people who are important to me may find out that I'm not as capable as they think I am.

- When people praise me for something I've accomplished, I'm afraid I won't be able to live up to their expectations in the future.

- I sometimes think I obtained my present position or success because I happened to be in the right place at the right time.

- I tend to remember the incidents when I have not done my best more than those times I have done my best.

- Sometimes I'm afraid that people will discover how much knowledge or ability I really lack.

Those who score high on this scale tend to have low self-esteem and frequently experience negative emotions, such as anxiety and fear. No surprises so far.

However, researchers keep finding something very puzzling. People who tend to experience chronic impostorism *don't necessarily actually believe* that others think more highly of them than they think of themselves.[65] Instead, the research suggests that people who score high in ongoing impostorism tend to view their own capacities negatively and also tend to think that others think poorly of them as well. A substantial number of people who report feeling like an impostor don't *really* think that others think positively about them. Consider how Obama describes her experience with impostorism: "It's sort of like 'you're actually listening to me?' It doesn't go away, that feeling of 'I don't know if the world should take me seriously; I'm just Michelle Robinson, that little girl on the south side who went to public school.'"[66]

Therefore, feeling inadequate is an aspect of impostorism, but many who report experiencing impostorism don't actually feel like impostors. Also curious is that a significant number of people who scored high on impostorism report that they would do poorly on an upcoming intelligence test only when they thought their responses would be known by other people. In a *private* response condition, they did not predict failure.

These findings, which have now been replicated across multiple studies, have led researchers to argue that impostorism can involve an aspect of *self-deprecating self-presentation*. People use many different self-presentation strategies to adjust others' expectations for them, and impostorism may be just one manifestation of the repertoire on offer among humans.

Again, impostorism is a real phenomenon, and many people genuinely feel like they are not as competent as they appear to others, and this belief leads them to feel like an impostor or fraud.[67] Yet a significant number of people who report high scores on impostorism scales are telling people they suffer from impostorism as a (probably automatic and nonconscious) strategy to *lower people's expectations* so that if they fail, they can say "I told you so!"[68] This allows them to avoid the negative evaluations and possible social rejection they might receive if it looks like they "fooled" people. As one group of researchers put it, "How ironic that 'impostors' may be merely pretending to be impostors."[69]

A number of studies show that impostorism is also correlated with another self-presentation strategy: "self-handicapping."[70] People who exhibit chronic self-handicapping tend to avoid effort and taking risks in order to decrease the pain and embarrassment of failure. They self-sabotage in the name of protecting their image in other people's eyes, along with their ego. It seems that people with low self-esteem may employ a variety of self-deprecating self-presentation strategies. (On the flip side, people who score high in grandiose narcissism may be more prone to using a variety of *self-enhancing* self-presentation strategies to protect their ego.) In line with this, my team found a strong correlation in our research between reports of chronic impostorism and vulnerable narcissism.[71] This is no surprise when you consider that core facets of vulnerable narcissism include contingent self-esteem and a strong motivation to seek validation from others.

Many pop psych treatments of impostorism encourage you to just remember how badass you really are! To simply self-affirm it away. But what if you actually *are* an impostor? I agree with Nathaniel Branden that, at least in part, "self-esteem is the reputation we acquire with ourselves."[72] You can try, but it's really hard to lie to yourself. (As research shows, when people with low self-esteem try to employ positive affirmations, they can actually feel worse.)[73] "Throughout the thousands of choices you make on a daily basis, being responsible toward reality or evading it, we establish a sense of the kind of person we are," notes Branden. "But deep in our psyche they are added up, and the sum is that experience we call 'self-esteem.'"

It may seem intuitive that being viewed positively by others would always be desirable and satisfying. However, a wealth of research on *self-verification theory* suggests that people often prefer to be viewed accurately rather than positively.[74] People want to feel consistency between their own self-views and the feedback they receive from others. Once you realize that the fear of "later discovery" is something that is deeply built in to all of us, it's easy to understand why feelings of impostorism are so widespread.

Maybe impostorism isn't something we should immediately try to overcome or view as always negative. Just like with the social protection system, feelings of impostorism can offer us valuable information. Perhaps we're *all* impostors to some degree. After all, we know ourselves better than anyone else knows us, so we hold a unique perspective. And it's understandable and pretty reasonable that—short of pretending to be someone we're not—we'd attempt to conceal the less flattering aspects of ourselves. So, maybe we should both cut ourselves some slack and take a closer look at what's really going on.

Whenever real impostorism rears its head—when you feel both inadequate and that people are overestimating your capacities—I urge you to take a breath and ask yourself the following questions:

How accurate is my self-view? Maybe I don't think highly of my abilities, but maybe I'm selling myself short. Maybe I need to recalibrate my perception so that it's more in line with the confidence others have in me. When enough people are believing in me, maybe *they* are the ones who are right, and it's my low self-esteem that is not in touch with reality.

Am I actually an impostor? As unpleasant as it feels to admit it, maybe I'm feeling like an impostor because I *am* one. At least right now. I did just start this new job, after all. I'm not there yet in my field, but that's okay! Everyone has to start some-where. I'll remain honest about what I know and what I hope to learn more about.

Is this impostorism moment I'm having something I need to hide? Perhaps I can simply point out to people that their perception of me isn't correct, but that I'll work hard and do whatever I can to live up to their expectations. Maybe I can even use this impostorism feeling as a motivating force to be better at what I do, and to become a better human. Healthy vulnerability for the win!

These reflections can help you put your impostorism in greater perspective and help calibrate your own self-views with the views of others in a way that doesn't make you feel so uncomfortable. After all, the real core of impostorism is that feeling of incongruence be-tween how you perceive yourself and how others see you. Instead of engaging in self-deprecation, lean on your learning goals! When you do that, your feelings of impostorism are sure to dissipate.

Cultivate Healthy Authenticity

Many will tell you that the solution to low self-esteem is to simply live your truth. That sounds good, right? Who among us wouldn't benefit from engaging with and sharing our authentic self? And yet, what if living your truth is hurtful or harmful, to yourself or others? I'm not talking about coming out to Grandma or letting your tattoos show at work. I'm talking about the idea that you get to do and be whatever *feels right* to you regardless of how it affects others.

Yes, I agree that you don't want to live a tightly controlled life where you constantly try to make others happy and meet cultural expectations, and yet some cultural expectations are reasonable and actually contribute to a better society. Being thoughtfully honest with people? Yes. Being purposefully hurtful because that's what's on your mind in the moment? Not so much. Also, what if *your* truth doesn't align with *the* truth? In other words, how worthwhile is your worldview if you haven't done the work to cultivate genuine self-awareness?

Authenticity is one of the most valued characteristics in our society. As children we're taught to just be ourselves, and as adults there's no shortage of self-help books that advise us to do the same. But what does that even mean?[75] Which self? We each contain multitudes. Does being authentic mean being congruent with your inner experiences, or your consciously chosen values, beliefs, and attitudes? Or are you most authentic when you're congruent with the various social roles in your life and what people expect of you? Were you being authentic that time you really gave the waiter a piece of your mind, or the time you didn't tell the waiter how you really felt because you were connected to your higher value of kindness? Looking at the political landscape these days, some of the most troubling figures are also the most authentic.

Let's go back to that self-awareness piece for a moment. When people describe their true self, they often show an *authenticity positive bias* (as I've described it) where they emphasize things like being generous, humorous, or creative—in other words, their positive and moral qualities.[76] We tend to see our positive behaviors as more authentic than our negative ones. That time we gave the bird to the old woman who swerved in front of us in traffic? That wasn't *really* us, we were just having a moment. Conveniently, we tend to be most aware of the parts of ourself that we value.

According to social psychologist Roy Baumeister, it's not enough to convince ourselves that we have positive traits; generally speaking, we also want others to view us in the same way.[77] On the flip side, Baumeister argues that when people fail to achieve their desired reputation, they tend to dismiss their actions as inauthentic and not reflecting their "true self."

Interestingly, research shows that we report feeling most authentic when we're acting in ways that are socially desirable. That's counterintuitive, because we often associate authenticity with going against the grain. The reality is that we often feel most authentic when we're spending time with close others, are in sync with our environment, or are garnering approval from others. When we're engaged in conflicts, feeling isolated, or in some way falling short of a standard, we tend to feel less aligned with ourselves. So, what we view as our true self could just be how we want to be seen.

What we view as our true self could just be how we want to be seen.

This would explain why people's evaluations of their authenticity are so strongly linked to their morality and most-valued goals and why merely reflecting on moral past experiences increases feelings of authenticity. After all, behaving in ways that are consistent with your "higher" goals—such as announcing your new humanitarian nonprofit—is typically perceived as more authentic by yourself and others than authentically watching Netflix while enjoying rocky road ice cream (even though both behaviors are really you).

While the idea of a single true self may be a convenient fiction, there is within each of us a *best self*, composed of aspects of you that are healthy, creative, and growth-motivated and make you feel most connected to yourself and to others. The more you can drop the façades and the defenses that you erect to protect yourself, the more you can open yourself up to greater opportunities for growth, development, and creativity.

An important step to healthy authenticity is being aware of your impact on yourself and the world. It's not about simply telling people everything you're feeling and thinking, which is obnoxious and could get you into social trouble. It's not about yammering about yourself and your greatness, which is narcissism. It's not about doing whatever you feel like doing no matter its effect on others, which is psychopathy. And it's also not about doubling down on all of your personal values and defending them come hell or high water, which is closed-minded and inflexible.

Instead, healthy authenticity is about self-accountability and self-acceptance. It's about taking responsibility for your whole self, using it as a lever to grow as a person and to develop meaningful relationships with others. Like self-actualization, authenticity is more of a process than an endpoint. It involves ongoing discovery, self-consciousness, and responsibility-taking that take place atop a secure foundation of a personality structure not dominated by an excessive need for validation. No problem, right? Don't let that description overwhelm you—it's all about baby steps, and every inch adds up over time.

The main components of healthy authenticity are the following: self-awareness, self-honesty, integrity, and authentic relationships. Here are some statements you can use to assess how you're doing in this moment with regard to healthy authenticity:

HEALTHY AUTHENTICITY SCALE[78]

SELF-AWARENESS

- I have a very good understanding of why I do the things I do.

- I understand why I believe the things I do about myself.

- I actively attempt to understand myself as well as possible.

- I am in touch with my motives and desires.

SELF-HONESTY
These items are all reverse-coded, which means that the less you endorse them, the more self-honest you are.

- I'd rather feel good about myself than objectively assess my personal limitations and shortcomings.

- I tend to have difficulty accepting my personal faults, so I try to cast them in a more positive way.

- I try to block out any unpleasant feelings I might have about myself.

- I prefer to ignore my darkest thoughts and feelings.

- If someone points out or focuses on one of my shortcomings, I quickly try to block it out of my mind and forget it.

INTEGRITY

- I try to act in a manner that is consistent with my personally held values, even if others criticize or reject me for doing so.

- I am willing to endure negative consequences by expressing my true beliefs about things.

- I find that my behavior typically expresses my values.

- I live in accordance with my values and beliefs.

AUTHENTIC RELATIONSHIPS

- I want close others to understand the private me rather than just my public persona or image.

- In general, I place a good deal of importance on people I am close to understanding what I'm really like.

- I want people with whom I am close to understand my weaknesses.

- My openness and honesty in close relationships are extremely important to me.

No matter where you currently fall on this scale, as long as you're working toward growth and moving in the direction of who you want to become, that counts as healthy authenticity in my book. The first step to healthy authenticity is shedding your positivity biases and seeing yourself for who you are, in all of your contradictory and complex splendor. Full acceptance doesn't mean you like everything you see, but it does mean that you've taken the most important first step toward actually becoming the whole person you most wish to become. As Carl Rogers noted, "The curious paradox is that when I accept myself as I am, then I change."[79]

BRINGING IT ALL TOGETHER

To summarize, the key to cultivating healthy self-esteem is not chasing it but rather fostering healthy authenticity in your daily life. This involves striving to accurately calibrate your social protection system.

To navigate the social world successfully, you need to understand how you're coming across to other people, the degree to which they value being connected with you, and when your perceptions are off-kilter one way or another. You don't want to be undercalibrated (chronically thinking you're worth less than you are) or overcalibrated (chronically thinking you're much better than you are). You don't want to be delusional about your capacities and social value; you want to have *authentic value*. You want to cultivate truly genuine relationships and authentic forms of mastery.

At the same time, you don't want to base your value entirely on the opinions of others or the accolades you may receive from them.

Admittedly, it's a delicate needle to thread. But with a commitment to reality and a fundamental belief in your own growth potential, it can be done! And as with many things, perhaps the real value isn't in the achievement of healthy self-esteem, since we're constantly evolving, but in the journey of self-discovery and self-honesty that allows us to live a fuller, richer, and more authentic life.

5

Don't Be a Victim
to Your Need to Please

Selflessness is the vainest form of selfishness.

—**Russian proverb**

The motivation to help others and to be of service is a fundamental drive. Everyone wants to feel useful. That's a good thing, right? Who would possibly want to criticize *that*? Well, like any other human drive, too much can be a bad thing. For one, overhelping can deplete us. Plus, we might focus on serving others or the world around us as a means of denying our own needs and avoiding caring for ourselves. At its most extreme, excessive helping (providing support or assistance when it's not wanted or needed) can become intrusive—both to our own well-being and to those who we insist need our help.

Some of the roots of excessive helping may be found in some rather mixed-up and, quite frankly, *messed-up* messaging from society or our families. One of the more damaging ideas we may be exposed to and could then internalize is that our only value comes from helping, and that joy, freedom, and a sense of belonging must be earned by supporting others. As children, we're often told that it's better to give than to receive, as though these are always opposite actions. You're either the giver *or* the receiver.

As we've already seen in previous chapters, dividing actions and emotions in this binary way is limited at best, and at worst it's damaging. It's an immature way of seeing the world and neglects the beauty and nuances of human complexity—the fact that we can be and feel more than one thing at the same time. We can be both givers *and* receivers. This is what helping looks like in a more relational or community-oriented model. The transactional view is more like an abusive model of employment: Our job is to give, and in return we get to be a part of the company. If at any moment we pull back, our status is in jeopardy.

We can be both givers *and* receivers.

It's time to stop this toxic meme, curb your excessive helping, and understand that you have an inalienable right to experience joy, freedom, and belonging regardless of your specific contributions. Let's be clear: Your contributions *are* needed and desired, but you need to understand when and what help is actually helpful.

Let's start by getting a better understanding of what excessive helping looks like and why we do it. In its most drastic form, excessive helping can turn into what psychologists call *pathological altruism,* a term coined by engineering professor Barbara Oakley.[1] That sounds weird, right? Not the fact that an engineering professor is studying excessive helping but the idea that altruism can be pathological. After all, isn't that kind of the definition of altruism—that it's a motivation to do good?

Well, our surface-level motivation or intention is one thing. But as you know by now, our actions can also have other, deeper motivations about which we're not fully aware. You may think you're doing something purely out of a wish to be helpful, but in reality, it's that deeper meme that's moving you. Giving can be motivated out of a desire to prove your worth or value, or to secure your spot in a group or a relationship. (And it can have other motivations that we'll delve into in a moment.)

Pathological altruism holds that giving can have a dark side. Recent research has begun to unravel the psychological aspects and consequences of altruism when it tips over from useful to intrusive.

Now personally, I'm not a fan of language that (at least in my view) overly pathologizes things. In my experience, it can contribute to the perception that everything is a major dysfunction and we're all hopelessly broken, and I don't buy into that. Broken? Sure—but in ways we can learn from and that can actually become our greatest strengths. Hopeless? Definitely not.

So, for the purposes of this book and what we're trying to do here, instead of "pathological altruism," I'm going to call it *excessive helping* or *intrusive helping*.

THE NEED TO PLEASE

Excessive helping can take many forms: It can look like codependency in relationships, abuse and victimization, narcissistic activism, self-righteousness, communal narcissism, narcissistic martyrdom, mothers-in-law (kidding! Just wanted to make sure I haven't lost you), narcissistic sainthood, chronic people-pleasing, animal hoarding, eating disorders, suicide bombing, and dark empathy. Wow, that's a lot.

Most likely, some of this list confused you. A few terms are probably unfamiliar, and others you're probably surprised to see here. (Like, how is an eating disorder considered a form of excessive helping?)* It's not the purview of this book to explore the full range of excessive helping behaviors, so I won't go into detail about all of them. However, as we start to look at the underpinnings of this behavior, you'll start to see the links.

In this chapter I'll focus on one of the most common underlying motivations for excessive or intrusive helping: *a compulsive need for approval*. It's normal and even good to want to do things that make others happy. But when your need to please goes overboard, it can lead to scenarios where we try to help others in ways that may not actually be useful and can be downright dangerous.

---

* If you're curious, this is a good review of that literature: Bachner-Melman, R., & Oakley, B. (2016). Giving 'till it hurts': Eating disorders and pathological altruism. In Y. Latzer & D. Stein (Eds.), *Bio-psycho-social contributions to understanding eating disorders* (pp. 91–103). Springer International Publishing/Springer Nature.

Also, overhelping can be harmful to *ourselves*, causing psychological strife and inner turmoil (the irony being that imposing our assistance on others is the thing we're doing to try to *avoid* strife and turmoil). Whether we're consciously aware of it or not, we know that when we overextend ourselves in this way, we're neglecting our own needs and that causes us to feel a loss of control. We feel unable to express ourselves authentically and give ourselves the care and attention we need. Ideally, we want to be able to give to others *and* ourselves.

In his 1966 book *The Duality of Human Existence*, psychologist David Bakan emphasized the importance of being able to toggle between two modes of human existence: agency and communion.[2] Agency involves the ability to protect and assert yourself, and to separate and isolate yourself from others when it serves you. Communion involves participation, openness, unity, singing "Kumbaya," and so on. Broadly speaking, you might think of them as individuality and connection.[*]

As Bakan argues, optimal mental health arises from a balance between both of these states. That doesn't mean that they need to be in perfect balance at all times but over the longer arc of our lives. For instance, parents of young children typically are heavily imbalanced toward serving others, but ideally in time, as the children grow older, parents are able to attend more to their own needs and interests. Our energy flows outward at some times, and at others we direct it more toward ourselves. Rabbi Hillel captures the importance of this balance beautifully when he asks, "If I am not for myself, who will be for me? But if I am only for myself, what am I?"[3]

Modern psychological research has found substantial support for this contention. Both agency and communion offer distinct, positive

---

[*] Similarly, the philosopher Martin Buber argued that it's important to live in *both* the worlds of "I-It" and "I-Thou." The I-It relationship is purely functional and agentic, and there is no mutuality, whereas the I-Thou relationship involves a real mutuality in which one's whole being is not only engaged with the world but is also *changed* by the world. Note that such a relationship does not necessarily involve interactions with other humans, but can also involve interactions with other animals, plants, trees, and the rest of nature. Buber argued that the I-Thou way of relating to the world is an ideal to strive for, but that one has to live primarily in the I-It world: "Without [living in the I-It world] a human being cannot live. But whoever lives only [in the I-It world] is not human." See Buber, M. (1937/2010). *I and Thou*. Eastford, CT: Martino Publishing.

implications for social functioning, relationships, health, and well-being.[4] Those with higher agency have greater independence and assertiveness, use anger more constructively, show less emotional distress and anxious attachment, and tend to be embedded in more supportive social networks. That last point is especially interesting, as we may think of people who demonstrate greater independence as having little or no social support ("I don't need anyone!"), but that's not the case. Someone who has more agency is more likely to act on their own behalf to meet their needs—whether those needs are more basic, like ordering a pizza, or higher-level, like pursuing a fulfilling career.

On the other hand, those with higher communion are more comfortable with social relationships and are less likely to experience problems with those relationships, and they're more likely to have support available when they're in distress. So, both of these dimensions are necessary and beneficial. If you were exercising, you wouldn't want to strengthen only your left arm, would you? Similarly, you want to be able to take action that's in your own best interests, and you also want to have generative and satisfying relationships and contribute to shared goals.

When we get too far toward one side (unmitigated agency) or the other (unmitigated communion), problems ensue, including serious consequences for health and well-being—both our own and others'. Both states are linked to poor physical health, issues with anger, and problems with relationships.[5]

In this chapter, we're zooming in on unmitigated communion, or—you guessed it!—excessive helping. People who score high in unmitigated communion tend to display problem behaviors because of their tendency to subjugate their own needs to the needs of others and their intense dependence on others for validation.[6] These excessive helpers demonstrate a willingness to place another's perceived needs above their own in a way that becomes intrusive to themselves or harmful to others (or both).

If you're wondering, "Is that me?" let's find out!

ARE YOU PRONE TO EXCESSIVE HELPING?

In the spirit of self-reflection, take a good, honest look at the following ten statements. Rank the extent to which you agree with them on a scale of 1 ("Nope, not at all!") to 7 ("Oh yeah, that's totally me.") Remember, there's no judgment here—we're just seeking out some data points so we can help you grow. (You can also take this test online at www.selfactualizationtests.com.)

EXCESSIVE HELPING SCALE[7]

1. I tend to sacrifice my own needs and interests so that I can devote myself to helping and serving others.

2. I am a total pushover when it comes to requests to help others.

3. I often feel a compulsion to help others, as though I can't help myself.

4. I am willing to place another's needs above my own in a way that may cause self-harm.

5. I am constantly trying to read, anticipate, or guess others' needs so that I can give them exactly what they want.

6. I have little time to myself because I am too busy helping everyone.

7. I often suffer from "empathy burnout"—helping others leaves me feeling exhausted.

8. I need to be needed.

9. I often feel run down due to the demands of others.

10. I often feel underappreciated for the work I do to help others.

Now, as I mentioned earlier, at some points, we may be in circumstances that necessitate some degree of imbalance, but hopefully these situations are temporary. This scale is meant to consider more of your general way of relating to life and to others. That said, if you went through these ten items and found yourself vigorously nodding in agreement, you may wish to take a step back and reflect.

Your proneness to excessive helping may be getting in the way of your own happiness and self-actualization, and it could be hurting others. In my team's research, we found that those who scored higher on this scale were more likely to report that their helping sometimes causes others harm. They also tended to agree with items such as, "People often tell me to stop helping them because they are overwhelmed with my constant helping."

As I mentioned before, the tendency toward excessive helping is likely to have originated at least in part in early developmental experiences. Specifically, those where the takeaway was that you should suppress your own needs and authentic expression in the service of helping others. In my research, people who scored high on this scale were more likely to strongly agree with the following statements:

- As a child, I was often encouraged by my family to substitute my own needs for their own.

- As a child, I was often encouraged by my cultural environment to substitute my own needs for their own.

When we looked at people's motivation for helping, we found a strong correlation between a tendency for intrusive helping and engagement with the ego.[8] In other words, helping behavior provided an ego boost (in psychologist-speak we call that "self-sacrificing self-enhancement"). Excessive helpers tended to agree strongly with the following statements:

- I try to show what a good person I am through my sacrifices.

- I help others in order to prove I'm a good person.

- I like to have friends rely on me because it makes me feel important.

- I feel important when others rely on me.

- Sacrificing for others makes me the better person.

Similarly, we found that a propensity toward excessive helping was related to an increase in pleasing others and receiving validation, such that people were likely to agree with the following statements:

- A major motivation why I give to others is to please them.

- A major reason why I help people is to gain approval from them.

- I often give to others to avoid criticism.

- I often give to others to avoid rejection.

Notice that these motivations for helping aren't actually focused on the real, felt needs of the other person. Also, we found a strikingly high correlation between excessive helping and vulnerable narcissism. And frankly, it makes sense.

Let's bring the house lights down for a minute. Look, when it comes to excessive helping, there's a tinge of entitlement. The belief is that if you're constantly "nice" and you're always helping others, then you're entitled to be liked and to receive love and approval from others. Basically, the thought is "Since I'm so nice, you *must* like me!" No wonder some people feel the urge to run away as fast as they can from intrusive helpers—that's a lot of pressure.

Not only did they not ask for your help, but you're also requiring them to receive this unrequested assistance in a way that validates you. And when they don't, you're likely to feel resentment. "What's wrong with them? Why are they so ungrateful? Poor me!" Let's have an empathy moment—no, not for you. *For them.* When you provide unwanted help, you're actually intruding on the other person's autonomy and their freedom to decide if and when they want assistance, and in what way. You're also directing them on who they're supposed to like and love. And you're putting the weight of your need to be needed and validated on them. That's not fun. It's like giving someone a gift that they didn't ask for and they might not particularly want, with strings all over it.

But also, this behavior doesn't serve you well, either. My research has found that a propensity toward excessive helping is related to a host of maladaptive ways of functioning—primarily an increase in fear and avoidance behaviors across multiple domains of life.[9] Excessive helpers were also significantly more likely to experience depression and less likely to experience high levels of life satisfaction and well-being.

In her memoir *Acceptance*, writer and software engineer Emi Nietfeld describes her experiences growing up with a troubled mother prone to excessive helping.[10] In addition to many other challenges, Nietfeld's mother struggled with hoarding, and the conditions in their home were so unsafe and unsanitary that Nietfeld's mother voluntarily placed her daughter in foster care but then interfered in her placements. She also attempted to control her daughter's behavior, ensuring that Nietfeld not share information that would make her look bad to the foster system, Nietfeld's doctors, or the schools to which she was applying. All the while, she made herself out to be a doting mother simply doing her best to care for her daughter.

I don't want to make Nietfeld's mother out to be a villain; it's important to hold compassion for everyone, and clearly she was facing many of her own challenges. At the same time, consider the impact her supposed caring had on her daughter. Nietfeld describes being in and out of not only foster homes but also psychiatric treatment facilities, where she received treatment for depression, disordered eating, and self-harm.

Psychologists Jennifer Crocker and Amy Canevello posit that humans have evolved two motivational systems: The *egosystem* desires positive impressions from others, while the *ecosystem* wishes to promote others' well-being and thriving and actively seeks to avoid harming them.[11] They argue that sometimes people who are more motivated by the egosystem act in prosocial ways—or ways that benefit others—"not because they genuinely care about others' well-being and want to be constructive and supportive, but instead as a strategy to manage others' impressions."

In other words, they provide others with care and support not for the benefit it brings them but so they can be *seen* as caring and supportive. Their research has found that people with truly compassionate goals create a supportive environment for themselves and others but only if they do not also have strong self-image goals.[12] In our research, we found that those who were oriented toward excessive helping were less likely to have genuine and growth-oriented motives for helping others. Growth-oriented motives were indicated by their responses to statements such as the following:

- I like helping others because it genuinely makes me feel good to help others grow.

- A main motivation why I give to others is a desire for personal growth.

- A main motivation why I give to others is to increase my openness to experience.

So here's a question you might ask yourself: If you find yourself wanting to help someone or offer assistance, would you still do it even if you couldn't tell anyone else about it? If you find yourself sharing all of your "selfless" efforts on social media, you may want to consider whether you're operating from your ecosystem or your egosystem. In a study published in the journal *Sociological Science*, researchers looked at 3,500 pledges of support made through HelpAttack!—an app that helps people donate to charity and offers the option to share their commitment on social media.[13] As it happened, those who put their intentions to give on blast were more likely to renege on their promise compared with those who didn't.

The same team of researchers also conducted a study in which they used Facebook (now Meta) ads and other means to drive donations to the charity Heifer International. Though the effort garnered 6.4 million Meta users, along with lots of shares and likes, only thirty donations were actually made. As the researchers told one interviewer, one implication of the studies is that charitable giving (or demonstrating the intention to give) can be motivated by a desire to have others see you in a positive light.

And this same desire to please and be valued for what you can offer others can make excessive helpers especially vulnerable to the wiles of people who score high in grandiose narcissism.

THE CODEPENDENCY TRAP

Excessive helpers are prime targets for the brand of manipulation that those high in grandiose narcissism (the kind of showy, self-important people we generally think of when we hear the word "narcissist") excel in. Why? Essentially, *they fulfill each other's needs*. Harsh, but true. Excessive helpers need to be needed, and grandiose narcissists tend to have an easy time exploiting and maneuvering such people to their advantage. Typically, the dynamic is toxic and codependent.

Excessive helpers tend to be rich in codependent behaviors including the following:[14]

> *External focusing:* They overattend to the behaviors, opinions, and expectations of others. They might agree with the statements "In order to get along and be liked, I need to be what people want me to be" and "I put on a show to impress people; I know I am not the person I pretend to be."

> *Self-sacrifice:* They neglect their own needs to focus on meeting the needs of others. They might agree with the statement "I often put the needs of others ahead of my own—it would be selfish to do otherwise."

Interpersonal control: They have an entrenched belief in their capacity to fix others' problems and control their behavior. They might agree with the statements "I feel compelled or forced to help people solve their problems or offer people advice" and "I feel that without my effort and attention, everything would fall apart."

Emotional suppression: They deliberately suppress or have a limited conscious awareness of their emotions until their feelings become overwhelming. They might agree with the statements "Feelings often build up inside me that I do not express" and "I push painful thoughts and feelings out of my awareness."

Grandiose narcissists eat codependents for breakfast. Recall that excessive helpers are prone to look outside themselves for validation. They're happy to heap onto grandiose narcissists the attention the narcissists long for, believing that being needed in this way secures their status. In some cases, excessive helpers can also revel in their own victim status—like the enabling partner of an addict who sees themself as saintly for sticking with their loved one. And yet the reality is that where there is one victim, there are often more.

> Grandiose narcissists eat codependents for breakfast.

I believe we need a more realistic and nuanced view of victimhood—one that looks past the classic setup of one very bad perpetrator and one angelic victim. Indeed, research shows that people often view those who are victims as more moral than people who behave similarly but are not victims. The phenomenon is called the *virtuous victim effect.*[15] In the case of codependency, there can be a real victim, *and* that victim can still be responsible—at least in part—for enabling the toxic relationship.

Now, if any of this hits too close to home (like, it came crashing into your window and landed next to you on the couch), that recognition probably doesn't feel very good. Maybe you've sensed there's a problem with your relationships but haven't been able to name it. Or perhaps you're already aware of your tendency toward codependency and you want to change it already. Well, the good news is that you can. As with any deeply ingrained behaviors, they require real work to shift, but over time and with practice, you can change your actions.

The first step toward ending this detrimental pattern is a tough one: You've got to be extremely honest with yourself about the ways in which you may be responsible for, or at least contributing to, the codependency. If you are someone who avoids difficult or uncomfortable feelings, this can be especially challenging (though to be fair, most of us struggle to recognize and admit to our own negative patterns—it's not just you!).

In her very insightful book *The Disease to Please*, clinical psychologist Harriet Braiker describes four ways that chronic people-pleasers can unwittingly set themselves up to be "nice" victims who are treated badly.[16] Importantly, she outlines steps you can take to change these behaviors.

STOP: Always being willing to take the blame.

Excessive helpers are quick to assume blame at the slightest hint of a problem in the relationship. By doing this, they reinforce and justify the anger that is coming toward them. They give the angry person permission to blame them, which fulfills the angry partner's need to externalize all the blame.

START: Sharing the blame.

In reality, blame is almost always shared. It may not be equally shared, but in a healthy relationship both parties will acknowledge at least some degree of responsibility for the problem that has arisen in the relationship. Admitting some of your share but also demanding that the other person take at least some of the responsibility makes it clear that you will not allow being made to always feel inferior, unworthy, or undeserving.

STOP: Becoming passive-aggressive when there's conflict.

Passive-aggression is its own form of hostility and includes pouting, sulking, refusing to talk, and even backhanded compliments. Because excessive helpers are so intensely uncomfortable with their negative emotions, they use a wide range of passive-aggressive strategies to do whatever they can to avoid displaying their anger overly.

START: Communicating honestly.

Passive-aggressive strategies are self-defeating and often provoke the angry person even more. Your extreme passivity combined with the denial of their real felt anger can become extremely frustrating to a partner. To be super clear: This doesn't mean that you're responsible for your partner's hostile reaction. Their reaction is their responsibility. But you can deal with your anger more effectively by communicating in an open and up-front manner about what you're really feeling.

STOP: Acting like a passive victim.

The grandiose narcissist needs someone they can control who will not challenge them directly. This allows them to maintain their dominance through intimidation, threat, and overt aggression.

START: Stating your needs.

You can break this cycle by asserting yourself effectively. I'm not talking about fighting overt aggression with overt or even passive-aggression. I'm talking about firmly stating one's needs and making it clear that certain behaviors are not okay! You can take responsibility for the way you deal with your anger and work on assertive skills to stand up for yourself and not be used as a verbal (or physical) punching bag.

STOP: Assuming that your partner is always right, and you are always wrong.

If the excessive helper is always resigned to the idea that they are the "wrong one," they will constantly feel guilty regardless of whether they are truly at fault. Allowing themself to be always wrong just so that the partner can feel superior and "right" will continually damage their self-esteem and limit them from taking risks, being creative, or trying new challenges where trial and error is essential and perfectionism will only get in the way.

START: Owning your mistakes.

You may try to cover up your mistakes to avoid your partner's disapproval, but this is likely to backfire because perfection isn't possible and it's human to make mistakes. Pretending that your partner is always right implies that you are always wrong, and there is no universe in which that can actually be true! When the inevitable mistakes of being human are revealed, you will lose the respect and trust of others and be double-faulted for both the mistake and your dishonesty in failing to admit it. So own your errors. If your partner criticizes you for them, tell them firmly and clearly that you're human, you've acknowledged what happened, and they need to get over it.

It's important to acknowledge that none of these shifts will change your partner—though changing your behavior could sufficiently upset the overall dynamic in the relationship such that your partner starts making different choices as to how they behave. When you stop fulfilling the needs of the grandiose narcissist, they tend to adjust their actions as a result. Or they may become bored or frustrated and simply move on. As much as that may hurt, you are better off without that energy in your life.

But let's not dwell too much on your partner—this is about you. Excessive helpers tend to overfocus on their partner in the first place, and what you want to start doing is considering yourself. That looks twofold. First, you want to look to your own needs and ensure that they're being met, and shore up your own sense of worthiness. I realize that's more easily said than done, but you do deserve to be treated well.

The second aspect of considering yourself is accepting responsibility for your own actions and the impacts they may have. You've got to assess what deposits *you're* making to your joint dysfunction bank account. And if you identify behavior that's potentially problematic, you've got to shift it.

Okay, there's actually a thirdfold. Once you're out of that behavior pattern, you want to broaden your awareness to other ways in which you might fall into a codependent entanglement. You want to learn how to identify potentially exploitative situations before you get involved with them in the first place. And you also want to avoid becoming the exploiter. Excessive helpers can be the victim or the victimizer (or both at the same time). Learning how to identify the various intrusive-helper types can help you avoid playing either role.

Unfortunately, some of these apparently kind and compassionate people can be exceptionally difficult to spot. Such is often the case with communal narcissists.

Communal Narcissists

If being seen as the best at being a sensitive helper were an Olympic event, the communal narcissist might just take the gold—not in actually helping others the most, necessarily, but in being *perceived* as helping. Communal narcissists engage in self-serving behavior while presenting themselves as extremely sensitive, compassionate, and self-sacrificial or altruistic.[17] However, they have the same core self-motives as agentic narcissists: grandiosity, esteem, entitlement, and power.

Here are some statements with which a communal narcissist is likely to vociferously agree:

- I am the most helpful person I know.

- I am going to bring peace and justice to the world.

- I am the best friend someone can have.

- I will be well known for the good deeds I will have done.

- I am the most caring person in my social surroundings.

- In the future I will be well known for solving the world's problems.

- I greatly enrich others' lives.

- I will be famous for increasing people's well-being.

Communal narcissists meet their self-motives through communal means (as the name implies) and may cloak their narcissistic motives under the guise of moral sainthood. Think of the celebrity who makes big contributions to charity, but only if there's a photo op. Or the spiritual luminary who is all peace, love, and light while the cameras are rolling, but treats their hardworking staff horribly. I've referred to it as *spiritual narcissism*, making the case that self-enhancement through spiritual practices can fool us into thinking we're evolving and growing when all we're really growing is our ego![18]

Indeed, communal narcissists commonly operate in the healing and spiritual sectors. Consider NXIVM, an organization (now widely branded as a cult) that brought participants in through a series of personal-development courses that promised to help them overcome limiting beliefs and realize their potential.[19] I'm not saying that everyone who works in personal development is a cult leader—far from it—just that any territory where vulnerability and finances come together is a fertile field for narcissism in many forms.

Again, discernment—on the part of the provider and the consumer—should be exercised. As with NXIVM, it's easy to look in the rearview mirror and see the problems. As *Esquire* writer Lauren Kranc describes, founder Keith Raniere "was hailed as an elusive, god-like savant within the company. . . . But rewiring your brain to learn Raniere's 'ethical framework for human experience' came at a

steep price. The cost for the first course, a 5-day intensive, was $2700."
When a forensic psychiatrist evaluated the organization, he concluded that the "scientific" technique taught in Raniere's Executive
Success Programs was actually a brand of mind control "aimed at
breaking down his subjects psychologically." Some participants reported experiencing hallucinations and psychotic episodes after especially grueling sessions. Yet others reported genuine breakthroughs
and even physical healing from the practices.

According to psychologists Delroy Paulhus and Oliver John, humans have two broad self-favoring biases that are self-deceptive: an
egoistic and moralistic bias.[20] The egoistic bias (or the *superhero* bias)
is a self-deceptive tendency to exaggerate one's social status, intellectual dominance, fearlessness, emotional stability, and intellectual
and creative prowess. The moralistic bias (or the *saintlike* bias) is a
self-deceptive tendency to deny socially deviant impulses and to
claim sanctimonious saintlike qualities such as compassion, dutiful-
ness, and moral restraint. For instance, one might swear off everything from alcohol to caffeine to refined sugar to processed food,
then claim a sort of moral superiority or greater "purity." People with
both the superhero and saintlike biases tend to show *pervasive self-
aggrandizement*. Yet superheroes self-aggrandize in more agentic
domains whereas saints self-aggrandize in more communal domains,
exaggerating their compassion, commitment to humanitarianism,
and superior self-sacrifice ("I have self-sacrificed more than anyone!").

Self-perception isn't always reality, however. Psychologist Jochen
Gebauer and his colleagues found that people scoring higher on the
communal narcissism scale were more likely to overclaim knowledge
regarding communal topics and were more likely to see themselves
as really communal even though they were seen as noncommunal by
observers.[21] Other research shows that even though communal narcissists view themselves as highly prosocial and declare themselves
interested in civic engagement and saving the environment, objectively speaking, communal narcissism has been found to be unre-
lated to prosociality as measured through actual behavior.[22]

Communal narcissists can genuinely see themselves as healers—

whether of individuals or the entire world—with unique abilities. Yet while their actions may actually provide some help, they can also hurt, and it can be difficult to separate the two to see what's really going on. And you can't always follow the money, because communal narcissists can find welcome homes within nonprofit and charitable organizations as well.[23]

According to psychologist Anne Fennimore, "the duplicitous nature of communal narcissism might mimic motivation toward public service by providing an outlet for self-aggrandizement."[24] Fennimore found that public service motivation and communal narcissism are significantly related to each other, and communal narcissists were prominent in leadership ranks with supervisory duties and in the nonprofit sector. Fennimore notes that "the service-oriented missions and values of many nonprofit organizations are perhaps congruent with compassion, self-sacrifice, and commitment to public interest dimensions."

In addition to attraction to public participation, communal narcissism was also associated with the self-sacrifice dimension of public service motivation. While Fennimore found that self-reported compassion was correlated with communal narcissism, the compassion-related items on her scale did not resonate as deeply with the communal narcissists as the self-sacrifice items and attraction to public participation. This suggests that communal narcissists may possess a "flexible" form of empathy that is used more strategically based on whether the situation will advance their ego.

Of course, self-sacrifice is a central motive for people desiring government and nonprofit sector engagement, and that's a good thing![25] But this can become pernicious if communal narcissists join public service to primarily self-aggrandize rather than benefit the collective.* Founding a nonprofit may be particularly attractive to

---

* Within the nonprofit organizational context, there exists *founder's syndrome*, which occurs when organizations revolve around a prominent person's personality rather than the organization's mission. Organizational development expert Carter McNamara believes this becomes a syndrome when the founder becomes unconcerned by their asymmetrical power over the organization. See Carver, J. (1992). The founding parent syndrome: Governing in the CEO's shadow. *Nonprofit World, 10,* 14–16; McNamara, C. (1998). Founder's syndrome: How founders and their organizations recover. *Nonprofit World, 16*(6).

communal narcissists because of their authority to dictate the culture and have the power to select and control powerful boards and employees.[26] This can lead to a culture of totalitarian decision-making, a lack of delegation of tasks, a lack of accountability, abuse of power, micromanagement, stifling and even downplaying the valuable contributions of junior employees, and creating an overall stressful work environment in which burnout among employees is likely.[27]

The truth is, virtually any communal domain can be attractive to the communal narcissist—the more potential for ego enhancement, the more attractive the domain. Research shows that communal narcissists are also drawn to organizations with religious affiliations more strongly than those scoring lower in communal narcissism.[28] Since a communal worldview is strongly encouraged by virtually all world religions and religiosity provides a central means for self-enhancement, religious leadership might be a particularly attractive domain for communal narcissists.[29]

Another domain that is ripe for the communal narcissist to self-aggrandize is the political sphere of influence (but perhaps you already guessed that). My team and I published an analysis of the audio of speeches by 143 U.S. senators and found that dark traits such as narcissism, manipulativeness, and psychopathy were the most prevalent traits among the Senate and were associated with longer tenure in political office but less legislative success—a form of political success that undoubtedly requires cooperation more than charisma![30]

Before you start thinking the world is a terrible place (or that I'm just terribly cynical), let me iterate that of course not every sensitive soul who seems to be motivated by benevolence and the desire to help the collective is really just trying to enhance their status. For instance, I believe most people really do want to do good in the world and be of service to others. The problem is that this need can become so compulsive that they get addicted to the ego boost and neglect the real felt needs of others.

Another area where we see an abundance of narcissistic behavior (both grandiose and vulnerable)—and where this behavior can be hard to see for what it is—is among activists.

Narcissistic Activists

Without a doubt, activism can be extremely good for society. However, not all activism is useful, and how it's done can be harmful. When it's coupled with narcissism and excessive helping, activists tend to project either their deepest feelings of insecurity or their feelings of superiority on others under the guise of making the world a better place. The world of activism can be like a candy shop for people with exploitative personalities who are more concerned with advancing their own ego-based agenda rather than a genuine desire to contribute to the collective good.

In 2018, Wayne Pacelle, then CEO of the Humane Society of the United States—one of the largest animal welfare organizations in the country—resigned in the wake of sexual assault allegations from multiple employees.[31] An article in *Politico* discussing the allegations characterized Pacelle as both "charismatic" and "aggressive."[32]

Research supports links between activism, aggression, and manipulative behavior. In one seminal study, Anne Krispenz and Alex Bertrams found that people who endorsed *antihierarchical aggression*—a component of authoritarianism that is defined as "the motivation to forcefully overthrow the established hierarchy and punish those in power"—were more likely to score higher on measures of antagonistic narcissism.[33] Those with antagonistic narcissism may exploit others, display a lack of empathy, have a sense of entitlement, show strong arrogance, and exhibit manipulative behavior. People who more strongly supported violent revolution against existing societal structures tended to also report stronger ego-focused traits.

Now, if you're thinking, "Uh-huh—authoritarianism. I know what political party *that* is!," you're wrong. Research shows that this brand of authoritarianism can be found on both the left *and* right ends of the political spectrum.[34] Involvement in political activism is not solely attributable to political orientation but rather to the personality characteristics of the person on the radical left or right of the political spectrum.[35] Indeed, research shows that antagonistic narcissism is a predictor of both left-wing authoritarianism and a social dominance orientation, a trait often associated with right-wing authoritarianism.[36]

Let me be super clear: Activism per se is not narcissistic. Research suggests, however, that some forms of political activism can be particularly attractive to antagonistic narcissists. Based on their own findings, Krispenz and Bertrams concluded that some political activists do not actually strive for social justice and the support of underprivileged groups or people but rather endorse or express violence for the satisfaction of their own ego-focused and antisocial needs.[37] (For instance, we can reasonably suspect that among those who are involved in looting or rioting behavior connected to activist movements, there are *some* who are not trying to advance any other cause than their own.)*

This insight led Krispenz and Bertrams to propose the *dark-ego-vehicle principle*.[38] According to this principle, people with narcissistic and/or psychopathic personality traits are attracted to certain ideologies and forms of political activism. They then use activism as a vehicle to satisfy their own ego-focused needs instead of actually working toward social justice and equality.

The researchers conducted four studies showing support for their principle in the realms of anti-sexual-assault activism, LGBTQ+ activism, feminist activism, and environmental activism.[39] Across all studies they found that narcissistic personality traits such as acclaim-seeking, authoritativeness, grandiose fantasies, and a high need for exhibitionism were related to a stronger identification with these causes.

For the LGBTQ+ study, they found that greater involvement in activism was also related to higher levels of psychopathy. The researchers argue that involvement in activism may provide opportunities for psychopaths to act sadistically (such as by publicly shaming political opponents) and also enjoy the violence they observe and sometimes

---

* Still, some activists say that looting is completely defensible. In shaping your own conclusions, it's worth considering their opinions. Some arguments can be found here: Chotiner, I. (2020, September 3). Examining Osterweil's case for looting. *The New Yorker*. https://www.newyorker.com/news/q-and-a/vicky-osterweils-case-for-looting.

contribute to. For these individuals, LGBTQ+ activism may simply be a good vehicle for their narcissistic and psychopathic needs to be satisfied. Krispenz, who is herself bisexual, told me in personal correspondence that genuinely victimized and marginalized people should know that there is potential for narcissistic people to be involved in these forms of activism and derail their genuinely altruistic mission.

Many excessive helpers are already guilt-prone, so exploitative narcissists can use that fact to manipulate them even more. There's a whole research literature on *survivor's guilt*. The contemporary psychological literature defines survivor's guilt not only as having guilt about being spared from harm that others incurred but also *feeling guilty to have had any kind of advantage compared with others*, such as greater success, abilities, better health, greater wealth, a better job, or more satisfying relationships.[40]

There are so many genuinely empathetic and compassionate people who are attracted to activism. However, since the excessive helpers are more likely to feel survivor's guilt in everyday life, they can be prime targets for exploitation from antagonistic narcissists who make them feel guilty for having even the slightest advantages in life or having any joy of their own. This can create a very toxic dynamic in activism and make it less likely for the activism to actually be effective. Guilt-driven activism isn't as uplifting and motivating as other-focused and change-focused activism.

So how can you tell the difference between people who genuinely want to help and those who are into it primarily for their ego? Take a closer look at some key behavior—namely, virtuous victim signaling.

VIRTUOUS VICTIM SIGNALING

When it comes to how to distinguish people with a genuinely altruistic motive from those who are using helping behaviors as a vehicle for ego enhancement, one indicator may be the prevalence of their signaling. In other words, how they characterize their victim status. A large body of research has documented the psychological and social costs of being a victim.

Most victims don't wish to keep ruminating on their suffering and would in fact like to move on with their lives and flourish.[41] Also, most victims often talk about their experiences as a way to help them heal and to raise important awareness about the condition that led to their victimization but aren't concerned with being seen as particularly outstanding or special. There is a key difference, therefore, between being a victim and *virtuous victim signaling*.

The antagonistic narcissist routinely engages in virtuous victim signaling in public and intentionally uses such signaling as a tactic to extract resources from others. They are aware of the fact that people tend to see victims as moral and trustworthy.[42] In a series of studies, Ekin Ok and her colleagues at the Immorality Lab (sounds like a fun place to conduct research!) at the University of British Columbia took a deeper look at those who seem to enjoy making a public spectacle of their suffering.[43] They found that the *virtuous victimhood signal*—incessantly talking about one's victimhood as well as one's many virtues—is a particularly effective mechanism for persuading others to transfer resources (such as money, effort, care, and concern) in a way that benefits the signaler.

Ok and her colleagues created a victim-signaling scale that measures how frequently people tell others about the disadvantages, challenges, and misfortunes they suffer. They found that individuals who scored higher on the "dark triad" traits—Machiavellianism (strategic exploitation and deceit), narcissism (entitled self-importance), and psychopathy (callousness, cynicism, and impulsivity)[44]—more frequently signaled virtuous victimhood, even after taking into account demographic and socioeconomic variables that are commonly associated with victimization in Western societies.

The personality trait of *amoral manipulation* was a particularly good predictor of the frequency of virtuous victim signaling. Amoral manipulation can be defined as "the willingness to disregard standards of morality and see value in behaviors that benefit the self at the expense of others."[45] An example is "I believe that lying is necessary to maintain a competitive advantage over others." The researchers additionally found that communal narcissism predicted virtuous

victim signaling (remember our good friend the communal narcissist?).

There were real practical implications. Frequent virtuous victim
signalers were more willing to purchase counterfeit products and
were more likely to cheat and lie to earn extra monetary rewards in a
coin flip game. Also, in one condition, study participants were asked
to imagine a scenario involving a competitive colleague in which
"something felt off" but the colleague actually behaved in a friendly
manner. High virtuous victim signalers were more likely to interpret
the ambiguous behavior in a discriminatory manner, making accusations about mistreatment from the colleague that was never in the
scenario, presumably to benefit themselves.

Tellingly, the researchers also found that those who scored higher
on this scale were more likely to talk about their strong virtuous
moral character while simultaneously placing less importance on
their moral identity. In other words, they were more interested in *appearing* morally good then actually *being* morally good.

To be fair, it doesn't help that society often encourages or even
requires people to signal their victim status to receive recognition
or resources. Emi Nietfeld recalls how, when trying desperately to
get accepted to and be awarded scholarships to attend an Ivy League
school (which she believed would assure her of a stable future), she
was told by a top college admissions counselor that she had to craft
her story in just the right way for her application essay.[46] She had to
share her experience so that people would be just alarmed enough at
what she'd been through to see her as a deserving victim but not so
horrified that they'd turn away from her, repulsed. Plus, she had to
prove that she'd learned from her experiences, to be the "perfect, deserving" victim who was "hurt in just the right way."

Also, to be clear, there are people who display virtuous victim
signals at certain times in their life because they have experienced
legitimate harm. Not everyone who engages in virtuous victim signaling is using it to exploit others or is a dark triad individual. In fact,
there are plenty of "light triad" individuals—people who don't use
people as a means to an end, who believe in the fundamental good-

ness of humans, and who value the dignity and worth of each individual—who may signal virtuous victimhood at some point in their lives.* Indeed, speaking out or otherwise signaling when one has been victimized can be an effective tool of social influence and can lead to truly important changes. The point here is that some people employ these signals *constantly* as a duplicitous tactic to acquire personal benefits, not to productively help others.

These findings are especially important in the age of social media where "competitive victimhood" can run rampant (more on that in Chapter 10).[47] Again, I'm not trying to deemphasize the very real suffering many people have experienced. It's important to be able to share our experiences but with the aim of gaining meaningful support so that those who have been hurt can heal, and that collectively we can all learn and grow from these experiences.

So where does all of this leave us with regard to excessive helping behavior? Well, it's time to move out of the darkness and negativity of excessive helping and into the light! Because the good news is that there *is* an alternative. There is a generative and beneficial way to channel your excessive helping instincts—toward *healthy* selfishness.

PRACTICING HEALTHY SELFISHNESS

Any pleasure that does no harm to other people is to be valued.

—*Bertrand Russell*

In much of this chapter, I've focused on the negative impact that excessive helping can have on others. But excessive helpers deserve love, too—just as everyone does. People don't engage in these behaviors because they are fundamentally bad but because they are trying

---

* For more on the light triad, see Kaufman, S. B., Yaden, D. B., Hyde, E., & Tsukayama, E. (2019). The light vs. dark triad of personality: Contrasting two very different profiles of human nature. *Frontiers in Psychology, 10*, Article 476; Neumann, C. S., Kaufman, S. B., Brinke, L. T., Yaden, D. B., Hyde, E., & Tsukayama, E. (2020). Light and dark trait subtypes of human personality—a multi-study person-centered approach. *Personality and Individual Differences, 164*, 110121.

to meet a need. They're just doing it in maladaptive ways. So one way to stop this behavior is to find more positive ways to meet those needs. One such way is to practice healthy selfishness.

You see, we're often told that attending to ourselves in any way is selfish. But this thinking is terribly misguided. In the opening to his 1939 essay "Selfishness and Self-Love," Erich Fromm writes that "modern culture is pervaded by a taboo on selfishness."[48] Inspired by Fromm's essay, Abraham Maslow argued for the need to distinguish between *healthy selfishness*, which is rooted in psychological abundance, and *unhealthy selfishness*, which is rooted in psychological poverty, neuroticism, and greed.[49]

Both Maslow and Fromm held that *healthy self-love* requires a respect for oneself and one's boundaries, and affirmation of the importance of one's own health, growth, happiness, joy, and freedom. Self-actualizing people have healthy boundaries, practice self-care, and have the capacity to enjoy themselves. Healthy selfishness is rooted in psychological abundance, whereas unhealthy selfishness is rooted in psychological poverty. Healthy selfishness requires self-love. The person who is motivated by healthy selfishness is motivated by a desire to become a unique person, to learn, grow, and be happy. In contrast, unhealthy selfishness is motivated by neuroticism and greed. This person's needs are insatiable, and they rarely receive any long-lasting satisfaction.

So how's *your* healthy selfishness practice?

The Healthy Selfishness Scale

By now you should know that I love creating personality tests! Drawing on both Fromm's and Maslow's writings, I was inspired to create a Healthy Selfishness Scale (HSS) and investigate its correlates in the real world.[50] I defined healthy selfishness as "having a healthy respect for your own health, growth, happiness, joy, and freedom." That sounds like something we'd all enjoy, right?

Here are the items I came up with. See how much you agree or disagree with each of the following (and to actually take the assessment, go to www.selfactualizationtests.com):

- I have healthy boundaries.

- I have a lot of self-care.

- I have a healthy dose of self-respect and don't let people take advantage of me.

- I balance my own needs with the needs of others.

- I advocate for my own needs.

- I have a healthy form of selfishness (meditation, eating healthy, exercising, and so on) that does not hurt others.

- Even though I give a lot to others, I know when to recharge.

- I give myself permission to enjoy myself, even if it doesn't necessarily help others.

- I take good care of myself.

- I prioritize my own personal projects over the demands of others.

Don't worry if you rank low on some or even most of these. The good news is that you can learn and improve upon each of these skills, and reading this book is a good start!

When we tested the HSS in the real world, we found that healthy selfishness was a strong positive predictor of high self-worth, well-being, and life satisfaction and was a strong *negative* predictor of depression. We also found that the scale predicted adaptive psychological functioning above and beyond other personality traits that have traditionally been studied in psychology (such as the Big Five personality traits—openness, conscientiousness, extraversion, agreeableness, and neuroticism).

In particular, healthy selfishness was positively related to a sense of self-competence (the perception that you're reaching your goals in life) and authentic pride for one's accomplishments.* Healthy selfishness was also negatively correlated with vulnerable narcissism, which as we've discussed is strongly linked to excessive helping. Individuals with high levels of healthy selfishness also tended to show themselves greater self-compassion (which I described in Chapter 2). We also found that healthy selfishness was negatively related to intrusive and overbearing child-rearing practices where the child's needs take a back seat to the needs of the parent.

Finally, it may seem paradoxical, but our research also revealed that people who scored higher in healthy selfishness were less motivated to exploit others for personal gain and were more likely to genuinely care about others and report genuine motives for helping others ("I like helping others because it genuinely makes me feel good to help others grow"). Healthy selfishness was negatively related to more vulnerably narcissistic motives for helping others ("A major reason why I help people is to gain approval from them" and "I often give to others to avoid rejection").

Fromm conceptualized love as an attitude, a way of being in the world where you have a healthy respect for the health, growth, happiness, joy, and freedom of others.[51] Our research suggests that the light of love can shine in any direction—outside to others but also inside to help develop one's own self.

---

* For more on authentic pride, see Weidman, A. C., Tracy, J. L., & Elliot, A. J. (2015). The benefits of following your pride: Authentic pride promotes achievement. *Journal of Personality, 84,* 607–622; Tracy, J. L., Cheng, J. T., Robins, R. W., & Trzesniewski, K. H. (2009). Authentic and hubristic pride: The affective core of self-esteem and narcissism. *Self and Identity, 8,* 196–213; Kaufman, S. B. (2012, July 16). Pride and creativity: How is pride related to creative achievement? *Psychology Today.* https://www.psychologytoday.com/us/blog/beautiful-minds/201207/pride-and-creativity.

PART II

Empower Yourself

6

Find the Light Within

Darkness cannot drive our darkness; only light can do that.
Hate cannot drive out hate; only love can do that.

—*Martin Luther King Jr.*

Picture it: You're a young kid growing up in inner-city Baltimore. You're surrounded by poverty and addiction. Your school is in disrepair. You're dealing with generational struggles along with institutional racism. Then you look on TV and it seems like everyone else in the world is living the good life. Social media offers the same story, with people's feeds looking like unending highlight reels. But in your own life, when you look around, all you see is struggle. Given this setup, it's natural to act out. As Atman Smith observes, "How are you supposed to care about learning, want to clean up your community, or have empathy for you classmates when you don't even care about yourself?"[1]

That lack of self-connection is exactly what Atman, along with his brother Ali and their friend Andrés González, set out to change.[2] To do that they invoked a perhaps unlikely set of tools. Growing up, the trio were schooled in meditation and other consciousness-based practices by Ali and Atman's father and, later, their godfather. After college, the three moved to the Smith family home in West Baltimore and decided to apply their learning to help underserved communities. The result is the Holistic Life Foundation, an organization that teaches yoga and other wellness practices to at-risk youth.

As Atman explained when we spoke, the physical practices help the kids regulate their nervous systems. By releasing excess energy and coming into a more centered place, their body becomes a safe space—something most of them have never experienced before. Breathwork practices are similarly designed to slow down their minds and help them self-regulate. They use meditation to tap into a sense of inner peace and develop loving kindness.

All of that might sound unremarkable if you've been exposed to these practices before, or if you're from the 'burbs. But imagine the experience of a child who has never experienced peace within or around them. Envision what it's like to discover that at virtually any time, the stillness and safety they seek can be found inside them. That's transformational.

And that's exactly what Ali, Atman, and Andrés have seen—that when kids truly embrace the practices, their lives change. *They* change, because they grow to understand that no matter what life has dealt them, their circumstances are not a reflection of their worth. As Ali says, they see that "this happens to be my physical reality, but it's not who I am." They start to value themselves and, as such, to demonstrate more self-love and empathy, and that becomes contagious. Atman describes it as a "positive zombie effect. They infect others with that understanding and insight."

As the work of Ali, Atman, and Andrés demonstrates—along with the countless kids who've adopted these practices—your life experiences do not have to limit your outcomes. Yes, we're all shaped and influenced by what happens to us, but it doesn't have to hold us back. (And you can learn more about the work of the Holistic Life Foundation in their book *Let Your Light Shine: How Mindfulness Can Empower Children and Rebuild Communities*.)

This is how Atman describes the process of empowerment:

> *If you have a victim mentality, like thinking that you won't ever achieve, that's what you'll believe. You connect with those constructs. If you can start to catch these ideas as they bubble up inside you and then shift them, that positive identity is what you'll*

start to identify with. The yoke of that victim mentality will un-bind and it will instead tighten up around your inner divinity.

We all have times when we feel broken at our base, myself included. But I can assure you that as wounded or dysfunctional as you may feel, there is something beautiful and perfect deep inside you that nothing can ever damage. That's what Ali, Atman, and Andrés teach their kids to connect with, and you can do the same.

Acupuncturist and wellness teacher Thea Elijah calls this light inside us our "pilot light."[3] When we locate that light and then focus on it, over time it will become brighter and will start to shine from within us in ways that change our entire outlook on life. It shifts how we see ourselves and others. And connecting with that light is what this chapter will help you do.

LOOK BEYOND YOUR BROKENNESS

Poet Jalal al-din Rumi once wrote, "The wound is the place where the Light enters you."[4] Many of us are familiar with that beautiful sentiment, and it's true. As you've now heard me say in many different ways, our hurts can provide some of our greatest opportunities for growth. At the same time, there's another concept that we need to understand if we're going to develop beyond those wounds. It's the idea that there are also parts of us that *cannot* be wounded.

It's this combination of brokenness and perfection that defines what it is to be human. If we want to not only heal but also bring out the best in ourselves, we need to recognize both of those truths. Yes, see and love your messy, complicated, battered-by-life self. But see your perfection as well—the pieces that exist outside anything that has ever happened to you.

Niall Breslin knows all about early wounds. As he described to me on my podcast, growing up in a primary school environment where he was forced to endure ongoing physical abuse caused Breslin to cut himself off emotionally from the world.[5] He went on to become outwardly successful, first as a professional rugby player, then a musician. Yet behind the scenes he struggled with his mental health, at times suffering debilitating panic attacks. But through much work and therapy Breslin discovered, remarkably, that there were aspects of himself that remained untouched by trauma. That recognition helped him to shift the way he sees himself. To engage with life from a space of personal empowerment and courage.

As Breslin told me, "To me, bravery is that acknowledgment that there's something in you that no matter how dark or difficult things get, or how intense life can feel sometimes, there is a part of you that no one's ever got to, and no one's ever wounded." To access your own bravery, he says, "You've got to find the parts of you that aren't broken."

To be sure, there are positive memes out there about what it means to have been shattered by life. Some people describe having been *broken open*. That's a healthy way to view our difficult experiences. The problem comes when we overidentify with this perception and see ourselves as perpetually or unavoidably dysfunctional. And society often rewards us for this, with its attention and accolades. As a result, we may start to subconsciously highlight these aspects of ourselves to continue to receive support, reassurance, and applause.

It's okay—and healthy—to acknowledge these parts of ourselves, but we don't want to let them define us. That's always been my issue with one-word labels, even if they're positive. When someone describes themself exclusively or primarily as a "survivor," for instance, they are inextricably linked to *that thing* they have survived. It defines them. I want more for you. I want you to be able to identify and appreciate *all of you*, and that means recognizing your "symphony of selves," as James Fadiman and Jordan Gruber describe it.[6]

EMBRACE YOUR MANY SELVES

Walt Whitman once wrote, "I contain multitudes."[7] Well, he's not the only one. Many psychologists and self-help gurus speak of the importance of developing a "healthy self." Yet Fadiman and Gruber say that, rather than seeing ourselves as a single, unified self, we'd be better served by acknowledging the many different identities that compose each of us.

We're familiar with the idea of the inner critic. That's the voice inside us that diminishes our capabilities, that tells us we need to play small, or that chides, "You could never pull off that shirt!" But generally, that's as far as we go. There's you, and then there's this little nefarious being who loves to chastise you. In reality, though, there are many, many more selves operating inside you.

If all of this conjures the program *United States of Tara* and the idea of multiple personality disorder in general (or dissociative identity disorder, as it's technically termed), that's not far off. But DID is an extreme and dysfunctional version of what is, in reality, quite normal and healthy. That's the fact that we all have many distinct aspects of our personality that, together, make us who we are. We have selves that we can inhabit or lean into based on the situation. And recognizing this complexity is a useful tool in becoming more empowered.

One of our biggest challenges in developing a positive self-image—one where we can harness that bravery and courage that Niall Breslin spoke of—is that we paint ourselves with a single broad brush. For example, we are a victim *or* a survivor. Or consider a far less charged aspect of our identity: We are introverted *or* extroverted. As I explained previously, even our inherent traits possess nuance. Now layer on top of this the idea of multiple selves and it looks something like this. . . .

Let's say that most of the time, Sally the librarian is pretty introverted. (Yes, I'm aware that I'm trading on a cliché, but I love librarians so just go with me on this.) Yet on Friday nights at the club, something in Sally comes alive and she lets loose. Suddenly she's the life of the party, happy to have all eyes on her as she busts a move. So who is Sally, really? Is she the introverted librarian or the dynamic dancer? Of course, she's both. And many more things, as well.

Consider yourself in this light. In fact, here's a fun exercise: Take out a piece of paper or open your notes app and jot down all of the primary aspects of your personality. Picture an icebreaker session at a workshop where you've got only one minute to describe yourself to the group. What would you say? Now, look at that list and consider all of the *exceptions* to those qualities—times and places where there was something else that was true. Maybe you're typically quiet and re-

We are never just one thing.

served *unless* you see someone getting bullied or ha-rassed. In those circumstances, a more outspoken self emerges and you feel compelled to speak up. Or maybe you often come off as self-confident or personable, but when you're trying to ask someone out, you instantly freeze up. (I have no idea what that's like, personally. It's a completely random example.)

You get the idea. When it comes to our personalities there are few universal truths, and yet we often fall back on this idea that each of us is a single self. And that misunderstanding can be the source of much suffering and confusion. We struggle to figure out who we are—to isolate a static concept of ourselves—but in reality, we are never just *one thing*. I mean seriously, have you ever tried to write an online dat-ing profile that truly captures all of you? It's, like, impossible! But that's a wonderful thing. If we can learn to recognize and embrace our complexity, we can actually have more empathy and understand-ing for ourselves.

Our self may include pieces that have been wounded. Maybe you have a victim self inside you who needs your love and care. You can give that to them! Just don't let them take over. Don't let them become

When all you do is attend to what's broken, that's the only self you'll see.

a black hole for your attention, because when all you do is attend to what's broken, *that's the only self you'll see.*

And guess what? Whatever you've experi-enced, if you're reading this right now (which you obviously are), somehow you got through it. Maybe you're going through shit *right now*, but you're still here! That means that inside you there is also someone who is incredibly courageous and strong! Maybe they feel hard to lo-cate, or their voice seems small, but do the work to find them. Find that pilot light inside you that's still burning, then use your loving attention to amplify it.

As Ali Smith told me, "You can't be your best self if you don't know your true self." And while I don't believe there is only one "true self," I do agree that identifying and accepting the many pieces inside you, including your light, is an important part of the work. And once you find your light, you can tap into it again and again. One way we can do all of this is by harnessing our strengths.

HARNESS YOUR STRENGTHS

When I talk about strengths, it probably conjures something like StrengthsFinder. But I'm talking about a different collection of strengths that are often overlooked and undervalued—your *character strengths*. The problem is, far too many of us don't even know what these strengths are.

Part of the challenge is that when we think about strengths, we often think about our talents (like you're athletic or a good singer), our interests (you love sci-fi movies or you're involved in the environmental movement), or our skills (you're a great gardener or an amazing writer). We might also think about our external resources (you have a wonderful family or you have a bit of money in the bank). But rarely do we consider our character and things like generosity, kindness, social intelligence, humility, or humor. Yet these strengths matter a great deal when it comes to our quality of life.

The book *Character Strengths and Virtues: A Handbook and Classification* represents a three-year effort by more than fifty psychologists and researchers to identify and codify our universal character strengths.[8] The group came up with a list of twenty-four such characteristics, as displayed in the chart on the following page.

When we embody them, these strengths not only contribute to a sense of personal fulfillment, they also help to make the world a better place. And that's a virtuous cycle, because as we first tap into our light, then let it shine, we see the world around us brighten, and that makes us shine even brighter.

The thing about the human brain is that we have this so-called *negativity bias*, where we're more likely to notice the bad stuff over

The VIA Classification of Character Strengths and Virtues

VIRTUE OF WISDOM	**CREATIVITY** Original & Adaptive, Clever, A problem solver, Sees and does things in different ways	**CURIOSITY** Interested, Explores new things, Open to new ideas	**JUDGMENT** A critical thinker, Thinks things through, Open minded	**LOVE OF LEARNING** Masters new skills & topics, Systemically adds to knowledge	**PERSPECTIVE** Masters new skills & topics, Systemically adds to knowledge
VIRTUE OF COURAGE	**BRAVERY** Shows valor, Doesn't shrink from fear, Speaks up for what's right	**PERSEVERANCE** Persistent, Industrious, Finishes what one starts	**HONESTY** Authentic, Trustworthy, Sincere	**ZEST** Enthusiastic, Energetic, Doesn't do things half-heartedly	
VIRTUE OF HUMANITY	**LOVE** Warm and genuine, Values close relationships	**KINDNESS** Generous, Nurturing, Caring, Compassionate, Altruistic	**SOCIAL INTELLIGENCE** Aware of the motives and feelings of others, Knows what makes others tick		
VIRTUE OF JUSTICE	**TEAMWORK** Team player, Socially responsible, Loyal	**FAIRNESS** Just, Doesn't let feelings bias decisions about others	**LEADERSHIP** Organizes group activities, Encourages a group to get things done		
VIRTUE OF TEMPERANCE	**FORGIVENESS** Merciful, Accepts others' shortcomings, Gives people a second chance	**HUMILITY** Modest, Lets one's accomplishments speak for themselves	**PRUDENCE** Careful, Cautious, Doesn't take undue risk	**SELF-REGULATION** Self-controlled, Manges impulses and emotions	
VIRTUE OF TRANSCENDENCE	**APPRECIATION OF BEAUTY & EXCELLENCE** Feels awe & wonder in beauty, Inspired by goodness of others	**GRATITUDE** Thankful for the good, Expresses thanks, Feels blessed	**HOPE** Optimistic, Future-minded	**HUMOR** Playful, Brings smiles to others, Lighthearted	**SPIRITUALITY** Searches for meaning, Feels a sense of relationship with the sacred

the good.[9] When we mindfully engage our character strengths, we actually shift our focus. By leaning into our own positive attributes, we both *create* more good in the world and *notice* more good in the world. It's like putting on rose-colored glasses, and at the same time also planting more roses.

I'm aware that all of this might sound like a lot of feel-good hyperbole, but try it. Go through this list and highlight your strengths, then choose just one that you want to intentionally lean into for the next month. See what happens. (And when you do, share your results with me on social media. I'd love to hear about your experience!)

If you're having trouble identifying your strengths, which is common, there are several tools that can help you. For one, you can ask your friends or loved ones what they see as your strengths. Also, psychologists Ryan Niemiec and Robert McGrath have expanded on this original research in character strengths to create several resources, including the book *The Power of Character Strengths*, and several related tools, such as an online strengths survey (which you can access at www.viacharacter.org).[10]

Identifying and leaning into our strengths helps us improve our outlook on life and gives us a more positive self-view. But we can also use our strengths as a lever to empower ourselves and become more mindful in the process.

Strengths-Based Mindfulness

One of the reasons I keep coming back to mindfulness is that it's such a powerful tool to get us out of our unhelpful stories and into the present moment, where we can reconnect with our inner light. Yes, the wind is blowing, but our light is still there, glowing. (Hey, maybe if this psychology thing doesn't work out, I can score a job writing motivational lyrics for boy bands.)

As Ryan Niemiec describes in *The Mindfulness and Character Strengths Workbook*, we can purposefully employ our strengths for our own growth and development.[11]

Let's use a simple example of a challenge that many of us face—

losing our cool in traffic. There we are, rolling along on the way to a
doctor appointment when out of nowhere, cars begin to slow, then
stop. Anxiously you glance at your phone, checking the time. Then
you hear the sirens. "Oh great!" you think. "It figures. An accident
just has to happen when I'm already running late!" When you hear the
soothing, dulcet tones of your victim self start to amp up, you're at a
choice point. You can go with the doom spiral (maybe share your
woes on social media), or opt to shift your thinking. If you opt for the
latter, you can leverage your strengths to make that shift.

For instance, let's say one of your strengths is kindness. How can
you exercise kindness in this situation? For one, you can say a prayer
(or send out good vibes or healing thoughts—however you roll) to
those involved, and to the first responders. You can also show *yourself*
kindness by not chastising yourself for leaving late. Yes, note that you
need to leave earlier next time, because you want to incorporate the
learning that's available to you, but don't call yourself a dumbass. Instead, recognize that it was simply a misstep on your part. Another
kind thing to do is to call your doctor's office and let them know
you're running late.

Perhaps another of your strengths is curiosity. How can you engage that in this situation? Well, you could consider how you might
use your newfound time. Perhaps you could catch up on a podcast
you've been meaning to listen to. Or maybe you can practice some
breathwork or create a gratitude list, or think through that challenging problem at work. Suddenly the time doesn't feel like a loss. You
see how this works!

Anytime we start hearing that victim mindset raise its voice, we
can transition to a more empowered way of thinking and being with
the situation at hand. To be clear, that doesn't mean we're trying to
ignore or drown out that victim voice entirely—in some situations it
might have valuable things to say. For instance, it might be calling on
us to care for ourselves or to acknowledge a wrong or hurt that's been
done to us, and that's valid. Again, we just don't want to overidentify
with that one voice.

As Niemiec and McGrath explain:

When things are going well, we can use character strengths to help us see what is best in ourselves and others. When things are going poorly, we can use character strengths to give balance to the struggles we face, to shift our focus from the negative to the positive, to avoid becoming overly self-critical by thinking about our strengths rather than what's wrong with us.[12]

Admittedly, though, sometimes it can be difficult to zero in on our strengths when we're facing what feels like some very real weaknesses.

A Strengths-Based Approach to Disabilities

For those of us (myself included) who have ever grappled with disabilities, what we can't do—or have some difficulty doing—tends to take center stage in our minds. Sometimes it can be flat-out hard to imagine that we have any strengths. Yet the reality is that, interestingly, challenges and strengths often travel together.

Research on students with disabilities such as those with autism show that they also commonly have a range of strengths, many of which can surpass the abilities of their nondisabled peers. In other words, they can also be what we call "gifted" in educational circles. In just reading that, you can see how our typical framing of "disability" fails to paint an accurate picture. Instead, we now have a term that's far more appropriate in its description of what's at work here—the *twice exceptional* child. It's a Yes/And approach to how we view ourselves and others.

Yes, we may struggle to express ourselves, we may be argumentative or have trouble focusing, but we may also be exceptionally imaginative, curious, and resourceful. And this isn't just true of people who are diagnosed with a disability, but all of us. We all have "disabilities" or things that we struggle with, and we all have things we're naturally better at. So we can also take a strengths-based approach to our "disabilities," rather than let them dictate our self-view.

Interestingly, research indicates that adversity—such as the kind we experience when grappling with disabilities and other challenges—may actually be *responsible* for some of our strengths.

Strengths from Adversity

I have spent my entire career attempting to show that giftedness and talent aren't characteristics that you're just born with fully developed, or things that are purely individualistic devoid of context and opportunity.[13] In their book *Giftedness in Childhood*, my mentor Robert Sternberg and his colleague Ophélie Desmet echo that sentiment, arguing that giftedness is "an interaction among an individual, a task or set of tasks, and a situation or set of situations."[14] Why does this matter? Well, according to the authors, one of the things that can spark us to develop remarkable skills or abilities is *adversity*.

For instance, one study showed that people who experienced the death of one or both parents when they were young were "more likely to achieve eminence in their fields than those who did not."[15]

In their Hidden Talents Framework, Bruce Ellis and his colleagues posit that adversity may actually help us develop a kind of "adaptive intelligence."[16] Their model holds that "adversity can serve as a catalyst for developing adaptive skills and coping mechanisms, such as resilience, persistence, adaptability, and empathy."[17] If we approach adversity only from a "deficit perspective," we can easily overlook the gifts that can also accompany it.

This isn't just a nice pep talk, telling you to simply look on the bright side. Shitty experiences are still shitty, but that doesn't have to be all they are. Instead of looking exclusively on either the bright side or the dark side, we want to take in the whole picture, as Azim Khamisa has done.

Khamisa has endured one of the most difficult experiences one can imagine—losing his child to an incident of gang-related violence.[18] And in the wake of his staggering loss, he undertook a revolutionary act. Determined to find a way to make something positive out of his tragedy, Khamisa decided to forgive his son's murderer, Tony Hicks—who was only fourteen years old at the time of the murder—along with Hicks's family. But he went even further than that, creating a foundation dedicated to helping young people embrace forgiveness, nonviolence, and peacebuilding. Today, he and Hicks's family together speak to groups of kids, encouraging them to develop their own positive character strengths, including forgiveness. Over two decades, Khamisa and his daughter also developed a relationship with Hicks, whom they grew to see as the second victim of the crime. In 2024, Hicks was released from prison after the pair offered their support at his parole hearing. Hicks now serves on the board of Khamisa's foundation.

In opting to adopt a more empowered self-view, forgiveness may be one of the most important strengths for us to cultivate.

HARNESS THE POWER OF FORGIVENESS

Who you blame is who you give your power to.

—*Mark Manson*

"We live in a time where victimhood is currency, very literally," artist Kimi Katiti told me when we spoke.[19] "I fell for that narrative for a time. I found that it doesn't yield the sort of liberation you would think it would."

I asked Katiti to share with me some of her insights on the victim mindset. She has a unique perspective, having spent many of her formative years in Africa—growing up in formerly colonized countries including Uganda and Tanzania, as well as South Africa, where she lived through high school. Even though the South African apartheid had long since been abolished, "there was still healing to be done," she says. "There is still an ever-present ghost of apartheid."

Still, when Katiti came to the United States for college, she was unprepared for the characterizations of race and gender that she encountered. "I was dosed with this idea that everything is working against you."[20] As a result, she says, "I started to believe that every look I got, or if someone didn't say 'hi' back to me, it was racist or sexist." Over time, she noticed a decline in her mental health and well-being. She felt fragile, anxious, and "filled with so much darkness."

Unsure of what to do to rid herself of these terrible feelings, she leaned into her spirituality and prayed for insight. "The answer was clear," she says. "I had to forgive."

When she thought back to her time in South Africa, Katiti recalled that while the specter of apartheid still loomed, there was also much talk of forgiveness. It wasn't about forgetting but about not letting the terrors of the past overshadow the present.

So Katiti got out her journal and started writing down as many transgressions as she could recall. For a year, every time she remembered an experience of racism or sexism, she wrote it down, and she forgave it. "That was the beginning of feeling peace," she says.

I realized that all of these things I was trying to keep and hold on to for fuel, for fire. Now I still remember everything, but there's no pain attached to them. And I've never had this much control in my life emotionally and in my psyche. I had to reject that model of thinking. It's a burden that, I discovered, is totally optional.

Again, this isn't about throwing up your hands and saying, "Eh, no big deal!" As Katiti observes, "You have to forgive *an injustice*—meaning it was real. We need to acknowledge that racism and sexism exist, but when we release their hold on us, we release their power over us." This is how we change culture, Katiti says, by refusing to let these things control us and how we live. In many ways it's similar to Azim Khamisa's approach of using forgiveness to model another, more compassionate way of being. When we witness that kind of grace and strength in others, it changes us, showing us another way we can walk through the world.

But forgiveness isn't just a spiritual concept—its effectiveness is backed by science.

The Science of Forgiveness

As research shows, forgiveness doesn't just feel good, it also benefits our mental and physical well-being.[21] As Stanford psychologist Frederic Luskin has demonstrated, learning to forgive renders us emotionally stronger. That may not sound too surprising, but check this out: In his research, including work with families whose loved ones were murdered during the political turmoil in Northern Ireland, Luskin found that practicing forgiveness also makes us feel more confident and gives us a more optimistic outlook on life.

As writer Jeremy Sutton observed:

One of the groups included women whose sons had been tragically killed, often shot for no other reason than their religious or political upbringing. Understandably, these women—even years after their son's death—were suffering extreme pain and anger and felt their healing had been largely ignored. The forgiveness training offered by the team at Stanford had incredible, life-changing results. On arrival, the women averaged a hurt score of 8.5 out of 10. By the time they left, their self-reported hurt had reduced to 3.5. Also, longer term, the women reported fewer feelings of depression and increased optimism.[22]

To be fair, like so many things, forgiveness is simple as a concept but often difficult in practice (especially when it comes to group conflicts, as we'll see in the last chapter). Think of Kimi Katiti journaling for *a year*. It's a journey, folks! Dr. Tyler VanderWeele, co-director of the Initiative on Health, Spirituality, and Religion at Harvard, says, "Forgiving a person who has wronged you is never easy, but dwelling on those events and reliving them over and over can fill your mind with negative thoughts and suppressed anger. Yet when you learn to forgive, you are no longer trapped by the past actions of others and can finally feel free."[23]

One way to think of it is that forgiveness

Forgiveness helps to dispel the darkness that's obscuring our light.

helps to dispel the darkness that's obscuring our light. One practice that can help you do that is called the REACH method.

The REACH Method

There are many paths to forgiveness, but if you'd like a step-by-step map to follow, the REACH method is just that. It works as follows:[24]

Recall: The first step is to recall the incident. The goal here isn't to get yourself all worked up or to justify your feelings of hurt, anger, or betrayal. The point is simply to get a clear picture of the trespass. Let those negative feelings exist, but don't amplify them.

Empathize: Now, try to take the other person's point of view, understanding what their motivation may have been or what they may have been feeling at the time. For instance, they may have lashed out verbally because they felt defensive. They may have made a racist remark because that's how they were raised. This is not about justifying or minimizing their actions but trying to get an inkling of insight on their perspective or rationale, no matter how small. It's about seeing them as a fallible human being.

Altruistic gift: Next, consider a time when you acted in a way you regretted. The point here is to recognize that we all need forgiveness from time to time. From this perspective, we understand that forgiveness is an altruistic gift we can offer another person.

Commit: Now you make a commitment to actually forgive the person. Again, this doesn't mean you automatically release what happened or let go of your resentment—this isn't a magic trick, and as we'll see in the last chapter you can healthily integrate the resentment with your commitment to forgive. However, this commitment puts the control back in your hands, as you are *choosing* to forgive the person and move on with your life.

Hold: Finally, hold on to your forgiveness—meaning that at some point (maybe many points) you will be reminded again of the other person's transgression, and those old feelings of anger or resentment may bubble up and feel strong. That's fine; this is a process. The ultimate goal isn't necessarily to shed all anger and resentment forever, it's to go through this cycle again and again as needed so that you can lead a healthier existence.

When you release someone from the prison of judgment you've been keeping them in—however much they may deserve to be there—as Kimi Katiti and Azim Khamisa experienced, you release yourself as well.

Forgiveness can take practice, and some methods may resonate with you more than others. That said, here's another approach that can help.

Connect with Healthy Self-Love

Whether you're struggling with forgiveness or just need to tame your reactivity, this simple but profound practice from the Holistic Life Foundation can transform how you see yourself and others.

As Atman Smith describes it: "If you find yourself cursing someone out, hating someone, blaming someone, getting worked up, meditate on how much you love yourself. Refocus on the light within yourself. *Then* look back at them."

More often than not, when you hold that space of love and acceptance around yourself, you transfer it to others. In other words, it's difficult to truly love yourself at the same time that you hate or blame someone else.

And that's what this chapter really boils down to, the idea that

Where you put your attention is where you put your life.

where you put your attention is where you put your life.[25] Yes, negative things will happen. Sometimes they're devastating. But if that's where we keep our focus, that's the lens through which we will view the world. And when that happens, as Kimi Katiti says, we rob ourselves of our peace.

Earlier in the chapter I noted that if all you focus on is your own victimhood, that's the only part of your identity that you'll see. Similarly, if all you *show* people is your victimhood, that's all *they'll* see. Yes, acknowledge your wounds—that's important. But also remember the part of you that's not wounded. The part that can't ever be broken, and see the world through *those* eyes. Show the world the whole you.

As Maya Angelou once said, "Nothing can dim the light that shines from within."

So connect with your light, and let it shine!

7

Channel Your Gifts
of Sensitivity

*The truly creative mind in any field is no more than this: A
human creature born abnormally, inhumanly sensitive. To
him . . . a touch is a blow, a sound is a noise, a misfortune is a
tragedy, a joy is an ecstasy, a friend is a lover, a lover is a god,
and failure is death. Add to this cruelly delicate organism the
overpowering necessity to create, create, and create—so that
without the creating of music or poetry or books or buildings or
something of meaning, his very breath is cut off from him. He
must create, must pour out creation. By some strange, unknown,
inward urgency he is not really alive unless he is creating.*

—*Pearl S. Buck*

Author Joseph Keon grew up in a household where he was plagued
by fear and anxiety. His father's physical violence put him on
constant alert. "I was trying to predict what the environment por-
tended in the next hours, days, weeks. And so, as a coping mechanism, what I did was I became a student of my father," Keon says. He
would watch for the slightest shifts in demeanor, tone, or language,
"anything that could help me forecast what was coming in the near
future and thereby potentially protect myself." He says, "I think that
experience also helped me in becoming increasingly sensitive as a
man in the world because I learned to pay attention to really subtle

cues." Wait . . . *Helped* him? How could something so traumatic be useful?

Well, as is so often the case (like in every single superhero origin story ever), the skills and abilities we develop to cope and to survive the most difficult circumstances can potentially serve us. As I mentioned in Chapter 1, upon deep reflection (and after lots of cognitive and somatic therapy), writer and producer Stephanie Foo was able to recognize that many of her most appealing qualities and strongest skills actually grew out of the soil of her abusive childhood.[1] And for the rest of us, the same can be true—the shit we endure can turn out to be tremendous fertilizer for future growth. This might be even more true for highly sensitive people, or HSPs.

Joseph Keon's story is featured in the documentary series *Sensitive Men Rising*, directed by award-winning Will Harper. It's a series in which I, too, was featured.* My entire life I have noticed that I feel everything deeply, notice subtle things in the environment, and can easily become overwhelmed by too much stimuli. When I discovered the psychological research on HSPs, it felt like such a relief to be able to better understand my experience.

Until relatively recently, however, few outside the research or clinical communities knew the acronym *HSP*. Today, however, it's relatively commonplace, even popping up in mainstream programming. One such appearance is in the first season of the blockbuster show *The White Lotus*, via the character Paula—a college student who accompanies her best friend on the latter's family vacation to Hawaii. And as the show depicts, being an HSP can be a double-edged sword.

In many ways, Paula is out of her element. She's a woman of color from modest means sharing a suite with the Mossbachers, an ultra-rich, ultra-white family. Underscoring Paula's standout status is her vast array of physical and mental health challenges. She seems allergic to, well, pretty much everything. She arrives on the island stocked

---

* https://sensitivemenrising.org

up with a cache of medications to quell her anxiety, help her sleep, and generally cope with the everyday demands of being alive.

One morning, Nicole, the Mossbacher matriarch, comes into the family living room, where Paula and her bestie, Olivia, are sleeping on the pullout. Nicole sweeps in and admonishes the pair for snoozing the day away. "Girls, let's get going. You don't wanna miss breakfast," she declares.

"Mom," Olivia scolds, "you can't just open the doors." When Nicole asks why not, Olivia responds, "Paula's an HSP."

"What's that?" Nicole asks.

Olivia groans at her mom's ignorance. "Highly sensitive person."

When Nicole protests that there's no such thing, Olivia counters that Paula's been clinically diagnosed.

"Really?" Nicole retorts. "Who's her physician? Lena Dunham?"

An incensed Paula asserts that she could suffer real damage from Nicole's incursion. "You could inflame my Morgellons," she deadpans.[2] For Paula, it's a subtle self-jab from the writers. Morgellons is a dermatological condition that many doctors characterize as psychosomatic.

This exchange highlights some of the misunderstandings about what it means to be highly sensitive (yes, Nicole, it *is* a real thing). And it also sheds light on how some people with this trait (along with some who *aren't* actually high in sensitivity) can lean on this identity too much, demanding special status or affordances in a way not conducive to growth and development.

Psychologist Elaine Aron, who pioneered the scientific study of HSPs, argues that the core of being an HSP is what scientists refer to as *sensory processing sensitivity*, or being acutely sensitive to sensory stimulation. While this may seem like a straightforward definition, as we'll see in this chapter, what it's like to be an HSP is much more complex. Let's turn back to Paula.

Though she's at first framed as somewhat frail, Paula also seems to have a sense of superiority and feels free to hastily and harshly judge others for their views and actions. Yet at the same time, it's clear that she has a strong intellect and is very insightful, often seeing things that others miss. For instance, she identifies some very real hypocrisies around her host family's behavior and is both aware of and obviously pained by the harm done to native Hawaiians by much of the tourist trade—something no other guest at the resort seems to notice or consider. In this way, she showcases some of the varied ways that those with high sensitivity can relate to the world around them.

If you look around social media, you'll see HSPs alternately venerated as special heroes with superhuman powers or infantilized and treated like helpless victims. So which is accurate?

High sensitivity can be a blessing *and* a burden.

High sensitivity can be a blessing *and* a burden. It's simply a temperament. And as with other traits, how we *choose* to both perceive and direct it is at least partly up to us. But we'll talk about that in a moment. First, let's take a closer look at what high sensitivity is.

WHAT'S IT LIKE TO BE A HIGHLY SENSITIVE PERSON?

As I mentioned, being highly sensitive can look different ways for different people. The following comments provide some insight into these varied experiences:

> "I think I was born with a great awareness of my surroundings and of other people. Sometimes that awareness is good, and sometimes I wish I wasn't so sensitive."[3]

> "It's that constant push-pull of going, How do I stay human and vulnerable and real, and how do I, at the same time, not let all this affect me?"[4]

> "[HSPs] feel different, but they don't know what it is. They feel more. Everything hurts. Everything. They're supersensitive. They see things that other people don't see."[5]

Being especially attuned to your environment can both be a powerful and empowering experience and present real challenges. As I mentioned, research on HSPs was pioneered by psychologist Elaine Aron, who developed the first self-assessment to gauge high sensitivity. Consider the following items, which are taken from Aron's quiz:[6]

- I am easily overwhelmed by strong sensory input.

- I seem to be aware of subtleties in my environment.

- Other people's moods affect me.

- I tend to be very sensitive to pain.

- I find myself needing to withdraw during busy days, into bed or into a darkened room or any place where I can have some privacy and relief from stimulation.

- I am easily overwhelmed by things like bright lights, strong smells, coarse fabrics, or sirens close by.

- I have a rich, complex inner life.

- I am deeply moved by the arts or music.

- I get rattled when I have a lot to do in a short amount of time.

- I become unpleasantly aroused when a lot is going on around me.

- I find it unpleasant to have a lot going on at once.

Maybe you don't really relate to any of these, or perhaps you feel that some of the statements describe you to some extent. Or maybe, like me, you're nodding vigorously to virtually all of them. If so, welcome to the HSP club!

It's estimated that roughly 15 to 20 percent of the population is highly sensitive.[7] Among this group, high sensitivity can look different ways but has some underlying characteristics that are relatively common.

As Aron writes in her book *The Highly Sensitive Child*:

> *One reason for the variation among HSPs is that temperament traits seem to be caused by several genes, each having small, cumulative effects. Thus each different flavor of sensitivity—sensitivity to the subtle, the overwhelming, the new, the emotional, the social, or the physical and nonsocial—may be caused by a different gene. Yet there is still something common to these sensitivities and they may be inherited together.*[8]

What's super interesting is that high sensitivity isn't just a trait among humans. In fact, it's been found in a wide variety of animals. But how do we know this? Did scientists observing sunfish find that some would get really annoyed by their finmates' constant loud swishing and would need to swim off for some alone time so they could decompress? Not exactly.

However, there *are* certain behaviors that humans share with other animals that indicate high sensitivity. For instance, among both primates and children, when both encounter a jungle gym for the first time, some will be happy to dive right in, while others will opt to hold back and study the structure before proceeding.[9] The latter behavior is associated with high sensitivity—among this group, both people and animals often proceed with caution in novel situations to give themselves time to process the new information and assess how they want to respond to it.

I characterize the highly sensitive person construct as comprising two highly related forms of sensitivity: being *open to life* and being *overwhelmed by life*. How can one person inhabit both of these spaces? I'll explain.

High sensitivity is characterized by a blend of two traits—neuroticism and openness to experience. This highlights some of the push-pull of high sensitivity, and why it can feel like both a blessing and a curse.

On the one hand, openness to experience is correlated with loads of positive attributes. I have been scientifically investigating the correlates of openness to experience for over fifteen years and have found that individuals who rate high in openness tend to score higher in creative achievement across the arts and sciences.[10] People who score higher in openness to experience have both the desire and the ability to explore the world cognitively through both their senses and their intellect.[11]

Modern research on openness can be linked to the concept of *overexcitabilities*, studied by the Polish psychiatrist Kazimierz Dąbrowski. According to Dąbrowski's theory of positive disintegration, overexcitabilities indicate a heightened activity of the nervous system and can lead to advanced moral and emotional development.

While acknowledging that overexcitabilities can make everyday life feel more intense, Dąbrowski very much viewed overexcitabilities as an aspect of "development potential." Through decades of experience as a clinician as well as his biographical studies of artists, writers, spiritual leaders, and developmentally advanced children and adolescents, he found over and over again that overexcitabilities were a key contributor to growth and development. Dąbrowski's overexcitabilities can be mapped onto different facets of the openness to experience domain of personality:[12]

- *Openness to fantasy* (imaginational overexcitability): having a rich fantasy life and proneness to vivid daydreaming

- *Openness to aesthetics* (sensual overexcitability): enjoyment and absorption in beauty and the arts

- *Openness to feelings* (emotional overexcitability): openness to a full range of feelings, both in variety and intensity

- *Openness to ideas* (intellectual overexcitability): having a ravenous curiosity, passion for learning, and need to understand ideas and the reasoning behind arguments

- *Openness to actions* (psychomotor overexcitability): love of novelty and getting out of one's comfort zone

On the other hand, when combined with a proneness to anxiety, worry, and rumination (as is often the case with HSPs), open people can be prone to avoidance behaviors, such as withdrawing in the face of challenge or overwhelm. They can tend toward devaluing themselves and their experiences, and they may be particularly sensitive to shame and apt to do whatever they can to avoid experiences that could cause shame. People-pleasing behavior is one of several potential maladaptive responses to this tendency. An abundance of neuroticism can tend to make HSPs more anxious, in general, without needing a distinct cause or source for their anxiety (other than being in their own brain, that is).

A distinct challenge of HSPs is that they (by which I mean *we*) have this quality of being open to what life has to offer, and yet when life offers, they can become quickly overwhelmed by all of the stimulation that they then have to process. It can seem like a bit of a cruel setup (and can feel that way quite often), but as I'll explain in a minute, it doesn't have to be that way.

In fact, I believe that high sensitivity offers far more gifts than drawbacks provided you learn how to work *with* it instead of *against* it. But before we get to that part, let's clear up some common misunderstandings about high sensitivity as a trait.

What We Get Wrong about High Sensitivity

One myth that's become prominent more recently is that high sensitivity is *caused* by trauma. Bzzzt! Hit the big buzzer, because this popular meme is simply not always the case.

Say it with me now: *Not everything is about trauma.* In other words, high sensitivity can and does exist separate from trauma.

Like everyone else, people who are highly sensitive may absolutely have experienced potentially traumatic events in their childhood and may have lingering trauma as a result. However, not all HSPs have had childhood trauma.

HSPs may be more likely to interpret adverse experiences as "traumatic" because they feel things so darn deeply. As a result of this interpretation of events, they may be more likely to develop longer-term issues as a result. But as you now know, high sensitivity is a *trait*, and all traits are a mix of nature and nurture. If you're highly sensitive, it's not because something's wrong with you, or because of something that happened to you—it's a part of your personality structure, trauma or no trauma.

Another common misconception is that high sensitivity is the same as introversion. When Elaine Aron first set out to study high sensitivity, she actually anticipated that this would be the case. Yet as she discovered, while there is a positive correlation between introversion and high sensitivity, they're not synonymous. In fact, roughly 30 percent of those who score as highly sensitive also score high in extraversion.[13]

Why the confusion? The perceived "shyness" that can be exhibited by those who are highly sensitive is often a component of the trait of neuroticism. Those high in sensitivity may be more *anxious* in new situations, but this isn't necessarily as much about shyness per se as simply wanting to hold back to assess the environment or the person before connecting. You see this frequently among highly sensitive kids—just because they might not like to dive right in, they can get tagged as shy. But those who know them better may simply characterize them as "slow to warm up," meaning they're often happy to interact if they get the lay of the land and decide they feel comfortable.

As I already mentioned, high sensitivity is also correlated with high degrees of creativity and imagination, which are often mistakenly linked with introversion. Many creative people—wherever they lie on the introversion/extraversion continuum—are deeply anxious *and* open people, who both worry a lot about human problems and are open to finding new meanings and interpretations.[14] In fact, I believe that a lot of people who think they are sensitive introverts are actually neurotic highly sensitive extraverts (yes, that personality configuration is possible)![15]

As you can see, there are many misunderstandings about not only high sensitivity but also introversion. People tend to believe that introversion and extraversion boil down to the degree to which you want to be social, but these are most likely just behavioral manifestations of the underlying mechanisms driving each.

Extraverts aren't just more social because they like people a lot, it's because they're more tuned to potential "appetitive" rewards in their environment—such as money, power, sex, and social status. It just so happens that among humans, social interactions evolved to be one of the best routes to these rewards.[16] For instance, gaining people's attention can be instrumental to acquiring friends, a romantic partner, a sexual liaison, money, or countless other appetitive rewards. So engage enthusiastically with the environment, garner the rewards.

Conversely, introverts are less energized by the possibility of these appetitive rewards. So it's not that they don't like people, or even that they necessarily have social anxiety (which has more to do with neuroticism than introversion) but rather that they aren't likely to expend energy on attention-seeking behaviors or to make new acquaintances (such as attending a networking event) because they just don't care as much about the potential dopaminergic rewards those things afford. Remember, too, that these traits are not light switches, they're dimmers. Each of us falls at some place along the spectrum between extraversion and introversion. Most people are actually *ambiverts*, who fall somewhere in the middle.

These traits are not light switches, they're dimmers.

Another common misunderstanding about HSPs is that they're sensitive to *everything*, but they haven't cornered the market on sensitivity. In fact, there are actually fifty shades of sensitivity (sorry, couldn't help myself).[17] All personality traits have an inherent sensitivity to *something*. Here are some examples:

- As you just learned, people high in *extraversion* are sensitive to appetitive rewards.

- People high in *agreeableness* are sensitive to other people's needs, goals, concerns, and feelings.

- People high in *conscientiousness* are sensitive to abstract or distant goals.

- People high in *vulnerable narcissism* are hypersensitive to criticism and evaluation.

- People high in *grandiose narcissism* are hypersensitive to cues of praise and acclaim.

Since HSPs typically have a blend of neuroticism and openness to experience, they tend to be highly sensitive to threat (neuroticism) and sensitive to the value of information for its own sake (openness to experience). That's why I refer to the openness brain pathway as the "nerdy dopamine pathway".[18] Instead of dopamine being projected to areas that signal the possibility of appetitive rewards (such as is the case with extraversion), HSPs often get energized by the possibility of learning something new.[19] As my friend and collaborator Colin DeYoung puts it, dopamine is the "neuromodulator of exploration," and this form of exploration can be directed toward both garnering appetitive rewards and gaining rewards from learning new information.[20]

Also, note that being an HSP doesn't necessarily mean you'll also be highly sensitive to the needs, goals, concerns, and feelings of other people—unless you're *also* high in agreeableness. And that's another myth about HSPs—that they inherently care more about others or are all "empaths." People with high sensitivity may be more attuned to others' suffering, but that doesn't mean they're necessarily more caring or compassionate than people who don't have this trait. It's the *blend* of personality traits that make the greater whole of a human personality. This can create interesting configurations of personality traits, such as the seemingly paradoxical dark healer—a brand of excessive helper (Chapter 5) that frequently falls into the HSP category.

Dark Healers

I know—the name sounds like an antihero out of a DC Comics movie, but dark healers really do walk among us. To be clear, not all healers are dark. In her beautiful book *Bittersweet: How Sorrow and Longing Make Us Whole*, my friend Susan Cain talks about the power of "wounded healers."[21] The term was first coined by Carl Jung in 1951, and it's one of humanity's oldest and most universal archetypes. You can find the wounded healer in Greek mythology, in cultures with shamanic traditions, and in Judeo-Christianity. Prominent examples of wounded healers include the Jewish Messiah, Christ, and Muhammad. In more recent times, we can look to luminaries such as Maya Angelou, who experienced parental abandonment, rape, and racism, only to triumph over her traumas and share her hard-earned wisdom with us.

To be fair, I don't want to make it sound like we can simply confront deep traumas and resolve them forever. Certainly, the process is not that simple. What Angelou and other wounded healers have been able to do that many of us struggle with is to make some kind of meaning from their suffering, developing wisdom and insight that help not only them but others as well.

According to Cain, wounded healers respond to loss by helping to heal in others the wounds they themselves have suffered. Such people are all around us, from the firefighter who as a child saw their own home go up in flames to the person whose father died of cancer when they were young and then went on to become a grief counselor. Wounded healers do exist, and what they offer can be tremendously positive. As the poet Dorianne Laux put it, "We're all writing out of a wound, and that's where our song comes from. The wound is singing. We're singing back to those who've been wounded."[22]

But it's important to underscore that wounded healers have done something that those obsessed with their victimhood have not—they have alchemized their suffering into learning and growth that can assist others.

Indeed, past suffering can make us more empathic and sensitive to others' anguish, and many excessive helpers are genuine empaths—people who are highly attuned to the emotions of others around them, who often feel what others are feeling—who self-label as such. On *Star Trek: The Next Generation*, Deanna Troi, who is gifted with telepathy and an ability to sense other species' emotions, functions as the ship's counselor. Yet people who are hypersensitive can also struggle to separate others' emotions from their own and may experience this attunement as a burden rather than a gift. Maybe, like Counselor Troi, they sometimes feel as if they can sense emotions from an entire planet away!

There is a very real need among "empaths" to learn strategies to self-regulate so they're not overwhelmed by what they feel. And yet for very different reasons, not all people with this skill set are *constructively empathic*.[23] In other words, they don't all use their powers for good. Enter the *dark healer*. (Dun-dun-dunnn!)

There can be a dark side to everything, even empathy. When we're convinced we know exactly what others are feeling, it can blind us to the real felt needs or experiences of others, especially if we are deeply attached to our identity as an empath.

New research validates the existence of dark healers.[24] Across a sample of 991 people, researchers discovered four basic profiles. Three of these were *typicals*, who were not especially empathic and did not score especially high on so-called dark traits, which include narcissism; *empaths*, who—you guessed it—scored high on empathy; and *dark traits*, or people who scored higher on traits such as narcissism.

While standard empaths composed just over 33 percent of the population, there was a second, smaller collection of empaths. In addition to being high in empathy, this group—the *dark empaths* (as the researchers referred to them)—also demonstrated elevated levels of narcissism, manipulativeness, and psychopathy. And unlike the typicals and the empaths (but like the dark traits group), they were more likely to show *indirect aggression*—making people feel guilty, excluding people socially, and using malicious humor. Like regular empaths, dark empaths may present as agreeable and polite, yet they may also exhibit these more negative behaviors.

So just being an empath doesn't necessarily render you willing or able to help others. (Plus, research shows that people who score high in emotional intelligence could actually use that astute awareness to manipulate others.)[25] And as psychologist Paul Bloom underscores in his book *Against Empathy: The Case for Rational Compassion*, one need not have *affective empathy* (to actually feel what people are feeling) to help others.[26] We can also operate out of something called *cognitive empathy*, or a rational sense of understanding, morality, and compassion.

Okay, yes—psychopaths tend to rate high in cognitive empathy and low in affective empathy, but just because someone isn't an empath, that doesn't mean they are necessarily a psychopath![27] Some people high in affective empathy seem to hold a kind of superiority around their empath status (there's that empathic ego again). However, when affective empathy is paired with an impairment in cognitive empathy, as I mentioned earlier, it can make it difficult to shift one's perspective away from those feelings, and even to distinguish one's own feelings from those of another person.

A sort of enmeshment ensues as empaths are unable to stop feeling other people's pain and may become depressed as a result. On the other hand, psychopaths are less likely to be concerned with other people's pain and suffering; however, they can use their acute perspective-taking skills to manipulate and exploit others. This may underpin a callous or remorseless nature in which, like the fictional character Gordon Gekko in the movie *Wall Street*, they are less bothered about hurting other people.[28]

The dark healer has high affective empathy but also scores high on measures of narcissism, manipulativeness, and psychopathy. They may seem to feel what others are feeling but also have the narcissistic confidence that they know *exactly* what they need to do to help the other person. However, they lack the perspective-taking ability to guide them in their helping. This can make it much more likely that their helping will be intrusive and not actually useful.

Consider this line from Walt Whitman's famous poem "Song of Myself": "I do not ask the wounded person how he feels, I myself become the wounded person."[29] While this sentiment is beautiful in one sense, when we consider it from another angle, it may not be the healthiest. (Walt, you need to establish some boundaries, my friend.)

I heard a rather disturbing story that can serve as a cautionary tale for both people with dark healer traits and those they encounter. A massage therapist I know was seeing a new client—someone who had formerly seen another therapist. In a quiet, barely audible voice, the client told the new therapist that she preferred light to moderate pressure. When the therapist assured the client that he would check in with her to gauge her comfort and wouldn't do anything she wasn't okay with, the client visibly relaxed. "Thank goodness," she said, "because the last therapist I had used a lot of pressure. Like, *a lot*. And when I told her it was too much, she told me that she knew what was good for me, and that I needed it." Tears came to the client's eyes. "She hurt me," the woman continued, "and when I asked her to stop, she wouldn't. She just kept saying that I needed it." If that doesn't sound like abusive behavior, I don't know what does!

Sadly, the specter of the dark healer looms large throughout the healing sector. If you're a self-help guru or a disciple of one, I'm looking at you. Yeah, you! Any time you engage in an experience or a framework where you're meant to be offering or receiving assistance with personal healing, it's essential to exercise discernment and deeply examine the motivations and methods involved. To the healer or guru, I encourage you to ask yourself:

- Am I empowering the people I work with, or disempowering them?

- Am I encouraging them to be an active participant in their own healing, or to believe that the only path to healing or personal development is through me?

- Do I encourage clients to give up their personal power and credit me with their healing?

- Do I see myself as special or uniquely capable of helping others?

To the devotee, ask yourself:

- Does this assistance come with an outsized financial commitment?

- Do I have a "golden projection" onto this person? Am I potentially seeing them as someone who is uniquely capable of "fixing" me, or are they helping me see myself as the source of my own healing?

- Is this person encouraging me to depend on them or encouraging me to be personally empowered?

Given their propensity for high empathy, it makes sense that HSPs compose a significant portion of the healing and personal development sector. Sadly, a subset of this population are dark healers. It probably won't come as a surprise, then, that research has also revealed connections between HSPs and vulnerable narcissism.

THE LINK BETWEEN SENSORY-PROCESSING SENSITIVITY AND VULNERABLE NARCISSISM

If you look on social media, you'll see a variety of messages about #HSPs. On one hand, there's a characterization of HSPs as having special abilities that make them unique. While this is true to an extent, I want to emphasize that *unique* is not necessarily *better*. In fact, research has found correlates between high sensitivity and some aspects of vulnerable narcissism.

Psychologist Emanuel Jauk and his colleagues noted aspects of self-importance and entitlement in the way that some people who self-identify as highly sensitive communicate about themselves.[30] Both are core features of narcissism.[31]

Let's be honest: Believing that "my sensitivity makes me superior to others" has the potential to veer into narcissistic territory. Conversely, HSPs sometimes characterize themselves as being victims of their own sensitivity who are constantly overwhelmed with the world. They therefore not only require but deserve special affordances.

Because they're deeply affected by their environment, they can expect everyone around them to at all times make every situation "welcoming" and "safe." And I bet at this point you know what *that* kind of attitude signals. You guessed it—*vulnerable narcissism.*

Here are some items on the Maladaptive Covert Narcissism Scale that may correlate with high sensitivity:[32]

- I can become entirely absorbed in thinking about my personal affairs, my health, my cares, or my relations to others.

- My feelings are easily hurt by ridicule or the slighting remarks of others.

- When I enter a room, I often become self-conscious and feel that the eyes of others are upon me.

- I feel that I am temperamentally different from most people.

- I tend to feel humiliated when criticized.

- I have problems that no one else seems to understand.

- I try to avoid rejection at all costs.

- Defeat and disappointment usually shame or anger me, but I try not to show it.

As I mentioned earlier, being sensitive doesn't necessarily make you a caring, kind, and cooperative human. It's entirely possible to be incredibly sensitive to all the stimuli in your environment *and* to criticism, and to even be heavily affected by others' moods and *still* be a colossal asshole! I'm reminded of the listicle "7 Signs Kanye West is Secretly an Introvert."[33] The article makes the case that Kanye really isn't a jerk, he's just a "highly sensitive introvert." Well, actually, you can be a highly sensitive introverted jerk! (In response to those kind of listicles about introverts, I wrote a cheeky article in *Scientific American* called "23 Signs You're Secretly a Narcissist Masquerading as a Sensitive Introvert.")[34]

Of course, many HSPs *are* exceptionally kind and empathetic; that may be *informed* by those people's high sensitivity, but it's not *because* of it. There are plenty of highly kind and caring people who do not score particularly high on the HSP scale. And let's be honest here: Some people with high sensitivity do act like total jerks.

Let's turn back to our friend Paula from *The White Lotus* for a moment. Spoiler alert! At one point in the show, Paula decides to exact revenge on the Mossbachers, who to her represent the epitome of white entitlement.[35] She convinces Kai, a hotel employee and native Hawaiian whom she's taken up with, to break into the Mossbachers' suite while they're out on a scuba trip and steal two of Nicole's expensive bracelets from the in-room safe.

Kai is extremely reluctant, but Paula pushes him, telling him that he's entitled to compensation for the land that was stolen from his family, and eventually he relents. It doesn't go well—Kai is caught and arrested, worse off than before thanks to Paula's misguided intervention. Her attitude is vulnerable narcissism on parade.

But I also want to point out something else here. Paula's sensitivity to Kai's situation was a very positive thing. The fact that she was aware of his and his family's suffering was commendable. It's what she decided to *do* with this awareness—the choice she made—that was the problem.

Let me be super clear: HSPs are not necessarily narcissistic. Jauk and his colleagues focused on correlations that only indicate a significant co-occurrence, but the correlations were far from perfect.

Nevertheless, their findings were informative. Jauk and his colleagues found a positive correlation between HSP scale items having to do with being *overwhelmed with life* (the *ease of excitation* and *low sensory threshold* subscales, to be exact) and the following specific dimensions of vulnerable narcissism: hiding the self, devaluing oneself, and having self-esteem contingent on external validation.

The items on the HSP scale having to do with heightened appreciation of beauty and aesthetics and feeling art and music more deeply were not as strongly correlated with these characteristics of vulnerable narcissism. That makes sense considering that aesthetic sensitivity is tied more to openness to experience than neuroticism, and it's the neuroticism that is particularly linked to vulnerable narcissism. Indeed, prior research has found that those scoring higher on the aesthetic sensitivity facet of the HSP scale tend to report greater positive emotions in their lives.[36]

These nuanced findings are elucidating. According to the researchers, "This shows that an irritability through external stimuli, paired with an attitude of own fragility . . . have not only theoretical but also substantial empirical overlaps with hypersensitive/vulnerable narcissism."[37]

Let's hit pause for a second and highlight that statement: A factor in whether HSPs also displayed tendencies toward vulnerable narcissism was *whether they saw themselves as fragile*. If you tend to be trapped in a victim concept about your sensitivity, you are more likely to exhibit these characteristics of vulnerable narcissism.

Also, while there was no correlation whatsoever between the HSP scale and a tendency to exploit others for one's own gain, there was a substantial correlation between the HSP scale and both entitlement rage and "vulnerable-based entitlement," which, if you recall from the Introduction, involves a pervasive sense of entitlement based on a past history of suffering or perceived fragility. Therefore, while HSPs may not show overtly antagonistic behaviors toward others, there does seem to be a significant correlation with covert antagonism that can serve as a defense mechanism to protect the self from being threatened. The researchers note that these findings indicate that some HSPs may hold an attitude of "I am fragile, so I deserve to avoid any discomfort."

The researchers were quick to point out that they were not

attempting to pathologize HSPs. Instead, they stated that high sensitivity has both adaptive and maladaptive qualities. "We believe that only a perspective facing both desirable and undesirable qualities of one's personality allows for individual growth."[38]

At the end of the day, it's only by seeing ourselves—including both our gifts and challenges—clearly that we can develop to our fullest potential. I mean after all, that's why you're reading this book, right? Personal growth requires facing one's own personality with radical self-honesty.

This research also highlights the potential downside of self-identifying too much as an HSP and tying that identity to a victimhood identity. Just because you have a disposition for high sensitivity doesn't mean that's *all* you are, or even that you must be highly sensitive *at all times*. Flexibility is key (more on that later in this chapter). It also doesn't mean that everyone should be a mind reader (or emotions reader?) and accommodate your every desire or forgive your every bad behavior simply because you "feel things more deeply" than other humans.

But we're not done yet. We have one more misunderstanding to dispel. It's about another group—those who *signal* sensitivity but who aren't necessarily HSPs.

Will the Real HSPs Please Stand Up?

By this point, you're acquainted with the idea of *signaling*, where we offer information in the hopes that it will help others understand or believe something specific about us. In and of itself, signaling isn't a bad thing. We might signal for beneficial reasons. For instance, teachers and business owners sometimes display a *safe space* sticker or rainbow flag to signal to members of the LGBTQ+ community that they're welcome. But signaling can also be used for less prosocial or inauthentic purposes.

Recall in Chapter 5 where I cited research on online giving, where people were quick to indicate their support of a cause but often didn't actually contribute. They received a social benefit by signaling their own generosity, but they didn't actually have to make good on their promise, and often they didn't. Just because we signal something doesn't mean it's *true*.

In the past, high sensitivity was largely misunderstood (and in many ways it still is). People saw sensitivity as a weakness, especially among men (again, plenty still do, unfortunately).[39] But more recently, as understanding about high sensitivity grows and people begin to see the upside of these acute abilities of perception, having empath or HSP status has gained some cachet. Thus, there are now some benefits of signaling high sensitivity.

In recent years, I've personally noticed a huge increase in *sensitivity signaling* on social media, in blogs and articles, and in my own classroom. Students often lean on their supposed sensitivity as a reason to not have to engage in challenging work. To be sure, anxiety is a genuine challenge faced by many highly sensitive people. Overstimulation and dysregulation of the nervous system are real and can be difficult to manage. But *signaling* high sensitivity isn't the same as *being* highly sensitive. In fact, many HSPs unfortunately feel shame over their temperament and hide it from others, to the detriment of their mental health.

As a kid, did you ever experience a stomachache and get sent to the nurse's office? Perhaps it prompted a caregiver to come pick you up from school. And that makes sense, because if you're sick, that's the priority—algebra can wait. But then, maybe there was a time after that when you felt a little anxious about turning in an assignment or taking a test, and maybe you *developed* a bit of a stomachache. Maybe it was faint and you were playing it up, or maybe it didn't even really exist, but you knew that this was a way of avoiding that challenge.

I'm not throwing stones here—I was a master at this particular tactic with my mom. I mentioned before that my mother was, shall we say, overly attentive. Okay, let's be honest—she coddled the hell out of me. Well, that often annoyed me. But eventually I realized I could also use it to my advantage. When there was a problem I didn't want to deal with, or if I simply felt like I wanted a little extra TLC, I sometimes leaned into this perception she had that I needed to be protected. You know the drill:

Cough, cough.

"Um, Mom? I don't feel so good."

"What? Oh, honey! Then you definitely need to stay home from school. Here, let me get your slippers."

Score!

Hey, I'm not proud of it, but I totally own that I did it. As a kid, I also sometimes used other people's low expectations of me to justify having low expectations of myself. The reality is, between my auditory processing issue, my mom's overprotectiveness, and feeling like a satellite receiving every little detail about the world around me, including everyone else's feelings, I faced some real obstacles.

Then, one day, that teacher happened upon me in my special education classroom and asked that fateful question: "Scott, what are you still doing here?" It was just the kind of gentle but firm nudge—the honest love—that I needed to step back and reevaluate my situation and my trajectory. When I did that, I realized she was right, and that I was capable of much more. I desperately wanted to grow.

Like me, others who are highly sensitive sometimes can signal weakness to get ourselves off the hook. Then there are those who *claim* sensitivity as part of a strategy of victim signaling. In these cases, identifying yourself as a victim isn't for the perfectly valid motivation of receiving genuinely needed assistance but because the idea of being a victim—in this case to one's high sensitivity—is actually desirable. In some circles it's in vogue to struggle with your sensitivity. People will rush to lavish attention and pity on you.

Yet as research shows, there's actually a very low correlation between *signaling* extreme sensitivity and actually *having* it. Psychologists Martyna Kajdzik and Marcin Moroń devised a scale to measure "signaling high sensitivity."[40] Here are some of the items it includes:

- I sometimes ask for privileges because of my high sensitivity.

- People treat me in a special way because they know how sensitive I am.

- When I mention that I am a highly sensitive person, others are more willing to help me.

- It is easier for me to persuade someone to support me if I admit that I am a highly sensitive person.

- Sometimes I avoid penalties for omissions/mistakes at work when I admit that I am a highly sensitive person.

- I sometimes tell others how difficult it is for me because of my high sensitivity.

- I sometimes say that I am a highly sensitive person so that people treat me better.

Now, here's the incredible part. When the researchers surveyed the results, they found zero—zip, zilch, nada!—correlation between those who actually had sensory processing sensitivity (as conceptualized by Elaine Aron and her colleagues) and those who signaled high sensitivity. While the latter group did not display the actual trait of high sensitivity, they did tend to display something else—higher rates of grandiose (not vulnerable) narcissism and psychopathic traits, such as a desire to exploit others for one's own gain. But wait, there's more!

Among the actual HSPs, their responses indicated activation of their behavior *inhibition* system, which is designed to help us avoid negative and fearful responses. Among the signalers, however, their actions were more related to the behavior *activation* system, which is about a motivation to approach others with the goal of receiving some kind of social reward (hello, extraversion).

To be extra clear, we're talking about people who signal high sensitivity as a strategy to obtain something: affordances, attention, and so on. As Moroń and colleagues put it, "Signaling high sensitivity could thus be an honest signal given by people with high sensory processing sensitivity, but also used instrumentally by narcissistic individuals to exploit others."[41]

If you're an HSP and you mention something on social media

about it, that doesn't necessarily mean you're a narcissistic sensitivity signaler. But if you do tend to talk about your high sensitivity *a lot*, especially in public spaces in situations in which you want something out of someone, perhaps notice how frequently you bring it up, the way in which you're doing it, and your motivation for doing so. Is it a genuine bid to create community and connection, or is it a bid for attention or a pity party, or an attempt to get a pass on having to negotiate the many everyday obstacles in life (I call them "everyday nuisances")?

The somatic practitioner Irene Lyon helps people deal with the effects of trauma on their nervous system. She says, "Acknowledging you've lived through trauma and survived it IS humanity [caps hers]. There's nothing special about it. When we make it extra special, we can fall into victim identification without even realizing it."[42] We can say the same thing about being highly sensitive.

High sensitivity does bring with it certain gifts, along with some very real challenges.

When you're highly sensitive, you can feel like a NASA-grade satellite dish taking in absolutely everything that's happening around you. Anxiety, depression, and some of the other negative emotional states that can accompany high sensitivity can be extremely difficult to deal with.

That's why you need to learn how to deal effectively with these challenges, so that you can harness the gifts of high sensitivity and use them for good—including *your own* good! Because I want to be clear—people with high sensitivity really are capable of great things, and Westernized culture, which is jam-packed with overstimulation, really can be rough. For instance, it isn't easy to walk through the world acutely aware of the pain and suffering that's all around you. But it can be done, and it's well worth the effort.

I'd be remiss if I didn't raise an important point here. If you scroll through the HSP blogs, you'll often see a common refrain—people's annoyance at being told "You're too sensitive!" I get it, that can be really irritating. I was often told as a child that I was always being "too sensitive" and I always hated it. It led to a feeling of shame for my highly sensitive temperament.

However, with a little more wisdom and maturity, I can see that at least once in a while, they kinda might have been right.

IS THERE SUCH A THING AS BEING *TOO* SENSITIVE?

News alert: You really can be *too sensitive*. But let me break down what I mean by that.

It may not seem "empathetic" of me to say so, but I think it's important for HSPs to take responsibility for their temperament and know when they really truly are being too sensitive relative to a situation.

For one, the abundance of input you receive can make you see slights that really aren't there. Maybe you see a neutral facial expression and perceive anger. Maybe someone offers a good and fair criticism of you and you break down and cry instead of listening to and considering their insights. That's not just being sensitive, that's being downright fragile.

Being overly sensitive isn't just irritating for others, it also keeps the world at arm's length. When your sensitivity prevents you from having meaningful interactions with others—the kind inherent in any adult relationship worth having—it holds you back. It becomes more important to wrap yourself in bubble wrap or demand that the environment change to accommodate you than to do the work of engaging. And I want better for you!

So, what do you do when you catch yourself acting over the top? Own it! Say to yourself, "I am being way too sensitive here. My knee-jerk reaction isn't warranted by this situation, and it isn't helping me at all. Let me take a minute to recalibrate and try again." I have this conversation with myself *all the time*. The good news is that with practice, it becomes easier to recognize when your immediate reaction is over the top, and you can correct yourself almost automatically.

Here's the thing: *You are not weak, and you are not a victim of your high sensitivity.* You are strong and capable, and it's time to claim that! Isn't that way more empowering?

> **You are strong and capable, and it's time to claim that.**

The essential thing here is *psychological flexibility* (remember that term?), and not using the label of HSP as a way to create a mental prison where you're sensitive in situations that don't call for it. And while you're at it, maybe you want to reframe that language. Referring to yourself as an "HSP" means you're affixing a permanent, limited label to yourself. In reality, high sensitivity is just one aspect of who you are. You don't really want to reduce your entire personhood to a single set of characteristics, do you?

For all of us, when we cling tightly to a fixed identity, we will fight to stay small because it's who we think we are. We'll reject anything that challenges this notion, including opportunities to see ourselves in beautiful new ways. So try to develop some psychological flexibility in your identity, and give yourself room to grow. You're not only more than an HSP, but you don't have to *always* be an HSP!

When we allow ourselves to "disintegrate" and re-form, it is an opportunity to embody a richer, fuller version of ourselves.[43] Highly sensitive people often wish they could change the world around them to make it more comfortable. While this isn't possible in the way we often picture it, it *is* possible in one very real sense—we can change how we *relate* to the world and to ourselves, and thus in many ways, the world as we experience it actually does change. How you conceptualize your sensitivity and how you shape yourself in light of it also reshapes your environment.

With that in mind, let's look at some ways you can embrace your sensitivity and help it work for you rather than against you.

USING YOUR POWERS FOR GOOD (FOR YOURSELF AND OTHERS)

Okay, it's time for the big reveal! Remember those quotes I shared at the start of the chapter—the ones that described some of the ways in which people experience high sensitivity? Now it's time to tell you who said them:

> "I think I was born with a great awareness of my surroundings and of other people. Sometimes that awareness is good, and sometimes I wish I wasn't so sensitive."[44] That was actor/producer/director Scarlett Johansson.

> "It's that constant push-pull of going, How do I stay human and vulnerable and real, and how do I, at the same time, not let all this affect me?"[45] That was actor/producer Nicole Kidman.

> "[HPSs] feel different, but they don't know what it is. They feel more. Everything hurts. Everything. They're supersensitive. They see things that other people don't see."[46] That was music producer Rick Rubin.

Each of these HSPs faced challenges because of their sensitivity, yet they were also able to engage its superpowers. As research shows, HSPs may be somewhat high-maintenance in their (our) needs, but that's not a bad thing. And when we learn how to properly tend to HSPs (or tend to ourselves), we can nurture some exquisite gifts.

Orchids and Dandelions

As I mentioned in Chapter 1, when it comes to genetics, we can really get it wrong. We look at temperaments and think of them as providing absolute advantages or disadvantages. But when it comes to actual outcomes, it's not about nature or nurture but how nature and nurture interact with each other over a lifetime. The same genes can lead to very different outcomes depending on your environment, and high sensitivity is one of the most significant examples of this.

Research shows that outcomes for highly sensitive people depend largely on their environment. Childhood, especially, can play an outsized role in how sensitivity plays out over the span of one's life.

Among virtually all children—HSPs or not—being in a positive, supportive environment has benefits, and being in a largely negative, unsupportive environment has drawbacks. This is actually more true for highly sensitive children, who are more affected by their environment. But if it sounds like a form of weakness or vulnerability to be so influenced by your environment, think again.

Psychologists W. Thomas Boyce and Bruce Ellis proposed a hypothesis that enhanced reactivity to our environment is a kind of biological sensitivity that has been perpetuated by evolution because it can offer a variety of benefits depending on the setting.[47] For instance, in stressful environments, it can help us stay alert to potential threats and dangers. In nonstressful situations, it can help us connect with others to gain resources and support.

I'm going to go back to the Counselor Troi example from *Star Trek: The Next Generation*. When encountering new life forms, Captain Picard would often call on the special sensitivities of the ship's resident HSP to detect whether the beings were friend or foe. If the former, Troi was often the one to make first contact, and if the latter, to attempt to broker peace.

Because of their acute sensitivity, HSPs can be among the most adept at sensing what's really going on in the environment (Alane Freund refers to HSPs as "canaries" because of this ability[48]) and at understanding situations and people in ways that are essential to forming authentic connections.

When a situation gets a little crazy, HSPs want everything to simmer down already! They need to dial down the stimuli so they can process everything that's going on, and that's a good thing. You know the expression "Let cooler heads prevail"? Those chilly noggins are often going to belong to the HSPs in the room. So when we see high sensitivity, we don't want to deride it, because there are some real advantages to having HSPs around; they play an important role in society.

When children's sensitivity to stimuli and reactivity is supported, it can steer them more toward the positive aspects of the trait, such as intellectual curiosity and excitement about learning and processing new things. But in a less supportive atmosphere, it can contribute to negative emotions, depression, and withdrawal.[49]

Adopting a Swedish metaphor, Boyce and Ellis describe "dandelions and orchids." Like the plant, dandelion children are those who can survive and even thrive in a variety of environments, including harsh ones. Conversely, orchid children need a lot of thoughtful tending in order to flourish. That may sound like a negative thing, but consider the results. When dandelions flower, they generate a yellow bloom that, though aesthetically pleasing, is rather pedestrian. Don't get me wrong—it's very powerful to be able to blossom regardless of the conditions. It's simply that when the orchid gets the special tending it needs, it also has more nuanced gifts to offer. "In conditions of neglect, the orchid promptly declines, while in conditions of support and nurture, it is a flower of unusual delicacy and beauty," Boyce and Ellis write.

Now admittedly, these two categories are broad and not everyone fits cleanly into one or the other. We can't just look at the entire population and say "Dandelion, dandelion, orchid, dandelion." But it's a useful metaphor when looking at highly sensitive children and the extent to which their outcomes are influenced by environmental supports, or lack thereof.

Many of our genes don't code for good or bad outcomes; they're more linked to the degree to which we're tuned to our environment: for better *and* worse. The same genes can be associated with people experiencing either extreme lows or extreme highs, and this is especially true for the HSP.

So, what if you're an orchid who was neglected? Does that mean there's no hope of flourishing? Absolutely not. The good news is that you have control *now*, and that matters. This entire book equips you with tools and resources to take control of your life.

HSP, Heal Thyself!

One of the great ironies and gifts of being highly sensitive is that you actually have access to an incredible tool that can help you grow from negative and even traumatic events. I'm referring to the creative abilities that are often linked with the trait of openness to experience.

One of the coolest things about the unique blend of traits that HSPs possess is that they tend to be exceptionally creative, which is why so many artists, actors, writers, and others are highly sensitive. And you can deploy this creativity not only for engaging or entertaining others but also for the purpose of your own healing.

To say that creativity has healing powers isn't just hyperbole. It's a common perception that artists and other creatives channel the energy of adverse experiences into their work.

Timothy Goodman, the graphic artist I mentioned in Chapter 2, says he constantly uses his struggles, including his traumatic childhood, to fuel his art.

Looking back, Goodman says, "There was this underlying, foundational creative person in me." When he started work on his first wall mural he grappled with what to do.[50] "I locked myself in this room for three days, and I sketched it all out with pencil, and I was crying, and it was intensive, and I didn't know what the hell I was doing, but I fucking did it somehow, and I never felt more stimulated in my life, creatively." Sounds like kind of a mess, right? But a beautiful mess. The kind from which incredible works of art emerge.

It was a transformative experience for Goodman. "I remember walking down the street. I asked myself a question. I said, 'This feeling I have right now, how do I make this the feeling I have for the rest of my life?'" From there, he realized that making such large-scale art didn't just serve himself, it served everyone who saw it. It had the capability of beautifying communities and actually influencing how others felt.

Goodman realized the impact he could have on the world, by learning not to suppress his sensitivity but to channel it. I should mention that Goodman is also a big believer in therapy. For those who've experienced trauma, healing is often a multifaceted process, and high sensitivity can actually help you heal.

As research shows, creative thinking and expression has inherent within it a meaning-making aspect that, according to research, can actually enable post-traumatic growth.[51] That's one of the reasons that writing, including journaling, along with art therapy can be so effective. It's been shown that writing consistently for fifteen to twenty minutes for a period of several days or weeks about a topic that's emotionally charged can help us both understand and express our feelings more effectively.[52] Such methods can provide us with an opportunity to sort through challenging thoughts and feelings in a way that decreases the sense of threat.

Mary Oliver would likely have agreed with this insight. The beloved poet was especially adept at tuning in to the gifts of high sensitivity, using them not only to deal with her own difficult past but also to create magnificent poetry. "I consider myself a reporter," Oliver once told interviewer Maria Shriver, "one who uses words that are more like music and that have a choreography."[53]

Oliver's high sensitivity is evident in her description of her childhood: "I spent a great deal of time in my younger years just writing and reading, walking around the woods in Ohio, where I grew up. . . . I very much wished not to be noticed, and to be left alone." This remained largely true for the poet throughout her life.

Like many highly sensitive artists, Oliver turned to writing in part for the opportunity it offered to become lost in her work. "With words, I could build a world I could live in. I had a very dysfunctional family, and a very hard childhood. So I made a world out of words. And it was my salvation," she told Shiver. And she invited us into that world, creating art that has touched so many.

That is one of the most profound gifts that HSPs offer: Through their own astute noticing and deep processing, they can help others see things through their eyes. Their offerings can help others connect more deeply and meaningfully with the world around them.

But you don't have to be an artist or "creative"—you can apply your own high sensitivity to virtually any endeavor. For instance, in my work as a researcher, professor, coach, and podcast host, my sensitivity gives me greater insight and a better understanding of those I work with. It also fuels my curiosity and motivates me to learn as much as I can about human behavior and potential. I get creative in how I pursue my research. I can often feel the vibe of my podcast guest or coaching client, and that vibe permeates my own being in a way that can help me connect with them and sometimes even see their greater potential.

Robin Wall Kimmerer, botanist and author of *Braiding Sweetgrass*, blends her background in science with her keen storytelling sensibilities, weaving a tapestry of science and story that both enchants and informs. Cellist Yo-Yo Ma deploys his high sensitivity to connect deeply with those around him. Close friends describe him as someone who is deeply feeling, who can bring a feeling of joy to a room or sit with people in their sadness and grief.[54] As someone who has been in his presence, I can personally attest to this. Clearly he channels his sensitivity into his virtuoso musical abilities as well.

So yes, being highly sensitive isn't the easiest gig in the world, but it can be incredibly powerful. It can contribute to a life of great meaning and purpose, where you engage your gifts not only to experience the world more richly, but to enhance others' lives as well.

It all starts with engaging an empowerment mindset. When you make that shift, you'll begin to see the world through a different lens, using your extraordinary powers of perception to take in all the ways that being an HSP can be a benefit rather than a hindrance. Instead of feeling like a constant victim to your sensitivity, you can view it as a gift to help you become a creative, deeply in-touch human who has a heck of a lot to offer to the world.

8

Harness Your
Underdog Motivation

The fact of being an underdog changes people in ways that we often fail to appreciate. It opens doors and creates opportunities and enlightens and permits things that might otherwise have seemed unthinkable.[1]

—*Malcolm Gladwell*

To say that Wilma Rudolph was an underdog is an understatement. Born premature in 1940, she weighed in at just four and a half pounds,[2] the twentieth of twenty-two children (no, that's not a typo) in her Clarksville, Tennessee, home. And while today off-grid houses are having a moment (at least among environmentalists and doomsday preppers), having a place with no electricity or running water was a result of her family's low socioeconomic status.[3] But we're just getting warmed up.

As a child Rudolph contracted double pneumonia and scarlet fever, then polio. As a result, she spent much of the first part of her life in bed. Though she managed to survive, the polio left her with a weakened leg and twisted foot, necessitating a leg brace.[4] It's hardly the start you'd imagine for a future Olympian, and yet Rudolph went on to become the first American woman to win three gold medals in track and field in a single Olympics.[5]

You've probably heard this story before because, well, we love an underdog story. They're like a hammer in a motivational speaker's tool belt. Nothing drives the point home that you can beat the odds like reading about someone else who's already done it. And yet these days, more and more people are likely to push back on such stories: to say some version of "That's nice for *other people,* but because of [insert circumstances or diagnoses] it's impossible for me to overcome my challenges."

To be sure, many of us face very real injustices on a structural level, adding real obstacles for individuals to overcome. Whether or not these structural issues affect us personally, at some point and in some manner, life will find a way to knock us around. To make us feel like an underdog. It's up to us to decide how we'll respond. Will we hang our heads and walk away, or will we double down, determined to show the world what we've got?

Will we give up, or will we rise above?

In this chapter, we'll explore how to do the latter.

Wilma Rudolph once boiled her mindset down to this simple recounting: "My doctor told me I would never walk again. My mother told me I would. I believed my mother."[6]

As research shows, one of the major determinants of whether we recoil from or rise to a challenge comes down to our beliefs.

THE POWER OF SELF-BELIEF

Whether you think you can or you think you can't—you're right.

—Henry Ford

When we think of underdogs, we think of people who have the deck stacked against them. Who have to expend all kinds of extra effort and energy climbing out of a hole just to reach a level playing field. Underdog status can also be merely a matter of perception—we may simply be underestimated.

Research in psychology and organizational behavior has largely underscored the idea that our performance tends to suffer when others voice low expectations of us.[7] If those around us have little to no faith in our abilities—and we know this—we tend to do worse or apply less effort than when people believe that we have what it takes to succeed. But this doesn't have to be the case. We don't *have* to internalize the expectations of others.

My buddy and fellow psychologist Samir Nurmohamed wasn't buying the false dichotomy that it's universally good when people expect a lot from us and bad when they expect less. After all, it seems clear at least anecdotally that being an underdog can sometimes have the opposite effect—it can energize us and inspire us to do better. But there was no research investigating whether this was actually true, and if so, how this *underdog effect* might work.

Nurmohamed set out to unravel the mystery (or at least start to) by asking this question: When someone expects us to underperform, what makes the difference between those who live down to expectations and those who bust through them? As he found, we have a lot more control over which category we fall into than we may think.

Investigating the Underdog Effect

In the first of three studies, Nurmohamed surveyed 371 employees of a packaged-goods company. Among the questions he asked them was whether others see them as an underdog.[8]

Seven weeks later, these same employees received performance evaluations from their supervisors. When the researcher compared these evaluations with the employee's self-assessments, he found a strong correlation between the perception that the employee was seen as an underdog and their performance. "In other words," he writes, "people who believed that others did not expect them to be successful were more likely to receive higher performance evaluations from their supervisors."[9]

The question, then, was *why*? What forces were at play? To gain further insight, Nurmohamed launched another study. This time he gathered 327 participants and randomly assigned them to one of three conditions. Some were told that they were not expected to succeed at the task, some were told that they had a high likelihood of succeeding, and others did not receive any insight as to how they were expected to perform.

The participants were told that the purpose of the study was to investigate their decision-making (sneaky, Samir!). As described to them, the task would have an observer and a participant—though the study participants all took the active role, and there was no actual observer.

The task in question required that the participant use a computer mouse to click as many rapidly moving circles as possible. After an initial "practice round," the participants received feedback from the supposed observer, Jaime. For the underdog group, they were told that based on their initial performance Jaime didn't think they were likely to do very well going forward compared with other participants. Then, the "real" task began. After five minutes of furious mouse clicking, the results came in. In the end, the underdogs outperformed both the high expectations group and the control group.

With this study, Nurmohamed had one more piece of the puzzle (which I'll describe in a moment). Yet it was still unclear why underdog motivation improved outcomes. So, on to study number three.

This time, 156 participants were assigned to one of two rooms—A or B—and were told that they were going to take part in a negotiation with someone in the other room. The lucky folks in room A were told that researchers had formulated questions that could determine their likelihood of success in negotiation tasks. Some of the participants were given the following feedback: "Based on your score, researchers do not expect you to perform better than other negotiators, and they suggest that you are an underdog in the upcoming negotiation." Others were told that they were expected do better than other participants, and a third group was told that they should do about as well as other negotiators.

After a few minutes of prep time in which they familiarized themselves with the nature of the negotiation, participants used an instant messaging platform to interact with their counterpart. After fifteen minutes, the negotiations ended, and the folks in room A were asked to fill out another questionnaire that included the following statements:

- I wanted to prove researchers wrong.

- I cared about proving to researchers that their expectations of me were wrong.

- I was energized by the opportunity to prove to researchers that they were wrong about me.

- I wanted researchers to know that their expectations of me were incorrect.

Sense a theme here? Once again, sure enough, the underdogs outperformed the others. But this time, Nurmohamed also had his *why*. You guessed it—to *prove others wrong*. Telling people they weren't expected to perform well sparked in them a desire to prove that they'd been underestimated, and it also helped them perform better.

You know, it's a common theme in personal development that we've got nothing to prove to others. That if we have a strong sense of self, we shouldn't care what others think of us. I blame these people for the fact that these days, plenty of folks seem to find it totally acceptable to do their grocery shopping in their pajamas—slippers and all! Aside from encouraging us to consider our personal presentation, caring what others think has other benefits, as well. As Nurmohamed describes it, research had previously demonstrated that "when people are focused on proving their capabilities to others, it can be beneficial for short-term performance as it heightens cognitive and affective engagement and sharpens focus on potential positive outcomes."[10] That's puzzle piece number two. When we're underestimated, many of us double down and dig deep—and we don't just *try* to turn in better-than-expected results, *we actually succeed*.

In his second study, Nurmohamed used the mouse-target task precisely because it required a combination of effort (and therefore motivation) and cognitive attention for participants to do well. When the underdog motivation kicked in, so too did a desire to prove others wrong, and that combination is what boosted performance—by jacking up cognitive and affective engagement. It created a high-stakes situation that forced focus and made study subjects bring their A game.

None of this would be news to basketball phenom Michael Jordan, who famously invented enemies.[11] When you're arguably the best in the game, sometimes you have to create someone to conquer—something to overcome. So Jordan would self-talk himself into a frenzy, getting himself to believe that others had a major beef with him. Okay, so some of these other players actually did have issues with Jordan, but instead of putting the friction aside and just focusing on the game, Jordan did the opposite. At least in his mind, and sometimes on the court, he amped up the conflict so he could harness that energy, channeling it into greater motivation, focus, and performance. To Jordan, every sleight, even *perceived* sleight, was "personal" motivation to get better.

And Jordan's not alone among well-known folks who've been bolstered by a desire to prove themselves. For instance, Howard Schultz, former chairman and CEO of Starbucks, says that others' beliefs that he would fail motivated him. In his words, "I was driven to prove that our company could achieve what others said was impossible."[12]

Psychologist Ciarán O'Keeffe links the power of the underdog effect to the *theory of desirable difficulties*, which "posits that successful individuals need to have those disadvantages because the struggle to succeed against seemingly insurmountable odds is important for growth."[13] Certainly, it does seem the case that if we come by things too easily, it tends not to be satisfying. More than that, it contributes little to nothing to our development.

Yet before we leave Dr. Nurmohamed and his research, we need to touch on one more critical element of his work that we've not yet covered. And this seems to be the key differentiator between those who falter under the weight of low expectations and those who actually transform them into fuel to blast past naysayers—*belief*. Not just about ourselves, but about the people evaluating us. Because it's clear that some people really do respond to dismal expectations by underperforming. So why is that?

In a fourth study, Nurmohamed demonstrated that a mediating factor in our response is *whether we perceive our evaluators as credible.* If we know that someone doesn't expect that we'll do well, and our reaction is some version of "You don't know me!," we're more likely to be motivated to prove them wrong. Yet if we deem that the person in question knows what they're talking about, we're more likely to move in the opposite direction. To underperform.

You can see how this might play out across a variety of scenarios. For instance, if you're new on the football team and the coach has barely seen you play, it's easier to dismiss his negative opinion of your potential. But if you're a senior who's been on the team for four years and he doesn't think you've got what it takes to make a critical play at crunch time, it's harder to access your underdog motivation.

Harder, *but not impossible.* After all, our beliefs are something we have some control over. But don't take it from me, take it from Wilma Rudolph. In the face of a dire medical diagnosis, she chose to believe her mother over her doctor. And as she ventured forward in life, again and again, she chose to believe herself over others. As she put it, "I believe in me more than anything in this world."[14]

We don't have much control over what we encounter in this world. In some cases, we have none. But what we can control are the stories we tell about our situation, and our ability to overcome it. We can shape our self-narrative.[15]

OWN YOUR STORY

Let's do a quick experiment. I'm going to give you two sentences, and I want you to say each out loud. Ready? Here's the first one:

- "I've encountered so many obstacles in life—my circumstances have definitely made me a victim."

Okay, shake that off. . . . Now, here's the second:

- "I've encountered so many obstacles in my life—my circumstances have definitely made me an underdog."

How did those feel in your brain, and in your body? Pretty different, right? Isn't it amazing how one word can make such a huge difference in framing? Well, imagine what an *entire life story* can do.

Whether we see ourselves as a victim or an underdog who can prove others wrong comes down to a choice in how we tell our own story. And it's easy to see which is both more empowering and likely to lead to better outcomes.

I'll say it again—this isn't about magical thinking, the idea that "if you can believe it, you can be it!" But we're throwing the baby out with the bathwater if we don't acknowledge just what a powerful force self-belief is in our lives. That includes whether we find our naysayers credible, and it includes what we believe to be true about the arc of our narrative. Are we on a doom spiral or a hero's journey? In many ways, it's up to us.

Or maybe this is the point when you realize that you've been letting someone else tell your story for you. That you've bought into the memes that say you're not capable of more, or better. Well, fortunately you can also choose to unplug from that narrative. Like I did.

In the Introduction, I talked about how, because of a challenge with auditory processing, I was perceived as ungifted and unlikely to succeed academically. After a very kind and attentive teacher inspired me to remove myself from special education, I embarked on a journey of trying every class and activity under the sun to discover what I was truly capable of. So that part we've covered. Now, cut to further along in high school. . . .

I'm now getting straight As in all of my classes—many of them honors classes—so I go to the school psychologist and announce that for my senior year, I'd love to be placed in the gifted program. He sees my grades and agrees that things look favorable, but then he does something else. He consults a file. Specifically, he looks up my IQ score from when I was eleven years old. That tells a different story. It tells him that I'm borderline intellectually impaired. (When I was given the test, I could barely hear a thing due to my auditory processing issues at the time.)

To break the news to me, he pulls out a piece of paper and draws a bell curve. Then he points to the far right. "That's where the gifted kids are," he says. From there, he keeps moving his pen to the left for what feels like forever, eventually stopping a bit to the left of the point he labeled *average*. "That's you," he says. "You don't qualify for gifted education."

My shoulders fall. *God*, I think, *at what point does my actual achievement get to outshine my potential?*

Fortunately, instead of buying into the finality of this declaration, I went the other way. The "You don't know me!" route, as Nurmohamed might call it. If I had to keep proving my ability, well, then prove it I would. And I'd invoke whatever means necessary to do so (on this side of the law, that is). Not only that, but I was going to go a huge step further. I set my sights on changing our entire system of measuring human potential.

As graduation approached, I applied to Carnegie Mellon to study cognitive science. I wrote a deeply personal statement outlining my vision for a new education system that redefined what it means to be smart and to achieve in life. And they welcomed me with open arms!

Just kidding. No, they didn't. Apparently, my SAT scores weren't high enough to redefine human intelligence. (Think about that one for a moment.)

So I took another tack. I looked at which schools within Carnegie Mellon didn't place such a premium on SAT scores and landed on . . . the opera department. I auditioned (singing my heart out with the song "Stars" from *Les Misérables*) and the music department accepted me on a partial scholarship.

A year later, I went to the psychology department and told the secretary that I'd taken a psych class, loved it, and wanted to become a minor in psychology (it's called the *foot-in-the-door technique*). My heart was beating so fast. I was terrified she was going to look at my IQ score from age eleven and tell me to go back to singing opera! Instead, she immediately smiled and said "Sure," sliding a paper across the table as she was finishing her lunch. I was so damn happy, I skipped back to my dorm room in my tights (I'd had dance class earlier). I remember thinking, *Wow, it's amazing what doors are open to you if you can persevere enough to get yourself in an environment where people already have high expectations for you.*

A semester later, I switched from a major in opera to a major in psychology. A few years later, I even added on a major in human-computer interaction from CMU's School of Computer Science, which is known to require some of the highest SAT scores in the world. From there, I was accepted on a full scholarship to Cambridge for my master's degree and Yale for a Ph.D. program. My dissertation topic? *A new theory of human intelligence.*

All this from a kid who was told he was ungifted. Yet I could have had a very different story. I could have believed what those teachers told me about my ability. I could have easily stayed in special education and accepted that I wasn't college material. And I could have taken Carnegie Mellon's initial no for a final answer.

But I didn't. And I am no more special than you are.

Yes, I did have some important advantages in terms of having a supportive family and not growing up poor, but that didn't open the doors for me that I wanted to open—I had to do that myself. I had to believe in myself more than nearly everyone else around me did. And let's look back at Wilma Rudolph and countless other severely disadvantaged people who, when faced with low expectations and active barriers, blew through them.

I know . . . *I know!* People have very real challenges—that's why they're underdogs! It is *not easy* swimming upstream. But I'd like you to consider something . . .

If you were to write your own story up to this point in your life, framing it as a memoir, how would it go? Now, keep in mind that in memoirs, the narrator is always a hero. It doesn't matter whether they've broken the law or done any manner of terrible things. It doesn't matter what they've suffered. In fact, the further down they're coming from, the bigger the payoff when they finally make that shift and start to come up. Being a hero doesn't mean you become Mother Teresa, it means you learn something. You figure something out. You make a change. Somehow you turn the tide. You overcome the odds.

You know what would make a really shitty memoir? *People told me I was a piece of crap, and I believed them.* THE END.

Or how about this: *I experienced a ton of trauma and other hardship, so I gave up.* THE END.

Sorry, neither of those is ending up on the Amazon bestseller list *because they are terrible stories.* And they don't have to be yours.

So ask yourself, from where you are in your life at this exact moment, what would be the most empowering choice for you, as the narrator of your own life, to make? What would make *your* story inspiring? What would bring someone else to tears or make them leap to their feet and shout "Yes!" Because I've got great news for you: There's still time.

Writer Bruce Feiler put it so eloquently when he wrote the following:

> We have a choice in how we tell our life story. We don't write it in permanent ink. There are no points for consistency, or even accuracy. We can change it at any time, for any reason, including one as simple as making ourselves feel better. After all, a primary function of our life story is to place difficult experiences firmly in the past and take from them something beneficial that will allow us to thrive in the future.[16]

Still, I get it. If you've told yourself a lifetime of stories about how hard the world is, it's tough to open up. It's hard to let go and try to see things differently. And I'm not saying that life *hasn't* been difficult. Just that you can leverage those experiences to lift you up. Because really, when you think about it, what else are you gonna do with your life? Shut yourself off forever? That's no life. I try to be really careful when I use this word, but it's appropriate here: You *deserve* better.

And this is where that healthy vulnerability comes into play—the kind of vulnerability that's in service of growth and connection.

Sometimes shifting our narrative requires that we do something really challenging—that we soften a shell that we've been carrying around for years. Long ago, we created this shell for a very good reason—because we needed the protection. We needed to be shielded from the possibility that we'd overexpose our sensitive nature and get hurt. Or we needed to be protected from the possibility of failure, from trauma . . . from so many things. But in many cases, that same armor that protected you then confines you now, and it's time to open up.

Another way that we need to shift our attitude is to raise our own expectations of ourselves.

EXPECT MORE OF YOURSELF

One of the greatest disservices of a victim culture is that the bar for everyone becomes perilously low, and we accept that. We buy into others' notions that because we have struggled, because we lack the advantages that others have, we will never achieve our goals or realize our dreams. I, for one, believe that an underappreciated narrative in the face of discrimination or trauma is to prove others wrong by succeeding.

As psychologist and writer Rob Henderson (who also happens to be a friend of mine) explains, when we see others (and ourselves) as victims, it's like a death sentence for our dreams. That's because most of us will do what we think is expected of us. Instead, to truly help others, we need to aim higher, and presume a better result, which is what Rob learned to do for himself.[17]

Like me, Rob managed to make his way to both Yale and Cambridge by a roundabout route, and also like me, it was not a path others expected he would—or could—take. Born into poverty in Los Angeles, Rob spent the first few years of his life with an abusive, drug-addicted mother and never knew who his father was.[18] Eventually neighbors called the police, and from there he was placed into foster care. He was just three years old.

Over the next few years, Rob was shuffled from one foster home to the next and from school to school. Eventually, Rob was adopted, but just a year later his new parents divorced, creating more up-heaval. Rob finally managed to graduate with just a 2.2 GPA and joined the Air Force. It was there that he first realized he might be able to make something of his life.

When Rob took a standardized exam to determine what military career path might suit him best, he was told his score was exceptionally high. With a little steam under him, he excelled in the Air Force and was rapidly promoted during his eight years in the armed forces. Along the way, though, he still dealt with his share of challenges, including a struggle with alcohol abuse.

After he left the Air Force, through the G.I. Bill and with some help from an organization that assisted vets in getting to college, Rob managed to be accepted to Yale, where he earned his undergraduate degree. He went on to earn his Ph.D. from Cambridge. Not bad for a South Korean-Mexican-American dude who came through the foster care system. Just to put that in perspective, studies show that roughly 3 to 4 percent of kids who come through the system earn a four-year degree.[19]

All of this is to say that when he talks about the kind of expectations that we want to have from people who've faced adversity, Rob Henderson knows what he's talking about. And this is what he says: It's not cruel or privileged to expect good things from people who've suffered. On the contrary, they *need* high expectations in order to succeed.

In a piece on his Substack, Henderson writes, "People think that if a young guy comes from a disorderly or deprived environment, he should be held to low standards. This is misguided. He should be held to high standards. Otherwise, he will sink to the level of his environment."[20]

Sure, he could engage his underdog motivation, just like we all can engage ours—and we should when faced with the tyranny of low expectations. But it's a high hurdle to have to overcome an assumption that you're incapable. It's both kind and helpful to assure people that you believe in them. And we can say the same thing to ourselves.

Give Yourself Wise Feedback

When I say "expect more from yourself," I don't mean you have to get all hardass or David Goggins on yourself. Though talk about underdog motivation—former Navy SEAL turned ultramarathoner Goggins has got it in spades.[21] As he writes in his book *Never Finished*: "If you catalogue your scars to use them as excuses or a bargaining chip to make life easier for yourself, you've missed an opportunity to become better and grow stronger."[22]

Expect more from yourself lovingly.

Now, you don't have to upbraid yourself or call yourself a lazy loser to get yourself motivated. I don't recommend that. Instead, you can expect more from yourself *lovingly*.

Think of a really caring parent or teacher giving you a pep talk. Imagine them looking you in the eyes and saying, clearly and firmly, "I *know* you can do this."

Claude Steele, Geoffrey Cohen, and Lee Ross demonstrated the power of something they called *wise feedback*.[23] A group composed of both Black and white students was assigned an essay on which a teacher provided feedback. On some of the papers, the feedback was accompanied by a Post-it note that read, basically, *Here, I'm giving you feedback*. But other students' notes said something different. They read, *I am giving you these comments because I have very high expectations, and I know you can meet them*.

While the white kids largely responded to the two notes similarly, with some students opting to revise and resubmit their essays and others not, for the Black students there was a big difference. Among those who received the *high expectations* note, far more opted to rework their essays. That simple phrase *I know you can meet them* could be enough to derail stereotype threat and encourage people— even those facing serious challenges such as racial discrimination—to rise to the occasion. Would we want less for them? Would we want to further limit their chances of success by discouraging them? By telling them that because of their circumstances, they're not capable of more?

Would you want that for yourself?

In the end, it all comes back to *belief*.

I know it's hurtful when others don't believe in you. At the same time, some people with the greatest disadvantages in life have used others' lack of faith in them to their own advantage. You've just read about several of them, and there are way more stories out there.

The world loves an underdog. But you've got to believe that you know yourself better than your critics know you. That you *can* succeed.

And if it helps, know this: I'm giving you this feedback because I have very high expectations, and I know you can meet them.

Look, we all have a choice. We can see ourselves as people with no chance and no hope, or we can frame our story as someone on the way up. As a person who's going to inspire great things in others someday.

Personally, I think you're the latter.

More importantly, what do *you* think?

9

Live Gratefully

To constrict, to turn away, to close our doors so that the losing of life or love will be less painful, so that there will be less longed for and therefore less lost—this is the life that fear beckons us to live—the life that, while feeling safe, is not truly lived at all.

—Kristi Nelson

By now I'm sure you've heard all about the power of gratitude, including advice on the many ways we should direct our attention toward thankfulness. But that idea can easily sound impossible to someone who is actively in the midst of physical or emotional pain. That was how Beth Knopik felt when someone handed her a gratitude journal. Just months before, her sixteen-year-old daughter, Leanna, had contracted a virus that, suddenly and inexplicably, traveled to her heart. After a weeks-long battle, doctors told Beth, along with her husband and their thirteen-year-old son, that Leanna would never recover, and the family made the excruciating decision to let her go.

Knopik, deep in grief, looked at the journal and thought, *What am I supposed to do with this?* Still, life had to go on. Eventually, she decided that she would try to find just one thing each day that was beautiful or just in some way positive. "Sometimes it would just be that the sun came up," she said in a personal interview.[1] She also looked at her son, who was on the rowing team and spending time with his friends. "He was showing me how to move forward," she recalls, "and I was grateful for that, and for the fact that I had to get up and get dressed to take him where he needed to go—otherwise I might have just stayed in bed." Her dogs, too, were something to be thankful for. Caring for them and for her son gave her a sense of purpose and put meaning in her days.

As Knopik discovered, "The activity of looking for just one thing you're grateful for changes your mindset from 'Woe is me' to something positive. It was one of the tools that helped me to shift out of such a dark place. You can't be depressed and grateful at the same time." But as Knopik observed, you have to *want* to get out of that dark place. If you never expend the effort, you may delay your recovery.

What Knopik advises isn't about telling people to "look on the bright side" when they're in the midst of crisis—that just denies reality and reads more like toxic positivity than actual gratitude (we'll discuss the difference later in the chapter). It's important to recognize when things genuinely suck. Yet as you'll soon read, being present with trauma and tragedy can actually help you feel more grateful.

As writer Jonathan Safran Foer writes, "You cannot protect yourself from sadness without protecting yourself from happiness."[2] You want to cultivate the ability to be with whatever life brings, which is typically a mix of things that feel bad and good. But often, as it turns out, the two go hand in hand.

SUFFERING MAKES US SEARCH FOR MEANING

Suffering is ever-present. Joy is ever-present.
They are here together and always will be.[3]

—Joe Primo

As leading gratitude scientist Robert Emmons of UC Davis writes, "Life is suffering. No amount of positive thinking exercises will change that truth."[4] And that's from a gratitude researcher! But as Viktor Frankl (reminder: this is a man who survived the Holocaust) observes, we can still have "tragic optimism." We can still find meaning in the midst of suffering, and in fact, our suffering is often what prompts us to search for meaning in the first place.

Think about it: When was the last time things were going well and you were perfectly content, but you suddenly stopped to ask yourself, "What's it all for?" In many ways, adversity is the chisel that shapes our lives into something beautiful, *if* we allow ourselves to engage with it that way.

Technologist and mountaineer Sylvia Vasquez-Lovado was cycling to work one day when tragedy struck—not once, but twice.[5] She was racing down Market Street in San Francisco when out of nowhere, a truck cut her off. As she swerved, her front tire caught on a trolley track and she was catapulted over her handlebars. When she regained consciousness, she was in an ambulance. When doctors examined her brain to determine the extent of her concussion, they discovered something else—a tumor at the base of her brain stem.

For Vasquez-Lovado, this was another in a series of extremely tough blows life had dealt her. During her childhood in her native Peru, she experienced ongoing sexual abuse by a family friend and she was beaten by her father. Later, when she came out to her family as a lesbian, they rejected her. Years after that, her partner died by suicide.

As she lay in her hospital bed, Vasquez-Lovado felt the cumulative effects of her grief. But then something else happened. She described the experience on the *Meditative Story* podcast:

> *My brain concussion is so severe the doctors keep me in the ICU for ten days. I have massive headaches. Friends visit. They cheer me up and make me laugh.*
>
> *In the quiet hours, I lie in the mechanical bed with scratchy sheets and let the gratitude come. It washes over me, stronger than the fluorescent lights. I remember the magical vistas I have seen, the dawns breaking over soaring peaks, the thin air sparkling with ice crystals. This is a softer feeling than I have ever experienced before. Yes, I am vulnerable. I've had a hell of a life. So much love. So much loss. Maybe it's time to go. Remembering the*

awe, the gratitude, I am opening. It doesn't feel scary. It feels won-derful.[6]

Fortunately, the tumor turned out to be benign and Vasquez-Lovado went on to summit Mount Denali, making her the first openly gay woman to climb the world's seven highest summits. As she describes in her memoir, *In the Shadow of the Mountain*, in many ways she embarked on this quest not in spite of but because of all the challenges she had experienced.

As researchers who study post-traumatic growth point out, it's not the traumatic event itself that lends itself to growth but how we process it and the meaning we make from it. For Vasquez-Lovado, one of the major shifts in her worldview was the recognition that "I can suffer without giving in to suffering."[7]

GRATITUDE AND SUFFERING GO HAND IN HAND

It is not happiness that makes us grateful. It is gratefulness that makes us happy.[8]

—*Brother David Steindl-Rast*

Scientists recognize that in the wake of trauma, gratitude can drive growth, and as both Beth Knopik and Silvia Vasquez-Lovado experienced, it can be an essential component of healing. Indeed, multiple positive mental health outcomes are associated with practicing gratitude on a regular basis, including a lower lifetime risk for depression, anxiety, and substance abuse disorder.[9]

In the wake of trauma, gratitude can drive growth.

Look, suffering doesn't feel good. Yet one could argue that we're built not only to endure it, but also to make it out the other side as better versions of ourselves. I'm not trying to imply that the process is quick, simple, or easy, but it's a very real phenomenon.

According to psychiatrist Kazimierz Dąbrowski and his theory of *positive disintegration*, experiences that force us to shift our identity or

reconsider our values—in other words, *disintegrate*—are actually necessary if we're to realize our full potential.[10] It's this coming apart that
enables us to construct ourselves differently, like a building that's
fallen in an earthquake being reengineered to be more flexible and
resilient. We learn to adapt, rebuilding a self that more closely re-
sembles who we truly are.

Interestingly, Dąbrowski believes that what we often see as indicators of mental illness—such as anxiety and neuroses—can, at least
in some cases, actually be indicators that a person is trying to move
toward their "personality ideal." You're feeling conflict or struggle because you're not where you want to be, and that's a good thing, even
if it doesn't *feel* good. (Don't mind me, I'm just rebuilding myself!)

Of course, you could just take the old bricks and try to reassem-
ble your original identity in the wake of tragedy, but those who go on
to thrive after trauma do so because they have altered their sense of
self, and therefore relate to life differently than before. But it takes
getting rocked in the first place to have the opportunity to rebuild.

As we discovered in Chapter 1, the human capacity for resiliency
is often underrated.[11] As researcher, psychologist, and trauma survivor Sherry Hamby notes, "Psychologists used to treat resilient people
like unicorns—remarkable and rare. But it turns out that resilient
people are like squirrels—we're everywhere!"[12]

A study that surveyed five hundred people from March to May
2020, just as COVID-19 was kicking off, found that even during those
especially scary first months of the pandemic, more than 56 percent
of people actually reported feelings of gratitude.[13] Those who experienced gratefulness were more likely to also report feelings of happiness. It wasn't because they were bypassing their emotions but
because they could widen their perception enough to take in the
beauty that was *also* present, even in the midst of anxiety and fear.

In his memoir *i am through you so i*, Brother David Steindl-Rast
described a similar experience of happiness arising in the midst of
pain when he recounted his early life as a young man in Austria during World War II. "Looking back I must say that for my friends and

me those terrible years of war were also years of true joy, a joy I wish never to lose. . . . We lived with such joy because we were forced to have death before our eyes constantly." In fact, Steindl-Rast went on to found an organization dedicated entirely to gratefulness and has been called the "grandfather of gratitude."[14]

As psychiatrist Paul Conti observed in conversation with neuroscientist Andrew Huberman, "When we observe happy people, consistently they have two things in common—they have a sense of agency, and a sense of gratitude." These factors actually bolster their resilience and keep them engaged in life in spite of challenges.[15]

In fact, I believe that struggle and suffering are an overlooked route to gratitude. Our extreme adaptability to relatively stable situations can cause us to take many things for granted—from the food in our refrigerator to the roof over our head. When something makes us wake up to our many comforts, it refreshes our sense of gratitude. Remember the first time you were able to get together in real life with friends or take your dog to the park when the COVID-19 restrictions began to lighten up? How much more appreciation did you have for those simple pleasures? Perhaps writer G. K. Chesterton said it best when he wrote, "Until we realize that things might not be, we cannot realize that things are."[16]

Multiple studies show that those who've experienced painful circumstances say their appreciation for life increased afterward. Similarly, among those who show the most gratitude, many have endured the most difficult times.

Living in Gratefulness

"I was never an ungrateful person before I got stage four cancer, but being diagnosed with such an advanced cancer stripped away all of my expectations," says Kristi Nelson.[17]

At thirty-two years old I was in a hospital bed for months, in isolation a lot of the time, going through all of these diagnostic procedures.

It was incredibly difficult, and the longer I was in the hospital the more I came to feel like, if this was it, if this was what I had left of life, how would I live it?

That was when I said what in a way was the first prayer I'd ever said, which was: 'If I die young, let my life be as potent as a long life would have been. And if I live, let my life be as potent as dying young would have been.' In other words, let my life and death have been meaningful no matter what. In that moment, I turned my life over to something outside of myself, and in doing that I also felt agency.

That kind of paradox, Nelson says, is a hallmark of gratefulness.

It was eighteen months from the time Nelson began her health odyssey to the time she completed chemotherapy and radiation. Then, every three months for the next two years, she underwent extensive imaging from her neck down through her pelvis to ensure that the cancer did not return. "You're in liminal land," she recalls. "You're done with the main treatment, but you're not really able to enter life because every three months you're gearing up to potentially hear this awful news."

But though that liminal space was difficult, Nelson says it was also "an opportunity to notice life like I'd never noticed before. I was seeing everything in sharp relief. Every beam of sunshine, every bird, every touch could bring me to tears. In not counting on things, they became more significant." But as for so many of us who experience a close call, the intense presence and gratitude she felt were fleeting. "After three years, I started counting on things again. I started taking things for granted. For me, that's the death knell for gratefulness— when we start feeling that entitlement for life and entitlement for things going our way."

So Nelson made a concerted effort to shift her perspective to grab hold of gratitude once again, this time for good. "I got really clear that being able to cultivate perspective in a moment, in a circumstance, was like developing what I call *spiritual musculature*." Now, when she starts to feel disconnected from life, or when resentment and expectation start to creep back in, she looks beyond her immediate sense of the moment to what else is there. She both broadens and deepens her sensing and her awareness. "Perspective became my lifeline to joy, to well-being, to resilience—to everything I needed."

Gratefulness is different from simply practicing gratitude. As Nelson describes it:

> It's an orientation to life that's not attached to conditions. You ground your gratitude in those things that you will have as long as you're alive, such as your breath and your presence here. It's like, even at times when your body is struggling, it's recognizing that there's so much that it's also doing exquisitely. In that way, gratefulness transcends your immediate circumstance.

Gratefulness is both a choice and an ongoing practice. "It's not just a passive exercise," Nelson explains. "You have to surround yourself with the things and put yourself in the places that bring you joy. For instance, if you choose to be around people who make you feel miserable, it's going to be a lot harder to be grateful."

Gratefulness is both a choice and an ongoing practice.

But sometimes we don't have a choice—life brings suffering to our doorstep. When she's really pressed, Nelson says she remembers all of the people she has loved and lost who would give anything just to be alive in that moment, "to experience this day, this pain, this struggle. I allow and sometimes push myself to remember these things when life feels challenging."

"Grateful living has become my way of life," Nelson says. So much so, in fact, that she went on to work for Brother David Steindl-Rast's organization, A Network for Grateful Living, and she authored the book *Wake Up Grateful: The Transformative Practice of Taking Nothing for Granted.*

It's a choice to see and experience the world this way, and sometimes that choice requires real work, but it's an option that's always available to us. As I've tried to underscore in this book, even in the face of experiences or predeterminations we cannot control, so much is still up to us. So much is still within our ability to direct it—as it turns out, even luck.

SEEING LIFE THROUGH THE
LENS OF GRATEFULNESS

I was waiting for something extraordinary to happen, but as the years wasted on, nothing ever did unless I caused it.

—*Charles Bukowski*

You might be wondering: What if it's hard to be grateful because you just have terrible luck? Psychologist and researcher Richard Wiseman was intrigued by questions of chance: the way our lives are influenced by random opportunities, catching a break, and being in the right place at the right time. So he set out to investigate. As he concluded, barring truly random circumstances, whether we're lucky or not is largely up to us.

In a series of experiments, Wiseman and his team put people who identified themselves as lucky or unlucky in a variety of circumstances, then tried to determine what influenced the difference in outcomes. He writes, "Over the years, I interviewed these volunteers, asked them to complete diaries, questionnaires and intelligence tests, and invited them to participate in experiments. The findings revealed that although unlucky people demonstrate almost no insight into the real causes of their good and bad luck, their own thoughts and behavior are actually responsible for much of their fortune."[18]

For instance, in one study, the researchers gave participants a newspaper and told them to count the number of photos in the paper. The unlucky people took about two minutes to complete the task, while the lucky required mere seconds. The reason? On the second page of the paper the scientists had pasted a message: *Stop counting. There are 43 photographs in this newspaper.* The self-identified lucky folks were more likely to notice the note, while those who felt unlucky in life looked right past it. As Wiseman notes:

Personality tests revealed that unlucky people are generally much more tense than lucky people, and research has shown that anxiety disrupts people's ability to notice the unexpected. . . . Unlucky people miss chance opportunities because they are too focused on looking for something else. They go to parties intent on finding their perfect partner and so miss opportunities to make good friends. They look through newspapers determined to find certain types of job advertisements and as a result miss other types of jobs. Lucky people are more relaxed and open, and therefore see what is there rather than just what they are looking for.[19]

His research shows that people who are lucky generate their own good fortune through four basic methods:

1. They're good at creating and noticing chance opportunities. For instance, lucky people tend to be more social, and having broader connections generates more lucky breaks, like hearing about a new job.

2. They generate good luck by listening to their intuition. In this case, intuition isn't a magical knowing but is informed by actual learning and experience.

3. Their generally positive attitude and expectations about life create self-fulfilling prophesies. They expect to do well or to gain opportunities, so they're actively looking for those good things.

4. Their more resilient attitude means that when bad things happen, lucky people are able to make lemonade by finding the good.

And as Wiseman's work also showed, the good news is that you can become a lucky person simply by acting like one, and adopting these ways of perceiving and reacting to the world.

To be clear, expecting good things to happen shouldn't be confused with entitlement. As Kristi Nelson notes, entitlement is kryptonite for gratefulness. And as studies have shown, people who experience entitlement are more likely to respond with anger rather than understanding when things don't go their way.[20]

Researchers Emily Zitek and Alexander Jordan predicted that "individuals higher in psychological entitlement, with their high expectations for personal outcomes and tendency to moralize them, would be more likely to experience anger after bad luck as compared to individuals lower in psychological entitlement."[21] They found that psychological entitlement was, indeed, positively correlated with anger and perceptions of injustice when the entitled people experienced bad luck. Additionally, "the relationship between entitlement and anger was specific to personally-experienced bad luck; entitlement was not correlated with anger when people recalled an unfair event or when they imagined that bad luck happened to someone else."[22]

In other words, when we feel morally superior and entitled to *some good things happening around here, already!*, we're more likely to get pissed off when they don't. Yet when we have that negative viewpoint, we're setting the stage for less good fortune to come our way. When we don't get what we want, we refuse to look through the lens of gratefulness and see what else might be present. All of these are choices.

Also, let me point out that when it comes to the luck of the draw, Beth Knopik, Silvia Vasquez-Lovado, Brother David Steindl-Rast, and Kristi Nelson were all dealt a pretty lousy hand. But they chose to play it out—to open themselves to the possibility that the extreme challenges they experienced were not all that life had to offer them; that perhaps they could even provide a stepping-stone to a richer way of living.

To be fair, when it comes to seeing life through rosier glasses, the cards are stacked against us lately. After all, how are we supposed to be positive when *everything is toxic*?

The Antidote to "Toxicity" Is Awe

The most fortunate are those who have a wonderful capacity to appreciate again and again, freshly and naively, the basic goods of life, with awe, pleasure, wonder, and even ecstasy.[23]

—*Abraham Maslow*

Toxic masculinity. Toxic bosses. Even toxic positivity. These days, everything and everyone is toxic. (And everyone is also *gaslighting* you!)

In Chapter 1, we looked at the drawbacks and even outright damage we cause when we label every negative experience as trauma. We encounter similar challenges when we're quick to call everything we either don't like or don't understand *toxic*. After a while, we start to believe that the world really is a bad place, and how are you supposed to live gratefully when *that's* your perspective?

As psychiatrist Grant Brenner writes in *Fast Company*:

> There is a difference between when something is truly harmful to us and something which we don't fully understand but feel uncomfortable with, even if deeply uncomfortable. There are times when our knee-jerk self-protective response is to label something toxic and then expel it from our lives and minds.
>
> Sometimes, we are projecting—a term psychoanalysts use to describe how we disavow parts of ourselves by putting them on something external. We then may "split," seeing ourselves as all good, and the object onto which we project as all bad.[24]

Brenner adds that being quick to dismiss what challenges us as toxic also robs us of the opportunity to reflect, learn, and grow. It makes us miss out on opportunities (as Wiseman's research demonstrates). It denies us the opportunity to practice and develop resilience. It also cuts us off from compassion.

In many ways, gratefulness is an antidote to seeing the world and everyone in it as toxic. It's true that people can behave horribly, and it's important to recognize when that's happening. At the same time, you don't have to be devoured by your hostility toward them. Plus, there are also really good people, and really good things happening, but if you're wearing your sludge-colored glasses all the time, it's extremely hard to see them.

One way gratefulness helps to counter toxicity is by connecting us with awe. Recall Kristi Nelson's description of how every moment took on new meaning—a sunrise or a touch could bring her to tears. When we really look for it, beauty can be found everywhere, and awe comes along with it.

Awe doesn't just feel *awe-some* (I had to do it!), it's good for us in other ways, as well. As psychologist and researcher Dacher Keltner has shown, "everyday wonder" can significantly improve our health and well-being.[25] And as Abraham Maslow observed, "The great lesson from the true mystics—from the Zen monks, and now also from the Humanistic and Transpersonal psychologists—is that the sacred is in the ordinary, that it is to be found in one's daily life, in one's neighbors, friends, and family, in one's back yard."[26]

So, in the same way that Kristi Nelson advised you to put yourself in the path of joy, go ahead and seek out some awe, as well. Go to a Grateful Dead (or okay, Taylor Swift) concert and sing along, sit under a tree and stare up-close at the miraculous architecture of a single leaf, check out an IMAX movie about the Grand Canyon (just try not to lose your lunch when they do that flyover thing with the camera). Do things that help you feel connected to something bigger and that boost your appreciation for what seems small.

What's Your Existential Gratitude Quotient (EGQ)?

When it comes to gratefulness, how are you doing? Gratitude researcher Lilian Jans-Beken and existential positive psychologist Paul Wong created an Existential Gratitude Scale to measure the tendency people have to feel grateful for *all* of human existence, not just the positive aspects.[27] Their scale includes items such as the following:

- I am grateful for my life even in times of suffering.

- I am grateful that my inner resources have increased as a result of overcoming adversities.

- I am grateful for the people in my life, even for those who have caused me much pain.

- I am thankful that I have something to live for, even though life has been very hard for me.

- I am grateful that every crisis represents an opportunity for me to grow.

- I have learned the importance of gratitude through suffering.

Pause and reflect on those statements for a moment. Perhaps you're experiencing a challenge right now that you might reframe from a perspective of gratefulness. If you develop the ability to shift your perspective (that *spiritual musculature*), research shows that you'll reap even more benefits than just momentary awe or joy.

Jans-Beken's team found that existential gratitude was associated with higher *spiritual well-being* (the perception of an individual's spiritual quality of life). This finding is important, considering that gratitude and spirituality have been shown to be protective factors against both anxiety and depression.[28]

A spiritual core of gratefulness is essential if gratitude is to be more than a tool for narcissistic self-improvement. A common misconception is that gratitude is necessarily self-serving, that it's all about appreciating *my* life and *my* blessings, in spite of the suffering of others. Some claim that it's impossible to be grateful while suffering, or that challenges occur anywhere on earth, and to be grateful means you're not paying attention.

Yet as Grateful Living CEO Joe Primo writes:

While joyfulness is not an easy path neither is joylessness. Indeed, there are all too many opportunities to be joyless thanks to grief,

trauma, tragedy, illness, the oppression of racism and economic
disparities, politics, environmental destruction, and on and on.

Absolutely, you can set perimeters for your joy and decide
you'll lean into it only once all energy is renewable energy, racism
is eliminated, socio-economic disparities are eradicated, no one you
love dies before you, your body holds strong until your 101st birth-
day, and humans finally figure out that everyone belongs and is
worthy of dignity and love. Yes, of course, you can wait for these
external variables—these conditions—which you cannot control or
change. But I wonder about all you will miss as you wait for the
right conditions. I wonder where you'll find bliss.[29]

In fact, gratitude can fuel not only joy but also the service that
will help to end all of this suffering. As Robert Emmons and psychoanalyst Robin Stern of the Yale Center for Emotional Intelligence
note, "True gratefulness rejoices in the other. Its ultimate goal is to
reflect back the goodness that one has received by creatively seeking
opportunities for giving."[30]

FROM GRATITUDE TO SERVICE

Some critics of gratitude (yes, even gratitude has detractors these
days) say that it creates too much self-focus—that as long as you think
things are good in *your* world, you won't care about helping others.
Fair enough. And Nelson agrees, observing that gratitude can be a
"self-satisfied panacea—a place to hang out where everything's just
about the feel-good of it all." But the way she sees it, "*gratefulness* is an
activator." As she says, "When my eyes fill with wonder and my heart
with love or joy, I do not betray my concerns for the world—I nourish
my capacity to attend to them." Living gratefully provides both the
motivation and the fuel to do good in the world.

In fact, for every story I've shared in this chapter, each person has
transformed their gratitude into giving. Beth Knopik now provides
outreach and support for those who are suffering a loss, and she
has written a book about her experiences in the hopes it will help oth-

ers experiencing grief and loss. It's titled *Beyond the Rainbow: A Mother's Journey Through Grief to Grace*.[31] Among other philanthropic efforts, Silvia Vasquez-Lovado created an organization to help young women who have survived sexual trauma. Her memoir, *In the Shadow of the Mountain*, describes her journey trekking to the base of Mt. Everest with a group of young women who were victims of sex trafficking and other forms of abuse. And I've already described some of the work by Brother David Steindl-Rast and Kristi Nelson.

Now, tell me again why *you* can't live gratefully?

To be clear, gratefulness is not the same as toxic positivity, which, in spite of my railing against overuse of the word *toxic*, is a real thing. It's where we sing tra-la-la in total ignorance of all that's crashing and burning around us, denying the real emotional pain within ourselves and others. Conversely, gratefulness is about recognizing all of what's happening in your life and in the world and using it as a lever for joy and appreciation, which, in turn, moves you to create positive change in the world.

As Kristi Nelson explains, "When we recognize the impermanence of everything, *that's* what wakes us up."

Life is precious and time is passing. So let's wake up now, together.

10

Help Empower Society

*Few will have the greatness to bend history itself; but each
of us can work to change a small portion of events. It is from
numberless diverse acts of courage and belief that human history
is shaped.*[1]

—*Robert F. Kennedy*

We love stories about how people in difficult situations came out on top: how they grappled with a massive challenge and not only found their way through but were changed for the better as a result. Or at least, we used to.

When Frank Bruni woke up one morning, immediately he knew something was wrong. His vision, which had been fine when he went to bed, was suddenly blurry. Extensive testing was inconclusive, leaving Bruni with only questions and no answers. Finally, it was discovered that for some unknown reason, Bruni had suffered a stroke of the optic nerve behind his right eye, causing permanent damage to the nerve. Because he is a journalist, Bruni's career relies heavily on his ability to read and process information. As he writes in his book *The Age of Grievance* (which offers a journalistic take on our current romance with victimhood), "My brain had to train itself to edit out the pointless efforts of my right eye, which warped and smudged what I saw."[2] Bruni became a slower reader, and writing became more difficult.

Bruni describes his initial feelings of victimization and self-pity: "But I soon realized what a danger and dead end that was. To focus and dwell on the obstacles that had been dumped in front of me . . . was attractive, understandable, warranted—and wholly unconstructive. . . . Measuring misfortune is no strategy for living."

Bruni began to write about his experience grappling with his vision issues, eventually penning a triumphant memoir, chronicling, as he describes it, "what I'd lost, what I'd gained, and how I'd worked to forge a relatively upbeat attitude about it all." The response wasn't what he anticipated. Though some were inspired by the book, more than a few reached out to Bruni to scold him. As they framed it, not everyone could access resilience. It isn't possible for everyone to be optimistic. Bruni was privileged, and it was heartless and cruel to share his hard-won optimism.

Frank, *I hear you!* It's like as a society, we can't just be *happy* anymore. Ever. About anything. Case in point: In 2022, when Jane Campion won a Critic's Choice Award for best director, she couldn't simply offer a hearty high five to the other women who'd been recognized that night. Accepting the award, Campion turned to attendees Venus and Serena Williams—who'd battled their way to the top of a mostly white sport, mind you—and said: "And Serena and Venus, you are such marvels. However, you do not play against the guys, like I have to."[3] Campion wanted people to know that her accomplishment was superior, because her struggle was superior!

It's like what Frank Bruni noticed through the lens of his own misfortune: So many of us construct our identities around our pitfalls and our struggles, and this has ripple effects. When victimhood becomes the currency of the land, it shapes culture. After all, if there were no cultural currency involved—no larger payout for touting one's victim status—we wouldn't do it.

Throughout this book I've provided you with insights and tools designed to help you overcome a victim mindset and embrace empowerment. And yet when society's against you, *it's hard*. As psychologist Mary C. Murphy notes in her book *Cultures of Growth*, mindset is not only individual and internal, it's also a feature of the environment. When the surrounding culture is oriented in the opposite direction, it's like swimming upstream.[4] It's still possible to embody the mindset you're aiming for, but the effort can be exhausting. It's hard not to adopt the predominant attitude. And yet that's exactly what I'm asking you to do. Because that's what we *need* to do if we want to see a move to a more empowered culture.

An empowered society begins with a shift in individual consciousness. A shift in *your* consciousness.

Gandhi once encouraged us to be the change we wish to see in the world. But that assumes that we have a clear vision in the first place. It's not always so obvious what change is necessary, and what methods will achieve those aims. And the evolution of society doesn't happen overnight.

It takes not only a vision and a plan but also a lot of humility and patience to make sustained long-term changes to the world at large. But what the hell—I say let's go for it! Because it's clear that some big changes are needed in our society right now. We're living in the age of the Victimhood Olympics, with not only individuals but *entire groups* competing for who has suffered most.*

PERPETUAL VICTIMHOOD IS NOT THE WAY

I'll say it again—it's true that, as a society, we need to make real structural shifts. There are groups that have historically been left behind, overlooked, or silenced, and corrective action is needed. Yet that on its own won't create a more empowered society. We also desperately need a shift in our *collective consciousness* to one where groups lead with empowerment—including their potential for strength, resiliency, autonomy, and agency. To get there will require moving victimhood from the center of a group's identity to the periphery.

---

* While Frank Bruni uses the phrase *Oppression Olympics* in his book, for the purposes of this book I use the phrase *Victimhood Olympics*. We're both talking about the same thing, though.

To the extent that real wounds have been incurred, we need to acknowledge that, metabolize it, and move on. But our current society does not allow that. Instead, it encourages *perpetual victimhood*, where emphasizing wounds nets societal rewards.

The majority of this book has focused on individuals and how a victim mindset is holding us each back from reaching our full potential. My original intention was that when I got to the conclusion of the book, I'd include a few observations on how victimhood works at the group level. Yet it became increasingly obvious to me with world events that something must be done at the collective level or else our precious planet will forever be caught in this victimhood trap.

So I dove into the voluminous literature on collective victimhood. I was blown away by the striking similarities with research on individuals. Almost across the board, the exact same mechanisms at work on the individual level apply to groups. And once all of these victims get together and form groups centered on their suffering, it can lead to intractable conflicts among groups, who compete for the title of the ultimate victim.

All of this seemed too important for a mere mention. After all, these group-level dynamics play a massive role in shaping our world, including our individual beliefs and actions. So I decided to add this concluding chapter, where I offer a science-backed approach to intergroup reconciliation and, dare I say, peace.

It's a lofty goal, to be sure. But, why not? Maybe this sounds a little pie-in-the-sky to you. After all, you're not a global peace negotiator. What do you need to know about intractable conflict? Except that in some ways, you are. We all are. My aim with this concluding chapter is to show you just how much your individual mindset and actions *matter* to collective behaviors and outcomes, so that you're inspired to make changes in your own life, knowing it will have knock-on effects in the world around you.

To start getting a handle on how the individual feeds the collective, let's recall the four main characteristics of interpersonal victimhood, which I mentioned way back in Chapter 3. They are:

- Incessant need for recognition

- Moral elitism

- Lack of empathy for others

- Frequent rumination about victimization

So what does all of this look like at the group level? For one, when we're primed to see ourselves as victims—remembering perceived or actual harms done to us—we show less empathy toward our adversaries.[5] Their suffering feels justified because *we* have suffered. When groups become preoccupied with their wounds, they can develop what psychologists describe as an "egoism of victimhood."[6] Members not only become unable to see things from their rivals' perspective, they also eschew responsibility for any harm—including atrocities— that their group inflicts on their enemies.[7] (We'll delve more into that research in a moment.)

Given that being a victim is not a positive experience and involves feelings of helplessness and a lack of agency, why do so many groups adopt a victimhood-centered identity? What's the appeal?

THE ALLURE OF COLLECTIVE VICTIMHOOD

For a victim identity to be so alluring to a group, there must be some need that it fulfills. As it turns out, psychologists have been studying this topic and have identified several potential benefits of collective victimhood:[8]

- *Entitlement and moral superiority.* When a group believes that they are the victims and others are the perpetrators, they feel both a sense of entitlement and moral superiority. They believe that it is their adversary's responsibility to remedy the wrongdoing and take steps toward reconciliation, while they wait.

- *Sympathy and support.* Collective victimhood is likely to elicit feelings of sympathy and gain support from noninvolved third parties. This can translate to political and social support. There is therefore a desire to make things out as cut-and-dried, meaning one party are clearly the victims (and therefore in need of support) and the other are the perpetrators (and in need of vilification).

Kurt Gray and Daniel Wegner's theory of *moral typecasting* is relevant here.[9] According to the theory, people generally hold an inverse relationship between *moral agency* (one's capacity to do right or wrong) and *moral patiency* (one's capacity to be a target of right or wrong). Across seven studies, the researchers showed that through the process of moral typecasting, "good- and evil-doers were perceived to be less vulnerable to having good or evil done to them." In other words, we tend to believe that people are either victims or perpetrators. Additionally, we tend to automatically perceive victims as weak, vulnerable, and moral, while we perceive perpetrators as aggressive and immoral.

- *Group cohesiveness.* Nothing brings a group together like collective grievance. When groups rally around their victimhood, they may feel united by a common cause. Emphasizing shared trauma is therefore a good strategy for leaders to gain the support of the masses. Just as "trauma bonding" is a real phenomenon among people in romantic relationships and friendships, it's also an effective way to increase group solidarity.

Every group where victimhood is central to their identity has their own "chosen trauma"—a traumatic historical event that they have chosen to single out, one that holds particular significance for the group. This event (which is often a very real event) becomes central in the group's collective memory and influences the group's self-view and relations with the outside world. A group's chosen trauma is transmitted from one generation to the next, discussed within families and in school settings, and expressed by cultural products in literature and film. This central element may lie dormant for periods of time, then reactivate during times of stress and insecurity.*

The Role of Collective Narcissism

There's something else that collective victimhood may provide—shared hubristic pride. And here's where the link with narcissism and the real damage of making suffering the central focus of the group comes in. Victimhood is especially alluring to groups that have become narcissistic.

As you'll recall from earlier in the book, not all individuals who operate with a victim mindset score high in narcissism. The same is true at the group level—not all victim groups are narcissistic or antagonistic. However, as with individuals, there are strong connections. Among groups that are narcissistic, they often demonstrate shared victimhood.[10]

To be clear, to be human is to be at least somewhat tribal. Social groups satisfy various individual needs and motives.[11] There is nothing narcissistic about wanting past wrongs to be recognized or even wanting some kind of correction or reparation. Narcissism comes in when groups see themselves as better or more worthy for having suffered, or they want special affordances—some of which may actually cause harm to other groups.

In *The Anatomy of Human Destructiveness*, humanistic philosopher Erich Fromm discussed the link between *group narcissism* and

---

* The Jewish Holocaust and the Palestinian Nakba are two prominent examples of chosen traumas that affect the ongoing conflict between these groups. Though modern-day Jewish Israelis for the most part were not direct victims of this horrifying event, it seems to be occupying an even greater bandwidth in many Israelis' minds now than in the past, suggesting that Israelis may be feeling a greater sense of threat than they have in a long while. See Klar, Y., Schori-Eyal, N., & Klar, Y. (2013). The "never again" state of Israel: The emergence of the Holocaust as a core feature of Israeli identity and its four incongruent voices. *Journal of Social Issues, 69,* 125–143.

personal pride. He writes, "Group narcissism . . . is extremely important as an element giving satisfaction to the members of the group and particularly to those who have few other reasons to feel proud and worthwhile."[12]

Psychologist Agnieszka Golec de Zavala pioneered the modern-day scientific investigation into group narcissism, which she calls *collective narcissism*.[13] She defines it as "a belief that the exaggerated greatness of one's group is not sufficiently recognized by others," where this thirst for recognition becomes the predominant focus of the group and is never satiated.[14] As she explained to me, the recognition doesn't only have to be the group's greatness but can also be a demand for acknowledgment of unique hardship that makes the group deserve special recognition above all other groups.[15]

To measure collective narcissism, de Zavala created the Collective Narcissism Scale, which includes statements such as "My group deserves special treatment" and "I insist upon my group getting the respect that is due to it." Notice that collective narcissism is less about concern for the well-being of the group's members and more about a constant need to receive recognition of a group's exaggerated superiority or suffering.[16] As she and her colleague Dorottya Lantos note, collective narcissism "is the form of 'in-group love' robustly associated with 'out-group hate.'"[17] They add, "The pervasive association between collective narcissism and intergroup hostility is driven by a biased perception of the in-group as constantly threatened and out-groups as hostile and threatening. Collective narcissism is associated with hypersensitivity to provocation and the belief that only hostile revenge is a desirable and rewarding response."

Extreme groups often thrive on their narcissistic understanding of their identity as a group. For example, incels as a group center their collective narcissism on gender, white supremacists on race, gang members on their particular gang, and aggressive sport fans on their team.[18] As research has shown, even college students at times have been shown to display high collective narcissism if they identify strongly with their college's sense of superiority.[19]

Perhaps not surprisingly, individuals who score high in vulnerable narcissism are more likely to fall into collective narcissistic thinking than those who don't.[20] If you're already feeling like you're a better person than others or you deserve more recognition or affordances because of past suffering, you're more likely to fall in with a group that feels similarly. It's like trauma bonding on steroids. But here's what's beneath it: Collective narcissists are obsessed with receiving group recognition because they personally feel deeply insecure about *their own value* and they desperately need validation.

Indeed, the negative consequences of collective narcissism result from its defensiveness and the frustration of an individual's basic psychological needs, including a sense of personal esteem. Collective narcissists need constant external validation of their positive self-image and are exquisitely sensitive when they feel criticized, or when others fail to adequately recognize their suffering.[21]

Collective narcissists don't actually get to enjoy the true benefits of healthy group membership, such as a sense of loyalty or fidelity. Instead, they bond over their shared prejudice and hostility toward those outside the group. In fact, narcissistic groups are likely to throw individual members under the bus when it suits them, or when members violate group rules, as they're not particularly loyal to one another.

As Golec de Zavala explained to me, collective narcissism is associated with low self-esteem (which, as I noted previously, I prefer to characterize as *uncertain* self-esteem), and by extension with low personal control. Individuals with low personal control (which in this context means a sense that you have little control over your life) tend to show in-group favoritism and negative out-group attitudes. They also tend to be derogatory toward critics in their in-group and display greater ethnocentrism.[22]

Lack of personal control can enhance collective narcissism because it undermines self-esteem. In other words, if you have low self-esteem, you're also likely to feel a low sense of personal control. When you feel you have low control over your life, it decreases your self-esteem, making you even more likely to want to be part of a narcissistic group. It's a vicious cycle.

This is just one way in which collective empowerment boils down to individual thinking and behavior. As individuals, together we create and reinforce the culture. If we want to live in a better world, creating that better world truly begins with each and every one of us. We start by making *our own world* better, and we do this by adopting new attitudes and strategies to cope with life's challenges. We learn to metabolize our own personal grief and suffering into grace, and we share that grace with others.

Collective narcissism is actually not a successful coping strategy, as it does not, in fact, improve personal esteem.[23]

The thing to note is that we *can all* be susceptible to collective narcissism at one time or another, especially when narcissistic beliefs become more widespread and normalized within our own groups. If you're part of a group that has victimhood as a central part of its identity, be on alert for these darker, narcissistic tendencies, which could actually derail the group's otherwise positive intentions. Something we especially need to be on the lookout for is *competitive victimhood*.

Competitive Victimhood

Individual victimhood fuels collective victimhood, which is a common element of collective narcissism. And this, my friend, is how we end up with an *intractable conflict*.

When you've got two or more groups that are opposed to one another, each wants to be seen as the biggest victim. That's because victimhood is a coveted psychological property.[24] And when each group is convinced that they are the supreme victims, they become mired in ongoing friction. Victimhood is like a renewable energy source for intergroup conflict.[25]

When we think of intractable conflict, we often conjure up thoughts of the Middle East. Though Israelis and Palestinians certainly have not cornered the market on long-term intergroup disputes, much of our research on competitive victimhood centers on this particular conflict. In one study, researchers observed dialogue groups composed of Israeli Jews and Israeli Arabs (Palestinians who are Israeli citizens).[26] The participants were instructed to discuss the relationship between their groups. As psychologist Arie Nadler observed, it was almost like there was a chair with a sign on it reading *The Real Victim* in the middle of the room, with the two groups fiercely competing to see who could occupy it.[27]

Both the Jews and Arabs framed their arguments through the lens of their chosen traumas. Jewish participants focused on historic antisemitism and the Holocaust and emphasized their demands for absolute and *total security*. The Palestinians focused on the wrongs they had suffered in the 1948 Nakba and underscored their demands for *total justice*. Notice the superlatives at play here with "total security" and "total justice." Nothing less would do. And unless and until the other group recognized the superior victimhood of the other and guaranteed these desired outcomes, there could be no progress.

When we focus only on the wrongs we believe have been done to us, everything else disappears.[28] And when we see ourselves as morally superior, we believe that violence and other forms of aggression against the other party are justified. As research from Boaz Hamieri and his colleagues demonstrates, when people see themselves as victims, they become more likely to support political violence.[29] They note:

> Prior work has established the importance of situational and dispositional predictors of political violence, such as search for significance and meaning and experiencing trauma. However, these predictors do not fully account for one of its most worrisome ingredients—the tendency to feel aggrieved and to express that grievance violently.

Victimhood is that missing link.

Yet to come to these conclusions, Hamieri and his team didn't turn overseas. Instead, they looked at groups of Americans—specifically, Democrats and Republicans. One study examined self-reported partisans who had participated in politically motivated violence. It found that "trait victimhood strongly predicted support for political violence—an association mediated through intergroup competitive victimhood beliefs."

In another study, when prompted to think about their own group's victimization, participants who were high in trait victimhood showed increased support for political violence. *This was true of both Democrats and Republicans.* It's important to underscore, once again, that competitive victimhood and collective narcissism can be found anywhere on the political spectrum. However, the latter seems particularly alluring to both populists and authoritarians (on the left and right).[30]

Competitive victimhood paves the road for disengagement from conventional rules of morality, with each group believing they are absolved of any wrongdoing because of their suffering. This results in a self-reinforcing cycle of violence.

This is strikingly similar to the concept of *vulnerable entitlement* at the individual level: Because a group has suffered, they are entitled to aggression and selfishness. Once a group's chosen trauma is activated, their higher values go right out the window.[31,*]

So we've established that competitive victimhood is a problem—a big one. And it keeps conflicts going indefinitely. But how can we finally break this cycle and escape this trap?

ESCAPING THE COLLECTIVE VICTIMHOOD TRAP

First, it's important to recognize that it's possible to have healthy ingroup love—where a member of a group feels a healthy pride in the genuine accomplishments of the group but isn't primarily focused on recognition of the group's superiority by others.[32] Healthy in-group

---

* In one study, Jewish Canadians who were reminded of the Holocaust accepted less collective guilt for their group's harmful actions toward Palestinians than those who had not been reminded of their in-group's past victimization. In another condition researchers found that when they were reminded of the attacks on September 11, 2001, Americans, but not Canadians, experienced less collective guilt for harm caused in Iraq. As the researchers note: "Consistent with a social identity perspective, when threatened by accusations of immorality, group members mount defenses that are aimed at protecting the ingroup's image, including lessening ingroup responsibly and legitimization of its harmful actions toward another group. Use of either or both of these strategies can effectively undermine feelings of collective guilt." See Wohl, M. J. A., & Branscombe, N. R. (2008). Remembering historical victimization: Collective guilt for current ingroup transgressions. *Journal of Personality and Social Psychology, 94,* 988–1006.

love is related to positive out-group attitudes and is therefore more likely to foster tolerance and openness to other groups.[33]

An example of a healthy in-group love could be breast cancer survivors who have united to raise awareness, provide support for others, or fundraise. Although having experienced cancer forms the central aspect of the group's identity, the group does not hold itself as superior to other groups who have experienced health challenges, nor does it try to target or act out against other groups.

Recall that individuals in narcissistic groups tend to feel they have little control over their life. It follows, then, that helping people have a greater sense of control and personal agency could help to shift them from *narcissistic activism* to *effective activism*.[34] Ultimately, healthy in-group positivity is more likely to contribute to effective activism. It also has important consequences with regard to personal well-being. Unlike collective narcissism, healthy in-group love has been associated with greater levels of life satisfaction, positive emotions, social connectedness, and gratitude.[35]

Sometimes though, the payoffs of collective victimhood and collective narcissism outweigh the benefits of healthy in-group positivity. Even when groups could opt to organize around positive beliefs and ideals, members sometimes push the more caustic and corrosive ideals of collective narcissism. In a dysfunctional sense, collective victimhood and collective narcissism may actually serve the group's goals, at least in the short-term. So how do we address that?

One thing that helps is to start young. Group-narcissistic beliefs can form early in life, but they don't have to. We can teach kids that their social identity doesn't have to be externally validated, and that they can get meaning from other sources. We can also help them to feel inherently worthy without feeling *superior*. We can also cultivate a healthier worldview and self-view as adults.

In the Introduction, I proposed the idea that just because challenging things have happened to you, that doesn't mean they have to limit you. You don't have to make trauma or grief the center of your identity. The same is true for groups. You may indeed have suffered unfairly. You may have been victimized and deserve to have that fact acknowledged. But that doesn't mean that you have to organize your group around a sense of entitlement or superiority or a desire for revenge.

In this section, I offer some science-backed pathways for breaking the cycle of competitive victimhood and increasing intergroup reconciliation. I take a *psychological needs approach*, which assumes that conflicts are often the result of a frustrated human need (lack of respect, loss of reputation, lack of autonomy, lack of agency, and so on) and that emotions such as anger, revenge, and the desire to maintain the image of supreme morality are key drivers of the conflict.*

Cultivating a Group Empowerment Mindset

As I previously discussed, a key aspect of an empowerment mindset is giving up hope for a better past. This may seem impossible to do, but the rewards are vast.

It's critical to emphasize that this doesn't mean forgetting the past. In fact, when wrongs have been done we want to remember them so that we can learn from them and prevent them from happening again. Also, metabolizing our shared traumas can benefit us. We can experience *post-traumatic group growth*!

The same principles we discussed in Chapter 1 are also helpful here at the collective level. We want to recognize that yes, terrible things have happened in the past, but that's not all we are. When we choose to have a broader perspective, we're exercising agency, and a belief in our own agency also helps to decrease the negative follow-ons associated with victimhood. We want to foster a sense that we have control in our lives. We can choose our behaviors and our path forward.

One of the ways we can become more personally empowered and

---

* This is in contrast to the "real conflict" approach, which assumes that intergroup conflicts are due to competition over scarce resources and that conflicts end when the two groups reach a rational agreement on how to divide limited resources. This approach is misguided because it ignores the role of need frustration and emotions in conflict. See Nadler, A. (2019). The social psychology of intergroup reconciliation: Moving beyond guilt and victimhood. In A. M. Biro & E. Verhas (Eds.), *International studies in human rights and identity: Populism, memory, and minority rights—CEE issues in global perspective*. Brill.

defuse intergroup conflicts is to engage in *healthy* groups. Agnieszaka Golec de Zavala and Dorottya Lantos found in their research that "the association between collective narcissism and intergroup hostility is weakened by experiences that fortify emotional resilience (such as positive identification with a community)."[36]

Now, the word *empowerment* on its own sounds positive, at least when it's included in a book on personal development. Yet it's critical to note here that there is a potential dark side of group empowerment. As we've seen, when groups bond over a chosen trauma and adopt narcissistic traits, they can become empowered, all right—empowered to act like assholes. Through a sense of empowerment, the victims can become the perpetrators.

On its own, empowerment is not enough. We need to be *positively empowered*. And we need to never forget what it was like to be victimized—not so we can enact revenge or feel superior, but so we can always have empathy for others who are in similar positions to what we once experienced.

Empowerment is not enough. We need to be *positively empowered*.

An incredible example of this is South Africa's move toward reconciliation after the end of apartheid. Nelson Mandela famously declared that his government would not enact revenge against their former oppressors. Instead, they would offer forgiveness. In his words, "You will achieve more in this world through acts of mercy than you will through acts of retribution."[37] As part of these efforts, Mandela encouraged South Africans not to see one another as white or Black but as fellow countrymen. As immortalized in the book *Playing the Enemy* by John Carlin and later the movie *Invictus*, one approach (of many) that Mandela employed was to encourage support for the country's rugby team. His goal was to inspire a new sense of group identity and national pride. (And one could say it worked pretty well, as South Africa won the World Cup that year.)

Empowering members of groups to believe in their potential for agency will not eradicate the memory of past wrongs, but it will render the role of collective victimhood less central in the group's collective identity. We can still recognize our collective victimhood, but we want to move our shared trauma from the center of our collective identity to the periphery. This puts us in a position where reconciliation is possible.

But *how* do we do this? For the rest of this chapter I will offer some options backed by research.[38]

Encourage Common Victimhood

You read that right—I'm actually encouraging you to embrace victimhood! Yet when I use the phrase *common victimhood*, it's about recognizing that both the in-group *and* out-group are victims of the conflict. Instead of insisting on a hierarchy of suffering, we can acknowledge that we both have suffered. (There's enough suffering to go around!)

In a study that demonstrated the powerful impacts of common victimhood, Israelis and Palestinians were shown a newspaper article that described both groups as victims of the conflict. These participants then demonstrated less competitive victimhood and more willingness to forgive members of the other group than did participants in a control condition.[39] Additional research showed that Israeli Jews who were prompted to see both groups as victims were less supportive of aggressive actions against Palestinians than were participants in a control condition.[40]

It doesn't directly have to do with victimhood, but I would add that another sentiment would help here as well. In complex situations, simply acknowledging the difficulty of finding a fair and equitable solution can also help.

The reality is, it's easy to take a polarized position on difficult topics if you're not truly engaged or interested in finding an actual *solution*, which is about more than simply having your side win. When we're thinking about actions and approaches that might actually work, we have to acknowledge complexity. Both that complex solutions are required, *and* the fact that typically, neither side is 100 percent right or wrong. Usually each has at least one point that is valid. A basic acknowledgment of that fact could create a toehold that might move the situation beyond one that's truly intractable.

Recognize Your Own Capacity to Be the Perpetrator

In any interpersonal conflict (whether at the individual or group level), all sides are motivated to maintain a positive moral self-image. This often creates two very different subjective realities, where the perpetrators tend to downplay the severity of their offense and their intent to offend, while victims tend to perceive the motivations of the perpetrators as arbitrary, senseless, immoral, and more severe than the perpetrator tends to view the situation.[41]

In psychology this is called the Capone Hypothesis: People with antagonistic personality characteristics perceive themselves as substantially more good than bad.[42] While this has been shown to be the case among psychology participants and even real-life prisoners,[43] it was named the Capone Hypothesis after Al "Scarface" Capone. Despite many of his victims regarding Capone as "pure evil," his view of himself was as follows:

> I have spent the best years of my life giving people the lighter pleasures, helping them have a good time, and all I get is abuse, the existence of a hunted man.[44]

Often the perpetrators can view themselves as victims, which complicates the waters and points to a deeper complexity in escaping the victimhood trap. Earlier, we looked at the idea of moral typecasting—the belief that people are either victims or perpetrators. Yet the reality is that the same person who is a victim in one case may be the perpetrator in another. A kid who's bullied can turn around and bully someone else.

Instead of categorizing people or groups as one or the other, or even categorizing *ourselves* as absolutely one of the other, we need to openly accept that all humans have the capacity to play either role. When we acknowledge this—that under the same circumstances, we might have done the same thing—we're more likely to show empathy and extend forgiveness.

In her book *The Blue Sweater*, Jacqueline Novogratz chronicles

her early work in various parts of Africa, including Rwanda. Novogratz worked with local women to found Duterimbere, an NGO
working to empower women to help eradicate poverty. She left
Rwanda prior to the 1994 genocide—a period of roughly 100 days
when ethnic minority Tutsi (along with more moderate Hutu) were
targeted and executed by armed militias from the Hutu ethnic group.
But it wasn't only soldiers who killed Tutsi. Hutu civilians also participated, caught up as they were in a tide of hatred and fear created
by militant Hutu leaders.

Novogratz returned to the country to find that the women she'd
worked with had all been swept up in the events in different capacities. She returned to Rwanda to speak with them in person, to try to
make sense of what had happened among these previously peaceful
women who had worked side by side just a short time before. She
writes, "What made my head spin was the fact that the women I'd
known and worked with for years . . . had played such dramatically
different roles in the genocide as victim, bystander, and even perpetrator."[45]

Human beings are neither angels nor demons. Given the same
circumstances, we do not know what we would do. When we recognize this, it becomes easier to offer compassion and forgiveness.

Acknowledge, Acknowledge, Acknowledge

John Lewis was fifteen years old when he first heard Dr. Martin Luther King Jr. speak.[46] When he was seventeen, he met Rosa Parks. At
eighteen, he met Dr. King. Lewis then became an activist himself,
peacefully protesting as part of the growing civil rights movement.

Lewis was on the bridge in Selma when protesters were beaten
by Alabama state troopers. Then, on the Freedom Ride in Rock Hill,
South Carolina, he and other protesters were beaten by members of
the KKK, who left them to die. Lewis survived and continued his
work, eventually becoming a congressman for the state of Georgia.

Commenting on how he kept moving forward in the face of such
hateful opposition, Lewis said, "You have to believe, somehow and

some way, in the possibility that we will reconcile to each other as humans. So you study. You meditate. And you forgive."

In 2009, two men came to Lewis's congressional office. As it turned out, one of them was a former Klansman from South Carolina, and he'd brought his son. The older man said, "Mr. Lewis, I'm one of the people that beat you and your seatmate. Will you forgive me? I want to apologize."

As Lewis recalled, both the man and his son began to cry. "They hugged me. I hugged them back. And the three of us cried together."

When facing a conflict with someone from a different identity group, you'd be surprised how a simple opening statement like "It is true, we played some role in your victimization" can go toward turning down the temperature. It's an incredibly powerful act to acknowledge that your group—whether presently or historically—was fully or partially responsible. As research shows, it also makes the victimized group more willing to engage in efforts toward reconciliation.[47]

That's not the only form of acknowledgment that matters, however. There is a difference between *acknowledgment of wrongdoing*, which implies responsibility, and *acknowledgment of suffering*, which does not carry a similar meaning. You may also be surprised to discover how powerful the words "It is true, you were victimized" can also be for quelling tensions.

While in reality victimhood acknowledgment by adversaries is rare, even a small positive gesture to your out-group can affect a readiness to reciprocate. In one study, Armenian Americans who read a text where Turkish scholars acknowledged the Armenian genocide felt better toward the Turkish people, compared with a group who'd been reminded of historic denial by the Turks of this event. In a separate study where American Jews were reminded of Germans' acknowledgment of the Holocaust, the participants felt not only more positive feelings toward the Germans but also greater psychological well-being.[48,*]

---

* In a series of studies, Boaz Hameiri and Arie Nadler found that the acknowledgment of Palestinian Nakba-sufferings by Israeli Jews and Holocaust-sufferings by Palestinians resulted in a greater willingness to make concessions on issues like the right of return, Jerusalem,

Acknowledgment of the other's suffering can have limited effects, however, in contexts where the collective has had a history of denying the other group's chosen trauma. Luca Andrighetto and his colleagues looked at citizens from societies entrapped in recent or ongoing conflicts—such as Bosnia and Herzegovina, Serbia, Palestine, and Israel—and found that while acknowledgment was effective in increasing trust toward members of the out-group—an important first step—it was ineffective in improving people's willingness to reconcile and stimulate hope for change if the out-group had a prominent narrative that denied their adversaries' chosen trauma.[49]

A third form of acknowledgment that goes a long way is simply expressing empathy for the group's suffering. A simple statement such as "We have empathy for what you are going through" can really go a long way.

These three forms of acknowledgment may seem basic, but for groups involved in intractable conflict, they can lead to real change. There's an underlying element here that I'd like to explore for a moment, and that's the importance of being able to quiet our own ego enough to channel empathy and humility.

Quiet Your Ego

Several years ago, a survey came out that showed that the words *humility* and *humbleness* are slowly disappearing from our books.[50] From 1901 to 2000, they endured a whopping 43 percent decline, indicating that we value these virtues less than we once did. The problem with this is that, as science shows, if we want to achieve a state of satisfaction and inner peace, it's *transcending* the ego—not enhancing it—that's gonna get us there.[51]

As psychologist Mark Leary explains, there are benefits of a

---

and giving back land for peace. See Hameiri, B., & Nadler, A. (2017). Looking backward to move forward: Effects of acknowledgement of victimhood on readiness to compromise for peace in the protracted Israeli-Palestinian conflict. *Personality and Social Psychology Bulletin*, *43*, 555–569.

strong sense of self, yet it can also cause us considerable problems.[52] Self-awareness, self-reflection, self-control . . . these are essential to helping us define and achieve our goals. Yet when our ego—our incessant need to see ourselves in a positive light—is loud and in charge, it can also trigger a conga line of defense mechanisms. We need a balance. We need what's called a *quiet ego*.

A quiet ego is not to be confused with a *silent* ego. As researchers Heidi Wayment, Kateryna Sylaska, and Jack Bauer (no, not the guy from 24) describe it, "The volume of the ego is turned down so that it might listen to others as well as the self in an effort to approach life more humanely and compassionately."[53] With a quiet ego, we have a solid sense of self, but we also consider others.

Wayment and Bauer identify the four components of a quiet ego as follows:[54]

Detached awareness: This is the ability to be focused on the immediate moment, without judgment over what should be happening. It is taking a nondefensive attitude toward whatever is happening, and it's associated with multiple aspects of psychological well-being.[55]

Inclusive identity: When we have an inclusive identity, we're not only concerned with what will help ourselves, we also care about others. We demonstrate compassion and are more cooperative in our approach.

Perspective-taking: Being able to understand another person's point of view helps us focus on the world outside ourselves. When we can consider others' perspectives, empathy is a natural follow-on.

Personal growth: We value learning and new experiences, understanding that they will help us grow. We focus more on continual development rather than any kind of finished product, and this helps to mute the ego.

Wayment, Sylaska, and Bauer found that although a quiet ego is generally associated with healthier self-esteem, it's also linked to *self-transcendence*.[56] In other words, if we want to create a better world, we need to honor both ourselves and our personal needs, but to some extent we also need to grow beyond them. *We need to get over ourselves!*

We need to not only expand our perception *beyond* ourselves, we need to also expand our perception *of* ourselves.

Embrace a Complex Human Identity

In order to interact more skillfully and compassionately with others, we need to develop a more complex and human identity for ourselves. Specifically, we need to see ourselves as inhabiting a range of ways of being that include some not-so-attractive—and even downright dark—characteristics. We need to embrace that we all have our moments when we're at our best, and when we're at our worst. (Remember the other day how you saw that old lady shuffling toward the elevator and you frantically clicked on the button to close the doors?)

When we recognize our own negative qualities, it makes it easier to cut others some slack. When we see others on their darker days (or years), it makes it easier to suspend our judgment and offer some grace instead. The same is true of the groups we're part of—they are also inhabited by an assortment of characters, from heroes to villains.

To be clear, this does not mean that we should give people or groups or nations a pass on abominable behavior. Remember that accountability is essential to reconciliation. It simply means that when we encounter nefarious behavior, we hold a space for the possibility of redemption, understanding that we could all use some compassion and forgiveness, at least once in a while.

Jean Améry's thinking on victimhood, forgiveness, and reconciliation is relevant here.[57] Following the occupation of Austria by Nazi Germany in 1938, Améry fled to Brussels, where he was identified as a Jew by Nazis and sent to multiple concentration camps, including Auschwitz. He would eventually return to Brussels, where he would write essays on his experiences in Auschwitz, the resentment that many victims felt, and the possibility of reconciliation with their perpetrators. Sadly, Améry committed suicide by overdosing on sleeping pills in a hotel room in Salzburg in 1978.

Améry observed that in many societies, forgiveness is often considered the morally superior option. As a result, victims are often pressured into granting "cheap forgiveness" to their perpetrators. He argued that genuine reconciliation can only come about when there is respect for the rights of the victim—particularly, the right of the victim to *be resentful toward their tormentors*. According to this view, a simple apology is not enough. Améry believed that going from cheap forgiveness to genuine forgiveness can occur only when the perpetrators integrate their past wrongs into their identity and genuinely convince the victim that the perpetrators view their wrongful actions as *part of who they are*.

Germany got this right by erecting monuments and museums acknowledging the atrocities they committed against German Jews. By doing so, they make modern-day Jews feel as though their right to resentment is honored. They don't try to deny that it happened; they actively incorporate it into their complex national identity. Imagine what it would be like to hear from a German public figure a statement such as the following: "Who are we? We are Beethoven, Schiller, Kant, and Hitler." Now *that* is a complex identity!

Ideally, we start to bake these concepts into our educational and family systems, so that we're raised with these higher ideals. As it is, socialization and education processes tend to perpetuate and even amplify ongoing hostilities among groups.

Teach Critical Thinking

In his article "The Enemy System," psychiatrist and professor John E. Mack writes:

Enmity between groups of people stems from the interaction of psychological, economic, and cultural elements. These include fear and hostility (which are often closely related), competition over perceived scarce resources, the need for individuals to identify with a cause, a tendency to disclaim and assign elsewhere responsibility for unwelcome impulses and intentions, and a peculiar susceptibility to emotional manipulation by leaders who play upon our more savage inclinations in the name of national security or the national interest.[58]

Whew! Got all that? No doubt you'll see embedded in Mack's words several of the concepts we just discussed. This description encapsulates Mack's concept of the multifaceted elements involved in creating a system of enemies, which, in far too many cases, leads to violent conflict. In his paper Mack quotes Vietnam veteran William Broyles, who wrote, "War begins in the mind, with the idea of the enemy."

And where do those seeds originate? From essentially the day we're born, we start to become indoctrinated with a system of beliefs held by the family we're part of and the culture that surrounds us. This includes a concept of the groups we're for and the ones we're against. Mack describes it with these stark and chilling words: "Ill-will and a desire for revenge are transmitted from one generation to another, and we are not taught to think critically about how our assigned enemies are selected for us."

Read that sentence one more time and really let it sink in. How many of *your* enemies were selected for you? What negative beliefs were imparted on you regarding other groups of people before you were aware enough to start thinking for yourself? It's worth reflecting on. In fact, it's essential that we all—each and every one of us—do some deep thinking about these questions if we are ever to inhabit the free, just, and peaceful society so many of us declare we want.

It's essential to understand that in intractable conflicts, all groups in some way indoctrinate future generations to apply a certain kind of zero-sum thinking toward one or more perceived adversaries. We not only have our own tunnel vision, we also lean down and put those same narrow-lensed glasses on our children, so that they see the world the way we do.[59]

As Maytal Nasie, Aurel Harrison Diamond, and Daniel Bar-Tal posit, political socialization of young children takes place in three ways:

Observations: Where they absorb information in the environment around them

Instructions: Talking, teaching, and debating with children the particular issues involved

Direct experiences of violence: By observing violent events, seeing people experience violence or loss, or experiencing it in their own family[60]

The group authored a paper examining messages that children in Israeli kindergartens and elementary schools receive around Jewish and national holidays (such as Passover and Holocaust Day). They found that common ideas frequently imparted to children centered on the following concepts:

- Justness of own goals

- Security

- Positive collective self-image

- Collective self-victimization (such as the idea that in every generation, people inevitably target Jews for extermination)

- National unity

- Patriotism

- Peace (meaning, framing Israelis as a peace-loving people)

When these children grow up to become the nation's decision-makers, well, you can see how intractable conflict continues. Again, it's essential to emphasize that although this specific paper focused on Israeli schools, *this kind of indoctrination happens on all sides of all intractable conflicts.* It is part of the inherent nature of such conflicts.

Building on work from Charles Sykes, Rahav Gabay and her colleagues observe, "When . . . feelings of entitlement are combined with a high individual-level tendency for interpersonal victimhood, social change struggles are more likely to take an aggressive, disparaging, and condescending form."[61] And that ain't gonna get us anywhere good.

So what can you do about this? As it turns out, there's *a lot* that can be done. Many skills in this book are relevant, such as teaching young people to regulate their emotions appropriately and become aware of their cognitive distortions. But learning to think critically is also essential.[62] Learn to question narratives. Learn to think for yourself. Learn to look at actual evidence and consider all sides. And crucially, people can be encouraged to *extend some grace*—to give people the benefit of the doubt, especially in those ambivalent situations. In his paper, Mack quotes Israeli sociologist Alouph Haveran, who said, "In times of conflict between nations historical accuracy is the first victim." Recognize that what you have been told about *those people* is likely not the full picture, and most certainly doesn't apply to everyone within that group. In my view, we need to go from cancel culture to *grace culture.*

Learn to question narratives.

And here's the promising news: If these socialization processes can so effectively instill a victim mindset in so many people and at such an early age, then surely we can take over this system of indoctrination and direct it more positively.[63]

We can seek to instill in young people and in our societies an empowerment mindset. We can teach people that trauma doesn't have to form the core of our identity, and that it's possible to grow through our most difficult experiences. We can demonstrate through our own actions that it's possible to have healthy pride for our in-groups, and that in-group love does not have to be linked to out-group hate. And we can teach that while no one is *entitled* to special affordances for having suffered, each and every one of us is *worthy* of being treated with care and compassion. We are all worthy of love and belonging.

One way we can do this is to not only teach historical facts (all of them—not just those that favor our side) and critical thinking, but emphasize the importance of *universalism values* and *moral inclusiveness*. As Shalom Schwartz writes:

> *Being helpful and forgiving are highly valued across most groups and societies. People also attribute high importance to justice, equality, and peace.*[64]
>
> *However, this consensus breaks down when we ask—helpful toward whom? forgiving of whom? justice for whom? Do people feel equally obligated to express these values to strangers as well as to friends? Do these values apply equally in relations with people of another religion or ethnicity, with the poor and weak, the rich and strong, and in relations with our extended family, friends, and others with whom we feel close? Phrased differently, how inclusive is our moral universe, the community to which we apply moral values?*[65]

In other words, our values must transcend the in-group. And yet, in many ways, we're currently teaching the opposite.

Empower DEI

The original intent of diversity, equity, and inclusion (DEI) programs was to increase a sense of belonging. I really like this spirit and think true inclusiveness makes *everyone* feel that they belong—ethnic and racial minorities and also people with alternative viewpoints and forms of neurodivergence.[66] As I often say, diversity is not just skin deep.

Somewhere along the way, though, many (though not all) DEI programs started to focus on our differences rather than what we all have in common. In particular, they began to emphasize a hierarchy of victimization,* losing sight of the broad spectrum of diversity on offer among humans and the fact that you never really know what someone is going through based on outward appearances. *Suffering is not a competition!* Indeed, a growing body of scientific research shows that many modern-day DEI interventions show few lasting effects and can even backfire when it comes to the motivation to reduce prejudice.[67]

Suffering is not a competition.

I don't want to give up on the good that such training can do, but we need to assess these programs more critically. The work of Karith Foster shows some of the true potential of DEI. Foster is the founder of Inversity Solutions, a company she says is the result of "diversity gone wrong."[68] Inversity Solutions is aimed at doing DEI differently, recapturing the positive essence of the concept, because what's happening now sometimes does more harm than good. As Foster describes it, "Division is exactly what we see happening when diversity is done poorly—that includes checking a box, wagging a finger or placing blame and shame."[69]

Ideally, as Foster told me, diversity programs don't focus on victimhood—especially competitive victimhood. Instead, they help *everyone* feel a sense of belonging.[70] Now, this isn't a commercial for Inversity Solutions, but the way Foster describes her work and her approach is one we can apply broadly, so I wanted to share it here. As she told me:

> *What I found was that the focus of most DEI programming was on what separates and divides us. That's the opposite of what the ultimate goal is, which is to bring people together. So my program is about celebrating our diversity—not only of our background and heritage and our sexuality, but also to include diversity of thought and ideas. The idea is to shift to what we have in common and how*

---

* The "privilege walk" is a good example of this explicit focus on a hierarchy of victimization. See https://www.eiu.edu/eiu1111/Privilege%20Walk%20Exercise-%20Transfer%20Leadership%20Institute-%20Week%204.pdf; https://medium.com/@MegB/why-i-dont-won-t-facilitate-privilege-walks-anymore-and-what-i-do-instead-380c95490e10.

we can be inclusive of one another, yet go beyond even that to be introspective and see your own value and worth so that you can see it in someone else.[71]

And this is really where each one of us comes in. As Foster sees it:

Most of DEI programming is trying to influence people from the outside in. Like, "You need to use this language and these words. You need to have this kind of thought process." Not, "You need to work on yourself so you treat yourself well, so you can treat others better." There's a really well-known book, and there's a line in it that says "Love your neighbor as yourself." People forget that part where you're supposed to love yourself. Most people don't. It's hard to be kind to other people when we're not kind to ourselves.[72]

Boom! Right? I agree with Foster that there is so much potential for DEI programs to be uniting and *empowering*. We can teach people to look beyond superficial characteristics that divide us to the deeper forms of suffering (such as loneliness and isolation) that we may all have in common,[73] as well as the unique strengths that all people can bring to the table. Programs that shift the consciousness of every individual toward those goals would be so valuable.* I'll say it again—all societal change starts *within.*

All societal change starts within.

Yet one of the biggest barriers to looking within is that we spend so much damn time looking outside ourselves, at social media! And that's also contributing to our messed-up perceptions of the world.

---

* Also see the work of Chloé Valdary, who also argues that conventional DEI isn't working. She created a "Theory of Enchantment" program that purports to increase employee inclusion, trust, and well-being (among other things). See https://www.theoryofenchantment.com.

Empower Social Media

As with DEI, many of the pitfalls of our online world—including its effect on our mental health and the mental health of our children—are by now well known.[74] Therefore, I won't belabor the point here. Yet I did want to take a moment to highlight how social media fuels division and the Victimhood Olympics.

As research has shown, if social media reflects the views of society, it does so through a funhouse mirror.[75] How many times have you had this experience: You're scrolling through your feed, and minutes (or hours) later, you're convinced the world is made up entirely of extremist wackos. And that's just from being on *my* social media accounts! Kidding, kidding. I try to broadcast a much more positive vibe out into the world, but as research shows, moderate and positive opinions tend to offer a weak signal in the online world. Algorithms are geared to boost posts that evoke negative emotions, such as animosity, fear, and outrage.

And who's creating these posts? Fewer people than you may think, actually. Research shows that it's an extremely small minority of worked-up agitators on either extreme of the political and social spectrums who are generating this ire. They simply get boosted, and so their views seem more prevalent than they actually are.

More thoughtful folks are afraid to voice their disagreement for fear of getting shouted down, or because of the perception that they're in the minority. But you're actually not! *Most people have more moderate views;* they simply don't feel empowered to voice them online. When they do, these more rational and open-minded posts tend not to be widely circulated. Most people would be truly surprised to know that their own private thoughts are more in line with the collective than what it may seem. Collective illusions abound.[76]

So guess what? *Not as many people are assholes as your feed would have you believe!*

And there's a related mechanism at work here that I think is worth delving into for a moment. As emotions expert Susan David framed it for me when we spoke, the massive amount of information and opinions we're exposed to these days is simply too much for our brains to process.[77] As a result, we have to institute a "flattening" process, whereby we strip out the complexity and nuance in various narratives. We simply don't have the bandwidth to process it.

We then take this more simplified information and do a kind of rapid sorting, dumping it into broad categories such as *agree* or *disagree, right* or *wrong,* and *good* or *bad.* You can see how all of that oversimplification and quick categorizing can create skewed perceptions of the world.

As David sees it, social media (along with our affinity for bonding-by-bitching) plays a critical role in this, as part of a formula for disaster that links these platforms with our propensity to see ourselves as victims. According to her calculus:

> *Pathologizing of normal human experience (the rapidity with which we label things as "trauma") + the addictive qualities of social media + co-rumination + social contagion = disastrous effects.*

That's some scary math!

Without a doubt, social media is a powerful instrument. In the same way that we can repurpose our methods of negative indoctrination of children, I fully believe we can use it for the good. But we need to start speaking up—to start voicing our more levelheaded and nuanced opinions. We need to boost stories of grace and forgiveness, and about people (and groups) who moved past preconceptions to create peace. We need to stop sharing anger, fear, and hate. We need to stop following people who act like assholes. We need to *boost love,* people! We need to show, through our actions, that this is the kind of positive content we want the algorithms to show us more of. It will take a real, sustained effort, but I believe we can do it.

Lastly, one of the most powerful ways we can counteract the negative effects of social media is to build real, meaningful relationships with real people in the real world. This includes people we currently characterize as the out-group.

Open Your Mind, Open Your Heart

As research has shown, one of the most powerful ways to engender forgiveness is to get to know your supposed enemy.[78] Too many of us have never actually conversed with people from the "other side," or the only interaction we've had is with extremists on social media or in the news. As you now know, these antagonizers almost never represent the feelings of the majority of their group. We need to expend real effort to get to know who people actually are and what they actually believe.

Open up your bandwidth and unflatten your thinking, because it is worth the work of doing some deep listening and learning. And if we ever want that peace we keep talking about, it's the only way we'll get there.

A Call to Empower Each Other

I acknowledge that many of the steps in this chapter for peace have their major hurdles—especially in situations where groups have a strong distrust for each other and where there has been a history of denial of the other group's chosen trauma. But at the end of the day, the science I reviewed gives us hope that change is possible. And it all starts with *you*.

We've discussed many tools throughout this book to overcome a victim mindset, empower yourself, and realize your full potential. Imagine if everyone adopted these tools. It would change how we all handle setbacks, how we treat one another, and how we empower others. Just as every challenge you encounter offers you an opportunity to grow, every person you meet offers an opportunity for you to empower someone else to be *their* best.

A world of collective empowerment is a world I want to live in. I deeply yearn for a humanistic society where we first and foremost treat each other as fellow humans and help each other see greater possibilities in life. A world in which we are self-actualization coaches for each other.

In a climate that rewards and breeds a victim mindset, even this message can be seen as controversial. Yet I hope the ideas and practices in this book can help change the collective consciousness and point us all toward a more transcendent and universal reality full of love, connection, and empowerment.[79] This will require rising above our egos, seeing ourselves and others as more than the worst thing that has happened to us, spotting the strengths and goodness in ourselves and others, having grace and tolerance for the ambiguities and complexities of being human, and considering the impact of our thoughts and actions on each and every person we meet.

I believe such a world is possible, and it all starts with *you*. Empower yourself, empower the world. I'm rooting for you.

Acknowledgments

This book has been a long time in the making, and a great number of people have contributed to my thinking, research, and morale over the years. First and foremost, I want to thank Kelly Madrone—my writing collaborator, thinking partner, and friend. I was committed to making this book accessible, and I learned so much from her about how to convey what I want to convey to as broad an audience as possible. I know that the book benefited greatly from her help and writing chops. Thank you, Kelly!

Second, I must thank my literary agent, Jim Levine, for cheerleading the book proposal and Marian Lizzi for accepting the proposal and betting on me and the book. I'm very grateful to both of you for continually believing in me!

Third, there's a long list of researchers and authors who reviewed drafts of sections of this book and offered helpful suggestions. In alphabetical order, thanks to the following people: Susan David, Colin DeYoung, R. Chris Fraley, Michael Gervais, Seth Gillihan, Agnieska Gorec de Zavala, Boaz Hameiri, Todd Kashdan, Mark Leary, Arie Nadler, Kristi Nelson, Ryan Niemiec, and Samir Nurmohamed. Thanks for your contribution to this book.

Fourth, thanks to those who agreed to be interviewed for this book. Your stories made this book better: Karith Foster, Andrés González, Kimi Katiti, Beth Knopik, Ali Smith, Atman Smith, and Kristi Nelson.

Lastly, thanks to my friends and family who have helped me keep up my morale throughout writing this book. Jordyn Feingold, Clare Sarah Goodridge, Dan Lerner, Elliot Samuel Paul, Krista Stryker, Lisa Sansom, Jordana Cole, Joshua Steinfeldt, and Alice Wilder ("Dr. Alice") have all been there for me during some of my biggest moments of self-doubt and have helped me overcome my own victim mindset. Thanks, guys.

As always, my parents, Michael and Barbara, have been there for me anytime I've needed it—no matter the day or time of day. They are the greatest example of unconditional love I've ever found.

Notes

Introduction

1. Brown, B. (2012). *Daring greatly: How the courage to be vulnerable transforms the way we live, love, parent, and lead.* New York: Avery.
2. Kaufman, S. B. (2013). *Ungifted: Intelligence redefined.* New York: Basic Books.
3. Kaufman, S. B. (2013). *Ungifted: Intelligence redefined.* New York: Basic Books.
4. Swift, T., and Antonoff, J. (2022). Anti-Hero [Song]. On *Midnights*. Republic.
5. Kaufman, S. B., Weiss, B., Miller, J. D., & Campbell, W. K. (2018). Clinical correlates of vulnerable and grandiose narcissism: A personality perspective. *Journal of Personality Disorders, 32,* 384.
6. Freis, S. D., & Hansen-Brown, A. A. (2021). Justifications of entitlement in grandiose and vulnerable narcissism: The roles of injustice and superiority. *Personality and Individual Differences, 168,* 110345; Hart, W., Tortoriello, G. K., & Richardson, K. (2020). Deprived and grandiose explanations for psychological entitlement: Implications for theory and measurement. *Journal of Personality Assessment, 102,* 488–498.
7. Freis, S. D., & Hansen-Brown, A. A. (2021). Justifications of entitlement in grandiose and vulnerable narcissism: The roles of injustice and superiority. *Personality and Individual Differences, 168,* 110345; Glover, N., Miller, J. D., Lynam, D. R., Grego, C., & Widiger, T. A. (2012). The five-factor narcissism inventory: A five-factor measure of narcissistic personality traits. *Journal of Personality Assessment, 94,* 500–512; Hart, W., Tortoriello, G. K., & Richardson, K. (2020). Deprived and grandiose explanations for psychological entitlement: Implications for theory and measurement. *Journal of Personality Assessment, 102,* 488–498; Hendin, H. M., & Cheek, J. M. (1997). Assessing hypersensitive narcissism: A reexamination of Murray's Narcissism

Scale. *Journal of Research in Personality, 31*, 588–599; Kaufman, S. B., Weiss, B., Miller, J. D., & Campbell, W. K. (2018). Clinical correlates of vulnerable and grandiose narcissism: A personality perspective. *Journal of Personality Disorders, 32*, 384.

8. Campbell, W. K., Bonacci, A. M., Shelton, J., & Exline, J. J. (2004). Psychological entitlement: Interpersonal consequences and validation of a Self-Report Measure. *Journal of Personality Assessment, 83*, 29–45.

9. Zitek, E. M., Jordan, A. H., Monin, B., & Leach, F. R. (2010). Victim entitlement to behave selfishly. *Journal of Personality and Social Psychology, 98*, 245–255.

10. Zitek, E. M., Jordan, A. H., Monin, B., & Leach, F. R. (2010). Victim entitlement to behave selfishly. *Journal of Personality and Social Psychology, 98*, 245–255.

11. Leonard, K., & Yorton, T. (2015). *Yes, and: How improvisation reverses "no, but" thinking and improves creativity and collaboration—lessons from The Second City.* New York: Harper Business.

12. Kaufman, S. B. (2020). *Transcend: The new science of self-actualization.* New York: TarcherPerigee.

13. Campbell, B. (2018). *The rise of victimhood culture: Microaggressions, safe spaces, and the new culture wars.* New York: Palgrave Macmillan.

14. Maslow, A. H. (1998; originally published in 1962). *Toward a psychology of being* (3rd ed.). New York: Wiley.

15. Kaufman, S. B. (2020). *Transcend: The new science of self-actualization.* New York: TarcherPerigee; Kaufman, S. B. (2023). Self-actualizing people in the 21st century: Integration with contemporary theory and research on personality and well-being. *Journal of Humanistic Psychology, 63*, 51–83.

16. Kaufman, S. B. (2020). *Transcend: The new science of self-actualization.* New York: TarcherPerigee.

17. Bridgman, T., Cummings, S., & Ballard, J. A. (2018). Who built Maslow's Pyramid? A history of the creation of management studies' most famous symbol and its implications for management education. *Academy of Management Learning and Education, 18*(1). https://doi.org/10.5465/amle.2017.0351; Kaufman, S. B. (2019, April 23). Who created Maslow's iconic pyramid? *Scientific American.* https://www.scientificamerican.com/blog/beautiful-minds/who-created-maslows-iconic-pyramid/.

Chapter 1: Don't Be a Victim to Your Past

1. Gibbons, S. (1944). *Cold comfort farm.* Penguin; Schlesinger, J. (1996). *Cold comfort farm* [Film]. BBC Films/British Broadcasting Corporation/Thames International.

2. Seligman, M. E. P. (1972). Learned helplessness. *Annual Review of Medicine, 23*, 407–412.

3. Frankl, V. E. (1959). *Man's search for meaning.* Beacon Press.

4. Maier, S. F., & Seligman, M. E. P. (2016). Learned helplessness at fifty: Insights from neuroscience. *Psychological Review, 123,* 349–367.

5. Tomasulo, D. (2020). *Learned hopefulness: The power of positivity to overcome depression.* New York: New Harbinger.

6. Hartman, S., Li, Z., Nettle, D., & Belsky, J. (2017). External environmental and internal health early predictors of adolescent development. *Development and Psychopathology, 29,* 1839–1849; Nettle, N., Frankenhuis, W. E., & Rickard, I. J. (2013). The evolution of predictive adaptive responses in human life history. *Proceedings of the Royal Society B, 280,* 1766.

7. Barrett, L. F. (2020). *7½ lessons about the brain.* Houghton Mifflin Harcourt.

8. Clark, A. (2013). Whatever next? Predictive brains, situated agents, and the future of cognitive science. *Behavioral and Brain Sciences, 36,* 181–204.

9. Fox, N. A., & Shonkoff, J. P. (2011). How persistent fear and anxiety can affect young children's learning, behavior and health. *Early Childhood Matters, 116,* 8–14.

10. Barrett, L. F. (2020). *7½ lessons about the brain.* New York: Houghton Mifflin Harcourt.

11. Schlenker, B. R., Chambers, J. R., & Le, B. M. (2012). Conservatives are happier than liberals, but why? Political ideology, personality, and life satisfaction. *Journal of Research in Personality, 46,* 127–146. https://papers.ssrn.com/sol3/papers.cfm?abstract_id=2239819.

12. Eurich, T. (2017, June 2). *The right way to be introspective (yes, there's a wrong way).* Ideas.ted.com. https://ideas.ted.com/the-right-way-to-be-introspective-yes-theres-a-wrong-way/; also see Eurich, T. (2018). *Insight: The surprising truth about how others see us, how we see ourselves, and why the answers matter more than we think.* New York: Crown.

13. Egar, E. (2017). *The choice: Embrace the possible.* New York: Scribner.

14. Egar, E. (2017). *The choice: Embrace the possible.* New York: Scribner.

15. Rumi, J. al-Din. M. (2023). *A community of the spirit.* The Line Break. https://thelinebreak.wpcomstaging.com/2013/01/10/rumi-a-community-of-the-spirit/.

16. Shiro, E. (2023). *The unexpected gift of trauma: The path to posttraumatic growth.* HarperCollins, p. xxi.

17. Viorst, J. (1986). *Necessary losses: The loves, illusions, dependencies and impossible expectations that all of us have to give up in order to grow.* London: Simon & Schuster, p. 295.

18. Nicole LePera [@Theholisticpsyc] (2023, April 2). *Culture doesn't celebrate trauma healing because it means we would wake up. It means we would no longer sleep walk through life accepting dysfunction as "normal."* [Tweet]. https://twitter.com/Theholisticpsyc/status/1642509653656363008?s=20.

19. Pandell, L. (2022, January 25). *How trauma became the word of the decade.* Vox. https://www.vox.com/the-highlight/22876522/trauma-covid-word-origin-mental-health.

20. Roll, R. (Host). (2023, July 27). Why Tim Ferriss is giving up on productivity [Audio podcast episode]. In *Rich Roll*. Rich Roll Enterprises, LLC. https://www.youtube.com/watch?v=B021ijTc0GY&t=272s.

21. Arroll, M. (2024). *Tiny traumas: When you don't know what's wrong, but nothing feels quite right.* New York: HarperOne.

22. Bonanno, G. A. (2021). *The end of trauma: How the new science of resilience is changing how we think about PTSD.* New York: Basic Books.

23. Bonanno, G. A. (2008). Loss, trauma, and human resilience: Have we underestimated the human capacity to thrive after extremely adverse events? *Psychological Trauma: Theory, Research, Practice, and Policy, 8,* 101–113. https://doi.org/10.1037/0003-066X.59.1.20; Kaufman, S. B. (Host). (2021, October 21). George Bonanno: The new science of resilience [Audio podcast episode]. In *The psychology podcast.* Stitcher. https://scottbarrykaufman.com/podcast/george-bonanno-the-new-science-of-resilience/.

24. Piper, B. [@healwithbritt]. (2021, September 17). *#ClonePhotos This trend but make it trauma responses. #fightflightfreeze #traumaresponse #traumacoach #traumahealing* [Video]. TikTok. https://www.tiktok.com/@healwithbritt/video/7009078728336674053; Palus, Shannon. (2021, October 6). *Why TikTok is so obsessed with labeling everything a trauma response.* Slate. https://slate.com/technology/2021/10/tiktok-trauma-response-why.html.

25. Reiner, R. 1987. *The princess bride* [Film]. Act III Communications/Buttercup Films Ltd./The Princess Bride Ltd.

26. Tse, J. S. Y., & Haslam, N. (2024). Broad concepts of mental disorder predict self-diagnosis. *SSM—Mental Health, 6,* 100326.

27. Conti, P. (2021). *Trauma: The invisible epidemic.* Louisville, CO: Sounds True Adult.

28. Conti, P. (2021). *Trauma: The invisible epidemic.* Louisville, CO: Sounds True Adult.

29. Kain, K. L., & Terrell, S. J. (2018). *Nurturing resilience: Helping clients move forward from developmental trauma—an integrative somatic approach.* North Atlantic Books; Payne, P., Levine, P. A., & Crane-Godreau, M. A. (2015). Somatic experiencing: Using interoception and proprioception as core elements of trauma therapy. *Frontiers in Psychology, 6*(93). https://doi.org/10.3389/fpsyg.2015.00093; Porges, P. W. (2022). Polyvagal theory: A science of safety. *Frontiers in Integrative Neuroscience, 16.* https://doi.org/10.3389/fnint.2022.871227; Lyon, I. (2023, May 14). *What it looks like to process survival stress (aka: trauma) when you are regulated. #nervoussystem* [Video]. YouTube. https://www.youtube.com/watch?v=dKwidMrM_ZE.

30. Bonanno, G. A. (2008). Loss, trauma, and human resilience: Have we underestimated the human capacity to thrive after extremely adverse events? *Psychological Trauma: Theory, Research, Practice, and Policy, 8,* 101–113. https://doi.org/10.1037/0003-066X.59.1.20.

31. Kaufman, S. B., & Feingold, J. H. (2022). *Choose growth: A workbook for transcending trauma, fear, and self-doubt.* New York: TarcherPerigee.

32. Van der Kolk, B. (2015). *The body keeps the score: Brain, mind, and body in the healing of trauma.* New York: Penguin.

33. Carr, D. (2023, July 31). Tell me why it hurts: How Bessel van der Kolk's once controversial theory of trauma became the dominant way we make sense of our lives. *New York Magazine.* https://nymag.com/intelligencer /article/trauma-bessel-van-der-kolk-the-body-keeps-the-score-profile .html.

34. Carr, D. (2023, July 31). Tell me why it hurts: How Bessel van der Kolk's once controversial theory of trauma became the dominant way we make sense of our lives. *New York Magazine.* https://nymag.com/intelligencer /article/trauma-bessel-van-der-kolk-the-body-keeps-the-score-profile .html.

35. Berry, S. (2023, May 15). Does the body keep the score? Our brains and bodies are more linked than we knew. *Sydney Morning Herald.* https:// www.smh.com.au/lifestyle/health-and-wellness/does-the-body-keep -the-score-our-brains-and-bodies-are-more-linked-than-we-knew -20230511-p5d7mc.html; Scheeringa, M. (2023) *Analysis of* The body keeps the score*: The science that trauma activists don't want you to know.* Kindle edition.

36. Huberman, A. (Host). (2023, October 15). Dr. Lisa Feldman Barrett: How to understand emotions [Audio podcast episode]. In *Huberman lab.* Scicomm Media. https://www.hubermanlab.com/episode/dr-lisa-feldman -barrett-how-to-understand-emotions; G. Bonanno, personal communication, August 15, 2023.

37. Editorial. (2023, November 8). Brain and body are more intertwined than we knew. *Nature, 623*(7986), 223–224. https://doi.org/10.1038/d41586-023 -03435-2.

38. Curran, L. (2012). *101 trauma-informed interventions: Activities, exercises and assignments to move the client and therapy forward.* Premier Publishing.

39. Tugade, M. M., Fredrickson, B. L., & Barrett, L. F. (2004). Psychological resilience and positive emotional granularity: Examining the benefits of positive emotions on coping and health. *Journal of Personality, 72,* 1161–1190.

40. Fraley, R. C., Gillath, O., & Deboeck, P. R. (2021). Do life events lead to enduring changes in adult attachment styles? A naturalistic longitudinal investigation. *Journal of Personality and Social Psychology, 120,* 1567–1606.

41. Mikulincer, M., & Shaver, P. R. (2016). *Attachment in adulthood: Structure, dynamics, and change* (2nd ed.). New York: Guilford Press; Wiebe, S. A., & Johnson, S. M. (2017). Creating relationships that foster resilience in Emotionally Focused Therapy. *Current Opinion in Psychology, 13,* 65–69.

42. Maté, G. (2024). *The myth of normal: Trauma, illness & healing in a toxic culture*. New York: Avery.

43. Dugan, K. A., Kunkel, J. J., Fraley, R. C., Briley, D. A., McGue, M., Krueger, R. F., & Roisman, G. I. (in press). Genetic and environmental contributions to adult attachment styles: Evidence from the Minnesota Twin Registry. *Journal of Personality and Social Psychology*.

44. Fraley, R. C., Gillath, O., & Deboeck, P. R. (2021). Do life events lead to enduring changes in adult attachment styles? A naturalistic longitudinal investigation. *Journal of Personality and Social Psychology, 120,* 1567–1606; Dugan, K. A., Kunkel, J. J., Fraley, R. C., Briley, D. A., McGue, M., Krueger, R. F., & Roisman, G. I. (2024). Genetic and environmental contributions to adult attachment styles: Evidence from the Minnesota Twin Registry. Manuscript under review.

45. Fraley, R. C., Gillath, O., & Deboeck, P. R. (2021). Do life events lead to enduring changes in adult attachment styles? A naturalistic longitudinal investigation. *Journal of Personality and Social Psychology, 120,* 1567–1606.

46. Pinker, S. (2003). *The blank slate: The modern denial of human nature*. New York: Penguin.

47. Moore, D. S. (2017). *The developing genome: An introduction to behavioral epigenetics*. Oxford University Press.

48. Teicher, M. H., Samson, J. A., Anderson, C. M., & Ohashi, K. (2016). The effects of childhood maltreatment on brain structure, function and connectivity. *Nature Reviews Neuroscience, 17,* 652–656.

49. Yalom, I. D. (2009). *Staring at the sun: Overcoming the terror of death*. Hoboken, NJ: Jossey-Bass.

Chapter 2: Don't Be a Victim to Your Emotions

1. livedownloads. (2012, May 29). *Philippe Petit: One man show—FEAR* [Video]. YouTube. https://www.youtube.com/watch?v=obsxMxLHgBI.

2. David, S. (2017, November). *The gift and power of emotional courage* [Video]. TED Talks. https://www.ted.com/talks/susan_david_the_gift_and_power_of_emotional_courage?language=en.

3. S. David, personal communication, March 28, 2024.

4. Rosmarin, D. (2023, July 28). Screening for anxiety will only make us more anxious: New federal guidelines set low bar for diagnosing anxiety disorders, encouraging doctors to see normal emotion as a medical problem. *The Wall Street Journal*. https://www.wsj.com/articles/screening-for-anxiety-will-only-make-us-more-anxious-21057f9c.

5. Parkes, C. M., & Prigerson, H. G. (2010). *Bereavement: Studies of grief in adult life* (4th ed.). Oxfordshire, England: Routledge.

6. David, S. (2017, November). *The gift and power of emotional courage* [Video]. TED Talks. https://www.ted.com/talks/susan_david_the_gift_and_power_of_emotional_courage?language=en.

7. Epstein, M. (2005). *Open to desire: The truth about what the Buddha taught.* New York: Penguin.

8. Schönbrodt, F. D., & Gerstenberg, F. X. R. (2012). An IRT analysis of motive questionnaires: The unified motive scales. *Journal of Research in Personality, 46,* 725–742.

9. Manne, K. (2015, September 19). Why I use trigger warnings. *The New York Times.* https://www.nytimes.com/2015/09/20/opinion/sunday/why-i-use-trigger-warnings.html.

10. Kamenetz, A. (2016, September 7). *Half of professors in NPR Ed survey have used "trigger warnings."* NPR. https://www.npr.org/sections/ed/2016/09/07/492979242/half-of-professors-in-npr-ed-survey-have-used-trigger-warnings; Palmer, T. (2017, March 29). *Monash University trigger warning policy fires up free speech debate.* ABC News. https://www.abc.net.au/news/2017-03-28/monash-university-adopts-trigger-warning-policy/8390264.

11. *The 2021 college free speech rankings.* (2021, September 21). The Foundation for Individual Rights and Expression. https://www.thefire.org/news/2021-college-free-speech-rankings.

12. Jaschik, S. (2017, March 3). *Middlebury students shout down lecture by Charles Murray.* Inside Higher Ed. https://www.insidehighered.com/news/2017/03/03/middlebury-students-shout-down-lecture-charles-murray.

13. Cashin, A. (2024, May 3). *Loneliness in America: How the pandemic has deepened an epidemic of loneliness—making caring common.* Harvard Graduate School of Education. https://mcc.gse.harvard.edu/reports/loneliness-in-america.

14. Koehn, N. (2018). *Forged in crisis: The making of five courageous leaders.* New York: Scribner.

15. Kaufman, S. B. (2024, February 20). Are trigger warnings actually helpful? *Scientific American.* https://blogs.scientificamerican.com/beautiful-minds/are-trigger-warnings-actually-helpful/; Manne, K. (2015, September 19). Why I use trigger warnings. *The New York Times.* https://www.nytimes.com/2015/09/20/opinion/sunday/why-i-use-trigger-warnings.html.

16. Gainsburg, I., & Earl, A. (2018). Trigger warnings as an interpersonal emotion-regulation tool: Avoidance, attention, and affect depend on beliefs. *Journal of Experimental Social Psychology, 79,* 252–263.

17. Wells, R. E., & Kaptchuk, T. (2012). To tell the truth, the whole truth, may do patients harm: The problem of the nocebo effect for informed consent. *American Journal of Bioethics, 12,* 22–29. Note: I'm not trying to suggest that anyone bypass informed consent—just reporting on these findings for the purposes of this discussion.

18. Bloom, P. (2010). *How pleasure works: The new science of why we like what we like.* New York: W. W. Norton.

19. Takarangi, M. K. T., Strange, D., & Lindsay, D. S. (2014). Self-report may underestimate trauma intrusions. *Consciousness and Cognition, 27,* 297–305.

20. Bellet, B., Jones, P., & McNally, R. J. (2018). Trigger warning: Empirical evidence ahead. *Journal of Behavior Therapy and Experimental Psychiatry, 61,* 134–141; Bridgland, V. M. E., Jones, P. J., & Bellet, B. W. (2023). A meta-analysis of the efficacy of trigger warnings, content warnings, and content notes. *Clinical Psychological Science, 12*(4) https://doi.org /10.1177/21677026231186625.

21. Bellet, B., Jones, P., & McNally, R. J. (2018). Trigger warning: Empirical evidence ahead. *Journal of Behavior Therapy and Experimental Psychiatry, 61,* 134–141.

22. Barrett, L. F. (2017, July 14). When is speech violence? *The New York Times.* https://www.nytimes.com/2017/07/14/opinion/sunday/when-is-speech -violence.html.

23. Beck, M. N. (n.d.). Goodreads. https://www.goodreads.com/quotes/120146 -emotional-discomfort-when-accepted-rises-crests-and-falls-in-a.

24. David, S. (2017, November). *The gift and power of emotional courage* [Video]. TED Talks. https://www.ted.com/talks/susan_david_the_gift_and _power_of_emotional_courage?language=en.

25. Deschene, L. (2018, April 2). Dealing with uncomfortable feelings & creating positive ones. *Tiny Buddha.* https://tinybuddha.com/blog/how-to-deal -with-uncomfortable-feelings/.

26. Bond, F. W., Hayes, S. C., Carpenter, K. M., Guenole, N., Orcutt, H. K., Waltz, T., & Zettle, R. D. (2011). Preliminary psychometric properties of the Acceptance and Action Questionnaire-II: A revised measure of psychological inflexibility and experiential avoidance. *Behavioral Therapy, 42,* 676–688.

27. Bond, F. W., Hayes, S. C., Carpenter, K. M., Guenole, N., Orcutt, H. K., Waltz, T., & Zettle, R. D. (2011). Preliminary psychometric properties of the Acceptance and Action Questionnaire-II: A revised measure of psychological inflexibility and experiential avoidance. *Behavioral Therapy, 42,* 676–688; Doorley, J. D., Goodman, F. R., Kelso, K. C., & Kashdan, T. B. (2020). Psychological inflexibility: What we know, what we do not know, and what we think we know. *Social and Personality Psychology Compass, 14,* 1–11.

28. *Suppressing negative thoughts may be good for mental health after all.* (2023, September 20). University of Cambridge. https://www.cam.ac.uk /research/news/suppressing-negative-thoughts-good-for-mental-health.

29. Grant, H. (2014, August 1). Do you play to win—or to not lose? *Harvard Business Review.* https://hbr.org/2013/03/do-you-play-to-win-or-to-not-lose.

30. Bach, P., & Hayes, S. C. (2002). The use of acceptance and commitment therapy to prevent the rehospitalization of psychotic patients: A randomized controlled trial. *Journal of Consulting and Clinical Psychology, 70,*

1129–1139; Vowles, K. E., & McCracken, L. M. (2008). Acceptance and values-based action in chronic pain: A study of treatment effectiveness and process. *Journal of Consulting and Clinical Psychology, 76,* 397–407.

31. Bond, F. W., Hayes, S. C., & Barnes-Holmes, D. (2006). Psychological flexibility, ACT, and organizational behavior. *Journal of Organizational Behavior Management, 26,* 25–54; Kashdan, T. B., Disabato, D. J., Goodman, F. R., Doorley, J. D., & McKnight, P. E. (2020). Understanding psychological flexibility: A multimethod exploration of pursuing valued goals despite the presence of distress. *Psychological Assessment, 32,* 829–850; Kashdan, T. B., & Rottenberg, J. (2010). Psychological flexibility as a fundamental aspect of health. *Clinical Psychology Review, 30,* 865–878; Wicksell, R. K., Lucas, J. J., & Moore, K. A. (2019). Psychological flexibility: Positive implications for mental health and life satisfaction. *Health Promotion International, 35,* 312–320.

32. Graham, C. D., Chalder, T., Rose, M. R., Gavriloff, D., McCracken, L. M., & Weinman, J. (2017). A pilot case series of brief acceptance and commitment therapy (ACT)-based guided self-help intervention for improving quality of life and mood in muscle disorders. *Cognitive Behaviour Therapist, 10,* Article e2; Vowles, K. E., & McCracken, L. M. (2008). Acceptance and values-based action in chronic pain: A study of treatment effectiveness and process. *Journal of Consulting and Clinical Psychology, 76,* 397–407; Wicksell, R. K., Ahlqvist, J., Bring, A., Melin, L., & Olsson, G. L. (2008). Can exposure and acceptance strategies improve functioning and life satisfaction in people with chronic pain and whiplash-associated disorders (WAD)? A randomized controlled trial. *Cognitive Behaviour Therapy, 37,* 169–182.

33. Kashdan, T. B., Disabato, D. J., Goodman, F. R., Doorley, J. D., & McKnight, P. E. (2020). Understanding psychological flexibility: A multimethod exploration of pursuing valued goals despite the presence of distress. *Psychological Assessment, 32,* 829–850.

34. David, S. (2016). *Emotional agility: Get unstuck, embrace change, and thrive in work and life.* New York: Avery, p. 6.

35. David, S. (2016). *Emotional agility: Get unstuck, embrace change, and thrive in work and life.* New York: Avery; David, S. (2017, November). *The gift and power of emotional courage* [Video]. TED Talks. https://www.ted.com /talks/susan_david_the_gift_and_power_of_emotional_courage?lan guage=en.

36. David, S. (2016). *Emotional agility: Get unstuck, embrace change, and thrive in work and life.* New York: Avery.

37. Huberman, A. (Host). (2023, October 15). Dr. Lisa Feldman Barrett: How to understand emotions [Audio podcast episode]. In *Huberman lab.* Scicomm Media. https://www.hubermanlab.com/episode/dr-lisa-feldman -barrett-how-to-understand-emotions.

38. Roll, R. (Host). (2020, January 9). Movement makes us human: Kelly Mc-Gonigal, Ph.D. [Audio podcast episode]. In *Rich Roll*. Rich Roll Enterprises, LLC. https://www.youtube.com/watch?v=ifw03u4IrS8.

39. Goodman, T. (2023). *I always think it's forever: A love story set in Paris as told by an unreliable but earnest narrator.* New York: S&S/Simon Element, p. 11.

40. Hayes, S. C. (2005). *Get out of your mind and into your life: The new acceptance and commitment therapy.* Oakland, CA: New Harbinger; Hayes, S. C., Luoma, J. B., Bond, F. W., Masuda, A., & Lillis, J. (2006). Acceptance and commitment therapy: Model, processes and outcomes. *Behavior Research and Therapy, 44,* 1–25.

41. Hayes, S. C., Luoma, J. B., Bond, F. W., Masuda, A., & Lillis, J. (2006). Acceptance and commitment therapy: Model, processes and outcomes. *Behavior Research and Therapy, 44,* 1–25.

42. Hayes, S. C., Luoma, J. B., Bond, F. W., Masuda, A., & Lillis, J. (2006). Acceptance and commitment therapy: Model, processes and outcomes. *Behavior Research and Therapy, 44,* 1–25.

43. Rinpoche, Y. M. (2024, April 25). *How I stopped my panic attacks.* Lion's Roar. https://www.lionsroar.com/how-i-stopped-my-panic-attacks/.

44. Quote Investigator. (2018, February 18). *Between stimulus and response there is a space. In that space is our power to choose our response.* https://quoteinvestigator.com/2018/02/18/response/.

45. Hayes, S. C., Strosahl, K. D., & Wilson, K. G. (1999). *Acceptance and commitment therapy: An experiential approach to behavior change.* New York: Guilford Press; Strosahl, K. D., Hayes, S. C., Wilson, K. G., & Gifford, E. V. (2004). An ACT primer: Core therapy processes, intervention strategies, and therapist competencies. In S. C. Hayes & D. Strosahl (Eds.), *A practical guide to acceptance and commitment therapy* (4th ed., pp. 31–58). New York: Springer.

46. Strosahl, K. D., Hayes, S. C., Wilson, K. G., & Gifford, E. V. (2004). An ACT primer: Core therapy processes, intervention strategies, and therapist competencies. In S. C. Hayes & D. Strosahl (Eds.), *A practical guide to acceptance and commitment therapy* (4th ed., pp. 31–58). New York: Springer.

47. Salzberg, S. (2024). *Real life: The journey from isolation to openness and freedom.* New York: Flatiron Books.

48. Brach, T. (2004). *Radical acceptance: Embracing your life with the heart of a Buddha.* New York: Bantam; Brach, T. (2024, January 31). *RAIN: Recognize, allow, investigate, nurture.* https://www.tarabrach.com/rain/.

49. Rinpoche, T., & Gere, R. (2012). *Open heart, open mind: Awakening the power of essence love.* New York: Harmony.

50. Rinpoche, T. (2024, April 5). *How to make friends with your beautiful monsters.* Lion's Roar. https://www.lionsroar.com/how-to-make-friends-with-your-monsters/.

51. As quoted in Salzberg, S. (2024). *Real life: The journey from isolation to openness and freedom.* New York: Flatiron Books, p.62.

52. David, S. [@susandavid_phd]. (2022, February 4). *Bothness is the idea that you can do something even if you are scared to do it. It's the idea* [Photograph]. Instagram. https://www.instagram.com/p/CZj6TA2J9Eb/.

53. Goodman, T. (2023). *I always think it's forever: A love story set in Paris as told by an unreliable but earnest narrator.* New York: S&S/Simon Element, p. 89.

54. David, S. [@susandavid_phd]. (2022, February 4). *Bothness is the idea that you can do something even if you are scared to do it. It's the idea* [Photograph]. Instagram. https://www.instagram.com/p/CZj6TA2J9Eb/.

55. Stevenson, S. (Host). (2022, June 28). Use these powerful tools to strengthen your emotional agility TODAY with Dr. Susan David (No. 595) [Audio podcast episode]. In *The model health show.* https://themodel healthshow.com/dr-susan-david/.

56. Collins, L. M. (2023, December 24). The best woman "big mountain extreme skier" has tips for conquering fear. *Deseret News.* https://www.de seret.com/2017/7/14/20615846/the-best-woman-big-mountain-extreme -skier-has-tips-for-conquering-fear.

57. Kashdan, T. B., Disabato, D. J., Goodman, F. R., Doorley, J. D., & McKnight, P. E. (2020). Understanding psychological flexibility: A multimethod exploration of pursuing valued goals despite the presence of distress. *Psychological Assessment, 32,* 829–850.

58. Watts, A. (n.d.). Lib Quotes. https://libquotes.com/alan-watts/quote/lbl2y9x.

59. Chödrön, P. (2016). *When things fall apart: Heart advice for difficult times.* Shambhala.

Chapter 3: Don't Be a Victim to Your Cognitive Distortions

1. Costello, W. (2020, August 6). Step your dick up: Why incels deserve better advice. Medium. https://williamcostello.medium.com/step-your -dick-up-why-incels-deserve-better-advice-307879d7c97b; Speckhard, A., Ellenberg, M., Morton, J., & Ash, A. (2021). Involuntary celibates' experiences of and grievance over sexual exclusion and the potential threat of violence among those active in an online incel forum. *Journal of Strategic Security, 14,* 89–121; Costello, W., Whittaker, J., & Thomas, A. G. (2024, April 8). Predicting harmful attitudes and beliefs among incels (involuntary celibates): how potent is the black-pill? https://doi.org/10.31219/osf.io /avhnf; Costello, W. (2023, May 23). The allure of inceldom: Why incels resist ascension. *Aporia Magazine.* https://www.aporiamagazine.com/p/the -allure-of-inceldom-why-incels; Kates, N. (2021, August 20). *What the media gets wrong about incels.* UnHerd. https://unherd.com/2021/08/what-the -media-gets-wrong-about-incels/; Jaki, S., De Smedt, T., Gwóźdź, M., Panchal, R., Rossa, A., & De Pauw, G. (2019). Online hatred of women in the Incels me forum: Linguistic analysis and automatic detection. *Journal of*

Language Aggression and Conflict, 7, 240–268; Costello, W., Rolon, V., Thomas, A. G., & Schmitt, D. P. (2023). The mating psychology of incels (involuntary celibates): misfortunes, misperceptions, and misrepresentations. *Journal of Sex Research, 7,* 1–12.

2. Gabay, R., Hameiri, B., Rubel-Lifschitz, T., & Nadler, A. (2020). The tendency for interpersonal victimhood: The personality construct and its consequences. *Personality and Individual Differences, 165,* 110134.

3. Suzuki, N., & Hirai, M. (2023). Autistic traits associated with dichotomic thinking mediated by intolerance of uncertainty. *Scientific Reports, 13,* 14049. https://doi.org/10.1038/s41598-023-41164-8; Sparks, B., Zidenberg, A. M., & Olver, M. E. (2023). An exploratory study of incels' dating app experiences, mental health, and relational well-being. *Journal of Sex Research,* 1–12. https://doi.org/10.1080/00224499.2023.2249775; Płatos, M., Wojaczek, K., & Laugeson, E. A. (2023). Fostering friendship and dating skills among adults on the autism spectrum: A randomized controlled trial of the Polish version of the PEERS® for Young Adults Curriculum. *Journal of Autism and Developmental Disorders,* 1–16. https://doi.org/10.1007/s10803-023-05921-y; Ribeiro, M. H., Blackburn, J., Bradlyn, B., De Cristofaro, E., Stringhini, G., Long, S., Greenberg, S., & Zannettou, S. (2021). The evolution of the manosphere across the web. In *Proceedings of the International AAAI Conference on Web and Social Media, 15*(1), 196–207. https://doi.org/10.1609/icwsm.v15i1.18053.

4. Reid, S. (2016, July 4). Brenda Martinez knocked off stride in women's 800 final at Olympic Trials. *Orange County Register.* https://www.ocregister.com/2016/07/04/brenda-martinez-knocked-off-stride-in-womens-800-final-at-olympic-trials/.

5. Stulberg, B., & Magness, S. (2019). *The passion paradox: A guide to going all in, finding success, and discovering the benefits of an unbalanced life.* New York: Rodale Books.

6. LetsRundotcom. (2016, July 8). *Brenda Martinez bounces back from 800 heartbreak to advance in Olympic Trials 1500* [Video]. YouTube. https://www.youtube.com/watch?v=OvByRlDP0-I.

7. Gabay, R., Hameiri, B., Rubel-Lifschitz, T., & Nadler, A. (2020). The tendency for interpersonal victimhood: The personality construct and its consequences. *Personality and Individual Differences, 165,* 110134.

8. Gabay, R., Hameiri, B., Rubel-Lifschitz, T., & Nadler, A. (2020). The tendency for interpersonal victimhood: The personality construct and its consequences. *Personality and Individual Differences, 165,* 110134.

9. Vangelisti, A. L., Young, S. L., Carpenter-Theune, K. E., & Alexander, A. L. (2005). Why does it hurt? The perceived causes of hurt feelings. *Communication Research, 32,* 443–477.

10. Nolen-Hoeksema, S., Wisco, B. E., & Lyubormirsky, S. (2008). Rethinking rumination. *Perspectives on Psychological Science, 3,* 400–424.

11. Gillihan, S. J. (2018). *Cognitive behavioral therapy made simple: 10 strategies for managing anxiety, depression, anger, panic, and worry*. San Antonio, TX: Althea Press.

12. Lackey, S. (2013, September 9). *Musturbation: Stop rubbing yourself the wrong way*. Albert Ellis Institute. https://albertellis.org/2013/09/musturbation-stop-rubbing-wrong-way/.

13. Kerry, N., White, K. C., O'Brien, M. L., Perry, L. M., & Clifton, J. D. W. (2023). Despite popular intuition, positive world beliefs poorly reflect several objective indicators of privilege, including wealth, health, sex, and neighborhood safety. *Journal of Personality, 92*(4), 1129–1142. http://doi.org/10.1111/jopy.12877.

14. Moser, E. (2023, September 6). *A positive worldview is less associated with privilege than expected*. Penn Today. https://penntoday.upenn.edu/news/primals-project-positive-world-beliefs-privilege.

15. Kerry, N., White, K. C., O'Brien, M. L., Perry, L. M., & Clifton, J. D. W. (2023). Despite popular intuition, positive world beliefs poorly reflect several objective indicators of privilege, including wealth, health, sex, and neighborhood safety. *Journal of Personality*. http://doi.org/10.1111/jopy.12877.

16. Chilcott, L. (Director). (2023, June 7). Athlete (Season 1, Episode 1) [TV series episode]. In L. Chilcott & A. Hughes (Executive Producers), *Arnold*. Defiant Ones Media Group; Invented by Girls.

17. Hibberd, J. (2023, July 15). Arnold Schwarzenegger gets candid on career, failures, aging: "My plan is to live forever." *The Hollywood Reporter*. https://www.hollywoodreporter.com/tv/tv-features/arnold-schwarzenegger-interview-netflix-fubar-terminator-conan-1235491977/.

18. Pinak, P. (2021, March 18). *"Hans and Franz" pump up America in timeless SNL skit*. FanBuzz. https://fanbuzz.com/national/hans-and-franz/.

19. Schwarzenegger, A. (2023). *Be useful: Seven tools for life*. New York: Penguin Press.

20. Chilcott, L. (Director). (2023, June 7). Athlete (Season 1, Episode 3) [TV series episode]. In L. Chilcott & A. Hughes (Executive Producers), *Arnold*. Defiant Ones Media Group; Invented by Girls.

21. Gillihan, S. J. (2022). *Mindful cognitive behavioral therapy: A simple path to healing, hope, and peace*. New York: HarperOne.

22. Gillihan, S. J. (2018). *Cognitive behavioral therapy made simple: 10 strategies for managing anxiety, depression, anger, panic, and worry*. San Antonio, TX: Althea Press.

23. Gillihan, S. J. (2018). *Cognitive behavioral therapy made simple: 10 strategies for managing anxiety, depression, anger, panic, and worry*. San Antonio, TX: Althea Press.

24. Schwarzenegger, A. (2023). *Be useful: Seven tools for life*. New York: Penguin Press.

25. Kabat-Zinn, J. (2005). *Wherever you go, there you are: Mindfulness meditation in everyday life*. New York: Hachette Books.

26. Gillihan, S. J. (2018). *Cognitive behavioral therapy made simple: 10 strategies for managing anxiety, depression, anger, panic, and worry*. San Antonio, TX: Althea Press.

27. Hayes, S. C. (2005). *Get out of your mind and into your life: The new acceptance and commitment therapy*. New York: New Harbinger.

Chapter 4: Don't Be a Victim to Your Self-Esteem

1. Kaufman, S. B. (2020). *Transcend: The new science of self-actualization*. New York: TarcherPerigee; Maslow, A. H. (1998; originally published in 1962). *Toward a psychology of being* (3rd ed.). New York: Wiley.

2. Leary, M. R. (1999). The social and psychological importance of self-esteem. In R. M. Kowalski & M. R. Leary (Eds.), *The social psychology of emotional and behavioral problems: Interfaces of social and clinical psychology* (pp. 197–221). American Psychological Association.

3. Rosenberg, M. (1965). *Rosenberg self-esteem scale (RSES)*. APA PsychTests.

4. Kaufman, S. B. (2024, February 20). Narcissism and self-esteem are very different. *Scientific American*. https://www.scientificamerican.com/blog/beautiful-minds/narcissism-and-self-esteem-are-very-different/.

5. Baumeister, R. F., Campbell, J. D., Krueger, J. I., & Vohs, K. D. (2003). Does high self-esteem cause better performance, interpersonal success, happiness, or healthier lifestyles? *Psychological Science in the Public Interest, 4*, 1–44.

6. Crocker, J., & Park, L. E. (2004). The costly pursuit of self-esteem. *Psychological Bulletin, 130*, 392–414.

7. Kaufman, S. B., Weiss, B., Miller, J. D., & Campbell, W. K. (2018). Clinical correlates of vulnerable and grandiose narcissism: A personality perspective. *Journal of Personality Disorders, 32*, 384.

8. Day, N. J. S., Townsend, M. L., & Grenyer, B. F. S. (2020). Living with pathological narcissism: A qualitative study. *Borderline Personality Disorder and Emotion Regulation, 7*, Article 19; Fatfouta, R., & Rogoza, R. (2024). Playing the victim? Facets of narcissism, self-perceived victimhood, and the mediating role of negative affect. *Advances in Cognitive Psychology, 20*, 92–97; Fatfouta, R., & Schröder-Abé, M. (2017). I can see clearly now: Clarity of transgression-related motivations enhances narcissists' lack of forgiveness. *Personality and Individual Differences, 105*, 280–286; McCullough, M. E., Emmons R. A., Kilpatrick, S. D., & Mooney, C. N. (2003). Narcissists as "victims": The role of narcissism in the perception of transgressions. *Personality and Social Psychology Bulletin, 29*, 885–893.

9. Jauk, E., & Kaufman, S. B. (2018). The higher the score, the darker the core: The nonlinear association between grandiose and vulnerable narcissism. *Frontiers in Psychology, 9*, 1305; Jauk, E., Ulbrich, L., Jorschick, P.,

Hofler, M., Kaufman, S. B., & Kankse, P. (2021). The nonlinear association between grandiose and vulnerable narcissism: An individual data meta-analysis. *Journal of Personality, 90,* 703–726; Kaufman, S. B., & Jauk, E. (2020). Healthy selfishness and pathological altruism: Measuring two paradoxical forms of selfishness. *Frontiers in Psychology, 11,* Article 1006.

10. Kealy, D., Tsai, M., & Ogrodniczuk, J. S. (2012). Depressive tendencies and pathological narcissism among psychiatric outpatients. *Psychiatry Research, 196,* 157–159.; Pincus, A. L., Cain, N. M., & Wright, A. G. C. (2014). Narcissistic grandiosity and narcissistic vulnerability in psychotherapy. *Personality Disorders: Theory, Research, and Treatment, 5,* 439–443; Rogoza, R., Cieciuch, J., & Strus, W. (2022). Vulnerable isolation and enmity concept: Disentangling the blue and dark face of vulnerable narcissism. *Journal of Research in Personality, 96,* 104167.

11. Bernardi, R., & Eidlin, M. (2018). Thin-skinned or vulnerable narcissism and thick-skinned or grandiose narcissism: Similarities and differences. *International Journal of Psychoanalysis, 99,* 291–313; Rogoza, R., Cieciuch, J., & Strus, W. (2022). Vulnerable isolation and enmity concept: Disentangling the blue and dark face of vulnerable narcissism. *Journal of Research in Personality, 96,* 104167.

12. Dixit, J. (2009, May 13). Greg Giraldo on failure. *Psychology Today.* https://www.psychologytoday.com/us/blog/brainstorm/200905/greg-giraldo-failure.

13. Radosław, R., Cieciuch, J., & Strus, W. (2022). Vulnerable isolation and enmity concept: Disentangling the blue and dark face of vulnerable narcissism. *Journal of Research in Personality, 96,* 104167; Kealy, D., & Rasmussen, B. (2012). Veiled and vulnerable: The other side of grandiose narcissism. *Clinical Social Work Journal, 40*(3), 356–365.

14. Caligor, E., Levy, K. N., & Yeomans, F. E. (2015). Narcissistic personality disorder: Diagnostic and clinical challenges. *American Journal of Psychiatry, 172,* 415–422; Cieciuch, J., & Strus, W. (2022). Vulnerable isolation and enmity concept: Disentangling the blue and dark face of vulnerable narcissism. *Journal of Research in Personality, 96,* 104167.

15. Crowell, S. E., Beauchaine, T. P., & Linehan, M. M. (2009). A biosocial developmental model of borderline personality: Elaborating and extending Linehan's theory. *Psychological Bulletin, 135,* 495–510; Finzi-Dottan, R., & Karu, T. (2006). From emotional abuse in childhood to psychopathology in adulthood: A path mediated by immature defense mechanisms and self-esteem. *Journal of Nervous and Mental Disease, 194,* 616–621; Riggs, S. A. (2010). Childhood emotional abuse and the attachment system across the life cycle: What theory and research tell us. *Journal of Aggression, Maltreatment & Trauma, 19,* 5–51.

16. Bishop, J., & Lane, R. C. (2002). The dynamics and dangers of entitlement. *Psychoanalytic Psychology, 19,* 739–758; Cieciuch, J., & Strus, W. (2022).

Vulnerable isolation and enmity concept: Disentangling the blue and dark face of vulnerable narcissism. *Journal of Research in Personality, 96,* 104167.

17. Leary, M. R., & Guadagno, J. (2011). The sociometer, self-esteem, and the regulation of interpersonal behavior. In K. D. Vohs & R. F. Baumeister (Eds.), *Handbook of self-regulation: Research, theory, and applications* (pp. 339–354). New York: Guilford Press.

18. Miller, J. D., et al. (2017). Vulnerable narcissism is (mostly) a disorder of neuroticism. *Journal of Personality, 86,* 186–199.

19. Orth, U., Robins, R. W., Trzesniewski, K. H., Maes, J., & Schmitt, M. (2009). Low self-esteem is a risk factor for depressive symptoms from young adulthood to old age. *Journal of Abnormal Psychology, 118,* 472–478.

20. r/AmItheAsshole? (n.d.). [Online forum]. Reddit. https://www.reddit.com /r/AmItheAsshole/.

21. Sutton, B. (n.d.). Asshole Rating Self-Exam (ARSE)—Are you a certified asshole? *Electric Pulp.* https://www.electricpulp.com/guykawasaki/arse/.

22. Bollinger, R. R., Barbas, A. S., Bush, E. L., Lin, S. S., & Parker, W. (2007). Biofilms in the large bowel suggest an apparent function of the human vermiform appendix. *Journal of Theoretical Biology, 249,* 826–831.

23. Robertson, T. E., Sznycer, D., Delton, A. W., Tooby, J., & Cosmides, L. (2018). The true trigger of shame: Social devaluation is sufficient, wrong-doing is unnecessary. *Evolution and Human Behavior, 39,* 566–573.

24. Robertson, T. E., Sznycer, D., Delton, A. W., Tooby, J., & Cosmides, L. (2018). The true trigger of shame: Social devaluation is sufficient, wrong-doing is unnecessary. *Evolution and Human Behavior, 39,* 566–573.

25. M. Leary, personal communication, July 7, 2023.

26. Kirkpatrick, L. E., & Ellis, B. J. (2003). An evolutionary-psychological approach to self-esteem: Multiple domains and multiple functions. In J. O. Garth & M. S. Clark (Eds.), *Blackwell handbook of social psychology: Interpersonal processes* (pp. 409–436). Hoboken, NJ: Wiley.

27. Baumeister, R. F., & Leary, M. R. (1995). The need to belong: Desire for interpersonal attachments as a fundamental human motivation. *Psychological Bulletin, 117,* 497–529.

28. Leary, M. R. (1999). The social and psychological importance of self-esteem. In R. M. Kowalski & M. R. Leary (Eds.), *The social psychology of emotional and behavioral problems: Interfaces of social and clinical psychology* (pp. 197–221). American Psychological Association; Leary, M. R., & Guadagno, J. (2011). The sociometer, self-esteem, and the regulation of interpersonal behavior. In K. D. Vohs & R. F. Baumeister (Eds.), *Handbook of self-regulation: Research, theory, and applications* (pp. 339–354). New York: Guilford Press.

29. Leary, M. R. (1999). The social and psychological importance of self-esteem. In R. M. Kowalski & M. R. Leary (Eds.), *The social psychology of emotional and behavioral problems: Interfaces of social and clinical psychology* (pp. 197–221). American Psychological Association.

30. Leary, M. R., Haupt, A. L., Strausser, K. S., & Chokel, J. T. (1998). Calibrating the sociometer: The relationship between interpersonal appraisals and state self-esteem. *Journal of Personality and Social Psychology, 74,* 1290–1299.

31. Vedantam, S. (Host). (2022, February 7). Mind reading 2.0: How others see you [Audio podcast episode]. In *Hidden brain.* Hidden Brain Media. https://hiddenbrain.org/podcast/mind-reading-how-others-see-you/.

32. Dangerfield, R. (2023, February 13). *"I got no respect the day I was born . . ."* [Video]. YouTube. https://www.youtube.com/watch?v=W3utS1w Y5e8.

33. Baumeister, R. F., Tice, D. M., & Hutton, D. G. (1989). Self-presentational motivations and personality differences in self-esteem. *Journal of Personality, 57,* 3.

34. Crocker, J., & Park, L. E. (2004). The costly pursuit of self-esteem. *Psychological Bulletin, 130,* 392–414.

35. Barrie, Z. (2015, July 16). *High on compliments: What it feels like to be addicted to validation.* Elite Daily. https://www.elitedaily.com/life/culture /feel-addicted-to-validation/1113336.

36. Baumeister, R. F., & Vohs, K. D. (2001). Narcissism as addiction to esteem. *Psychological Inquiry, 12,* 206–210.

37. Branden, N. (1995). *The six pillars of self-esteem.* New York: Bantam.

38. Prilleltensky, I., & Prilleltensky, O. (2021). *How people matter: Why it affects health, happiness, love, work, and society.* New York: Cambridge University Press.

39. Prilleltensky, I., & Prilleltensky, O. (2021). *How people matter: Why it affects health, happiness, love, work, and society.* New York: Cambridge University Press.

40. Flett, G. L., Nepon, T., Goldberg, J. O., Rose, A. L., Atkey, S. K., & Zaki-Azat, J. (2021). The anti-mattering scale: Development, psychometric properties and associations with well-being and distress measures in adolescents and emerging adults. *Journal of Psychoeducational Assessment, 40,* 37–59; Flett G. L. (2018). *The psychology of mattering: Understanding the human need to be significant.* New York: Academic Press/Elsevier.

41. Farmelo, G. (2011). *The strangest man: The hidden life of Paul Dirac, mystic of the atom* (Reprint). New York: Basic Books.

42. Flett, G. L. (2018). *The psychology of mattering: Understanding the human need to be significant.* New York: Academic Press/Elsevier.

43. Flett, G. L., Nepon, T., & Scott, X. (2022). The anti-mattering scale versus the general mattering scale in pathological narcissism: How an excessive need to matter informs the narcissism and mattering constructs. *Journal of Psychoeducational Assessment, 41,* 619–633.

44. Gervais, M. (2023). *The first rule of mastery: Stop worrying about what people think of you.* Boston: Harvard Business Review Press.

45. Collins, L. (2023, June 12). Pilvi Takala and the art of awkwardness. *The New Yorker.* https://www.newyorker.com/magazine/2023/06/19/pilvi -takala-profile.

46. Kaufman, S. B. (2020). *Transcend: The new science of self-actualization.* New York: TarcherPerigee.

47. Abraham Maslow echoed a similar idea in the introduction to *Toward a Psychology of Being*: "Does sickness mean having symptoms? I maintain now that sickness might consist of not having symptoms when you should. Does health mean being symptom-free? I deny it. Which of the Nazis at Auschwitz or Dachau were healthy? Those with stricken conscience or those with a nice, clear, happy conscience? Was it possible for a profoundly human person not to feel conflict, suffering, depression, rage, etc?"

48. Kishimi, I., & Koga, F. (2018). *The courage to be disliked: The Japanese phenomenon that shows you how to change your life and achieve real happiness.* New York: Atria Books.

49. Crocker, J., & Knight, K. M. (2010). Contingencies of self-worth: Implications for self-regulation and psychological vulnerability. *Self and Identity, 2,* 143–149.

50. MacDonald, G., Saltzman, J. L., & Leary, M. R. (2003). Social approval and trait self-esteem. *Journal of Research in Personality, 37,* 23–40.

51. Reiner, R. (Director). (1989). *When Harry met Sally* [Film]. Castle Rock Entertainment/Nelson Entertainment.

52. Kernis, M. H. (2009). Toward a conceptualization of optimal self-esteem. *Psychological Inquiry, 14,* 1–26; Kernis, M. H. & Lakey, C. E. (2009). Fragile versus secure high self-esteem: Implications for defensiveness and insecurity. In R. M. Arkin, K. C. Oleson, & P. J. Carroll (Eds.), *Handbook of the uncertain self-esteem* (pp. 360–378). New York: Psychology Press.

53. Stulberg, B., & Magness, S. (2019). *The passion paradox: A guide to going all in, finding success, and discovering the benefits of an unbalanced life.* New York: Rodale Books.

54. Mel Robbins. [@melrobbins]. (2023, July 24). *Stop letting people treat you like sh*t!! You can't control their behavior, but you CAN control how you react and* [Photograph]. Instagram. https://www.instagram.com/p/CvFZqUn SNgW/.

55. M. Leary, personal communication, June 16, 2023.

56. Neff, K. D. (2009). The role of self-compassion in development: A healthier way to relate to oneself. *Human Development, 52,* 211–214.

57. Neff, K. D. (2023). Self-compassion: Theory, method, research, and intervention. *Annual Review of Psychology, 74,* 193–218.

58. Neff, K. D. (2023). Self-compassion: Theory, method, research, and intervention. *Annual Review of Psychology, 74,* 193–218.

59. Neff, K. D. (2023). Self-compassion: Theory, method, research, and intervention. *Annual Review of Psychology, 74,* 193–218.

60. Maslow, A. H. (1998). *Toward a psychology of being* (3rd ed.). Hoboken, NJ: Wiley.

61. Neff, K. D. (2023). Self-compassion: Theory, method, research, and intervention. *Annual Review of Psychology, 74*, 193–218.

62. McElwee, R. O., & Yurak, T. J. (2007). Feeling versus acting like an impostor: Real feelings of fraudulence or self-presentation? *Individual Differences Research, 5*, 201–220.

63. Brown, M. (2018, December 4). Michelle Obama tells London school she still has impostor syndrome. *The Guardian.* https://www.theguardian.com/us-news/2018/dec/03/michelle-obama-tells-london-school-she-still-has-imposter-syndrome.

64. McElwee, R. O., & Yurak, T. (2010). The phenomenology of the impostor phenomenon. *Individual Differences Research, 8*, 184–197.

65. Leary, M. R., Patton, K. M., Orlando, A. E., & Funk, W. W. (2001). The impostor phenomenon: Self-perceptions, reflected appraisals, and interpersonal strategies. *Journal of Personality, 68*, 725–756.

66. Brown, M. (2018, December 4). Michelle Obama tells London school she still has impostor syndrome. *The Guardian.* https://www.theguardian.com/us-news/2018/dec/03/michelle-obama-tells-london-school-she-still-has-imposter-syndrome.

67. Leary, M. R., Patton, K. M., Orlando, A. E., & Funk, W. W. (2001). The impostor phenomenon: Self-perceptions, reflected appraisals, and interpersonal strategies. *Journal of Personality, 68*, 725–756.

68. Leonhardt, M., Bechtoldt, M. N., & Rohrmann, S. (2017). All impostors aren't alike—Differentiating the impostor phenomenon. *Frontiers in Psychology, 8*, Article 1505.

69. McElwee, R. O., & Yurak, T. J. (2007). Feeling versus acting like an impostor: Real feelings of fraudulence or self-presentation? *Individual Differences Research, 5*, 201–220.

70. Cowman, S. E., & Ferrari, J. R. (2002). Am I for real? Predicting impostor tendencies from self-handicapping and affective components. *Social Behavior and Personality, 30*, 119–126; Ferrari, J. R., & Thompson, T. (2006). Impostor fears: Links with self-presentational concerns and self-handicapping behaviors. *Personality and Individual Differences, 40*, 341–352; Kolligan, J., & Sternberg, R. J. (1991). Perceived fraudulence in young adults: Is there an "impostor syndrome"? *Journal of Personality Assessment, 56*, 308–326; McElwee, R. O., & Yurak, T. J. (2007). Feeling versus acting like an impostor: Real feelings of fraudulence or self-presentation? *Individual Differences Research, 5*, 201–220.

71. Kaufman, S. B. (2024, February 20). Are narcissists more likely to experience impostor syndrome? *Scientific American.* https://www.scientificamerican.com/blog/beautiful-minds/are-narcissists-more-likely-to-experience-impostor-syndrome/.

72. Branden, N. (1995). *The six pillars of self-esteem.* New York: Bantam.

73. Wood, J. V., Perunovic, E., & Lee, J. W. (2009). Positive self-statements: Power for some, peril for others. *Psychological Science, 20,* 860–866.

74. Swann, W. B., Jr. (2012). Self-verification theory. In P. A. M. Van Lange, A. W. Kruglanski, and E. T. Higgins (Eds.), *Handbook of theories of social psychology* (pp. 23–42). New York: Sage Publications.

75. Jongman-Sereno, K. P., & Leary, M. R. (2019). The enigma of being yourself: A critical examination of the concept of authenticity. *Review of General Psychology, 23,* 133–142; Kaufman, S. B. (2024, February 20). Authenticity under fire. *Scientific American.* https://www.scientificamerican.com/blog/beautiful-minds/authenticity-under-fire/.

76. Kaufman, S. B. (2024, February 20). Authenticity under fire. *Scientific American.* https://www.scientificamerican.com/blog/beautiful-minds/authenticity-under-fire/; Kaufman, S. B. (2020). *Transcend: The new science of self-actualization.* New York: TarcherPerigee; also see Strohminger, N., Knobe, J., & Newman, G. (2017). The true self: A psychological concept distinct from the self. *Perspectives on Psychological Science, 12,* 551–560.

77. Jongman-Sereno, K. P. & Leary, M. R. (2019). The enigma of being yourself: A critical examination of the concept of authenticity. *Review of General Psychology, 23,* 133–142; Baumeister, R. F. (2019). Stalking the true self through the jungles of authenticity: Problems, contradictions, inconsistencies, disturbing findings—and a possible way forward. *Review of General Psychology, 23,* 143–154.

78. Items taken from Kernis, M. H., & Goldman, B. M. (2005). From thought and experience to behavior and interpersonal relationships: A multicomponent conceptualization of authenticity. In A. Tesser, J. V. Wood, & D. A. Stapel (Eds.), *On building, defending, and regulating the self: A psychological perspective* (pp. 31–52). New York: Psychology Press; Wood, A. M., Linley, P. A., Maltby, J., Baliousis, M., & Joseph, S. (2008). The authentic personality: A theoretical and empirical conceptualization and the development of the Authenticity Scale. *Journal of Counseling Psychology, 55,* 385–399.

79. Rogers, C. R. (1995). *On becoming a person: A therapist's view of psychotherapy.* New York: HarperOne, p. 17.

Chapter 5: Don't Be a Victim to Your Need to Please

1. Oakley, B. A., Knafo, A., Madhavasan, G., & Wilson, D. S. (2011). *Pathological altruism.* New York: Oxford University Press.

2. Bakan, D. (1966). *The duality of human existence: Isolation and communion in Western man.* Boston: Beacon Press.

3. Rabbi Hillel, *Ethics of the Fathers,* 1:14.

4. Bakan, D. (1966). *The duality of human existence: Isolation and communion in Western man.* Boston: Beacon Press; Fritz, H. L., & Helgeson, V. S. (1998). Distinctions of unmitigated communion from communion: Self-

neglect and overinvolvement with others. *Journal of Personality and Social Psychology, 75,* 121–140; Ghaed, S. G., & Gallo, L. C. (2010). Distinctions among agency, communion, and unmitigated agency and communion according to the interpersonal circumplex, five-factor model, and social-emotional correlates. *Journal of Personality Assessment, 86,* 77–88; Helgeson, V. S. (1994). Relation of agency and communion to well-being: Evidence and potential explanations. *Psychological Bulletin, 116,* 412–428; Helgeson, V. S., & Fritz, H. L. (1999). Unmitigated agency and unmitigated communion: Distinctions from agency and communion. *Journal of Research in Personality, 33,* 131–158; Wiggins, J. S., & Trapnell, P. D. (1996). A dyadic-interactional perspective on the five-factor model. In J. S. Wiggins (Ed.), *The five-factor model of personality: Theoretical perspective* (pp. 88–162). New York: Guilford Press.

5. Helgeson, V. S., & Fritz, H. L. (1999). Unmitigated agency and unmitigated communion: Distinctions from agency and communion. *Journal of Research in Personality, 33,* 131–158; Helgeson, V. S., & Fritz, H. L. (2000). The implications of unmitigated agency and unmitigated communion for domains of problem behavior. *Journal of Research in Personality, 33,* 131–158; Kaufman, S. B., & Jauk, E. (2020). Healthy selfishness and pathological altruism: Measuring two paradoxical forms of selfishness. *Frontiers in Psychology, 11,* Article 1006.

6. Helgeson, V. S., & Fritz, H. L. (2000). The implications of unmitigated agency and unmitigated communion for domains of problem behavior. *Journal of Research in Personality, 33,* 131–158.

7. Scale adapted from Kaufman, S. B., & Jauk, E. (2020). Healthy selfishness and pathological altruism: Measuring two paradoxical forms of selfishness. *Frontiers in Psychology, 11,* Article 1006.

8. Kaufman, S. B., & Jauk, E. (2020). Healthy selfishness and pathological altruism: Measuring two paradoxical forms of selfishness. *Frontiers in Psychology, 11,* Article 1006.

9. Kaufman, S. B., & Jauk, E. (2020). Healthy selfishness and pathological altruism: Measuring two paradoxical forms of selfishness. *Frontiers in Psychology, 11,* Article 1006.

10. Nietfeld, E. (2022). *Acceptance: A memoir.* New York: Penguin Press.

11. Crocker, J., & Canevello, A. (2018). From egosystem to ecosystem: Motivations of the self in a social world. In A. J. Elliot (Ed.), *Advances in motivation science* (pp. 41–86). Elsevier Academic Press.

12. Crocker, J., & Canevello, A. (2008). Creating and understanding social support in communal relationships: The role of compassionate and self-image goals. *Journal of Personality and Social Psychology, 95,* 555–575.

13. Ercolano, P. (2016, April 7). *Social slacktivism: Some users share updates about online charitable giving without following through, study shows.* The

Hub. https://hub.jhu.edu/2016/04/07/donations-deleted-after-social-media-share/.

14. Dear, G. E., Roberts, C. M., & Lange, L. (2005). Defining codependency: A thematic analysis of published definitions. In S. Shohov (Ed.), *Advances in Psychology* (Vol. 34, pp. 189–205). Nova Science.

15. Jordan, J. J., & Kouchaki, M. (2021). Virtuous victims. *Science Advances*, 7(42).

16. Braiker, H. B. (2002). *The disease to please: Curing the people-pleasing syndrome.* New York: McGraw-Hill.

17. Gebauer, J. E., Sedikides, C., Verplanken, B., & Maio, G. R. (2012). Communal narcissism. *Journal of Personality and Social Psychology, 103,* 854–878; Rogoza, M., Marchlewska, M., & Rogoza, R. (2023). Towards integration of communal narcissism within the structure of the narcissistic personality traits. *Journal of Research in Personality, 102,* 104316.

18. Kaufman, S. B. (2024, February 20). The science of spiritual narcissism. *Scientific American.* https://www.scientificamerican.com/article/the-science-of-spiritual-narcissism/.

19. Kranc, L. (2022, October 17). How NXIVM seduced Hollywood stars and America's most powerful elite into a barbaric "sex cult." *Esquire.* https://www.esquire.com/entertainment/tv/a33658764/what-is-nxivm-sex-cult-celebrities-stars-the-vow-hbo-true-story/.

20. Paulhus, D., & John, O. (1998). Egoistic and moralistic biases in self-perception: The interplay of self-deceptive styles with basic traits and motives. *Journal of Personality, 66,* 1025–1060.

21. Gebauer, J. E., Sedikides, C., Verplanken, B., & Maio, G. R. (2012). Communal narcissism. *Journal of Personality and Social Psychology, 103,* 854–878.

22. Fatfouta, R., Ziegler-Hill, V., & Schröder-Abé, M. (2017). I'm merciful, am I not? Facets of narcissism and forgiveness revisited. *Journal of Research in Personality, 70,* 166–173; Naderi, I. (2018). I'm nice, therefore I go green: An investigation of pro-environmentalism in communal narcissists. *Journal of Environmental Psychology, 59,* 54–64; Nehrlich, A. D., Gebauer, J. E., Sedikides, C., & Schoel, C. (2018). Agentic narcissism, communal narcissism, and prosociality. *Journal of Personality and Social Psychology, 117,* 142–165; Rogoza, M., Marchlewska, M., & Rogoza, R. (2023). Towards integration of communal narcissism within the structure of the narcissistic personality traits. *Journal of Research in Personality, 102,* 104316; Yang, Z., Sedikides, C., Gu, R., Luo, Y. L. L., Wang, Y., Yang, Y., Wu, M., & Cai, H. (2018). Communal narcissism: Social decisions and neurophysiological reactions. *Journal of Research in Personality, 76,* 64–73.

23. Fennimore, A. K. (2021). Duplicitous me: Communal narcissists and public service motivation. *Public Personnel Management, 50,* 25–55; Rainey, H. G., & Steinbauer, P. (1999). Galloping elephants: Developing elements of a theory of effective government organizations. *Journal of Public Admin-*

istration Research and Theory, 9, 1–32; Ritz, A., Brewer, G. A., & Neumann, O. (2016). Public service motivation: A systematic literature review and outlook. *Public Administration Review, 76*, 414–426.

24. Fennimore, A. K. (2021). Duplicitous me: Communal narcissists and public service motivation. *Public Personnel Management, 50*, 25–55.

25. Kim, S., & Vandenabeele, W. (2010). A strategy for building public service motivation research internationally. *Public Administration Review, 70*, 701–709.

26. Fennimore, A. K. (2021). Duplicitous me: Communal narcissists and public service motivation. *Public Personnel Management, 50*, 25–55.

27. English, L., & Peters, N. (2011). Founders' syndrome in women's nonprofit organizations: Implications for practice and organizational life. *Nonprofit Management & Leadership, 22*, 159–171; Fennimore, A. K. (2021). Duplicitous me: Communal narcissists and public service motivation. *Public Personnel Management, 50*, 25–55; Jensen, U. T., Andersen, L. B., & Holten, A. L. (2017). Explaining a dark side: Public service motivation, presenteeism, and absenteeism. *Review of Public Personnel Administration, 39*, 487–510; Justice, D. (2010). Avoiding founder's syndrome in arts organizations: Studies of successful succession transitions in three established regional theatres [Doctoral dissertation, Texas Tech University, Lubbock]; Paulhus, D. L. (2014). Toward a taxonomy of dark personalities. *Current Directions in Psychological Science, 23*, 421–426.

28. Gebauer, J. E., Paulhus, D. L., & Neberich, W. (2013). Big two personality and religiosity across cultures: Communals as religious conformists and agentics as religious contrarians. *Social Psychological and Personality Science, 4*, 21–30.

29. Fennimore, A. K. (2021). Duplicitous me: Communal narcissists and public service motivation. *Public Personnel Management, 50*, 25–55.

30. Neumann, C. S., Kaufman, S. B., Brinke, L. T., Yaden, D. B., Hyde, E., & Tsukayama, E. (2020). Light and dark trait subtypes of human personality— A multi-study person-centered approach. *Personality and Individual Differences, 164*, 110121.

31. Bosman, J., Stevens, M., & Bromwich, J. E. (2018, February 2). Humane Society C.E.O. resigns amid sexual harassment allegations. *The New York Times*. https://www.nytimes.com/2018/02/02/us/humane-society-ceo-sexual-harassment.html.

32. Kullgren, I. (2018, January 30). Female employees allege culture of sexual harassment at Humane Society. *Politico*. https://www.politico.com/magazine/story/2018/01/30/humane-society-sexual-harassment-allegations-investigation-216553/.

33. Krispenz, A., & Bertrams, A. (2024). Understanding left-wing authoritarianism: Relations to the dark personality traits, altruism, and social justice commitment. *Current Psychology, 43*, 2714–2730.

34. Costello, T. H., Bowes, S. M., Stevens, S. T., Waldman, I. D., Tasimi, A., & Lilienfeld, S. O. (2022). Clarifying the structure and nature of left-wing authoritarianism. *Journal of Personality and Social Psychology, 122*, 135–170.

35. Zeigler-Hill, V., Destaney, S., & Paige, M. (2021). Through the eyes of Narcissus: Competitive social worldviews mediate the associations that narcissism has with ideological attitudes. *Self and Identity, 20*, 811–840.

36. Zeigler-Hill, V., Destaney, S., & Paige, M. (2021). Through the eyes of Narcissus: Competitive social worldviews mediate the associations that narcissism has with ideological attitudes. *Self and Identity, 20*, 811–840.

37. Krispentz, A., & Bertrams, A. (2024). Understanding left-wing authoritarianism: Relations to the dark personality traits, altruism, and social justice commitment. *Current Psychology, 43*, 2714–2730.

38. Krispentz, A., & Bertrams, A. (2024). Understanding left-wing authoritarianism: Relations to the dark personality traits, altruism, and social justice commitment. *Current Psychology, 43*, 2714–2730.

39. Bertrams, A., & Krispenz, A. (2024). Dark-ego-vehicle principle: Narcissism as a predictor of anti-sexual assault activism. *Current Psychology, 43*, 3585–3598. https://doi.org/10.1007/s12144-023-04591-4; Krispenz, A., & Bertrams, A. (2023). Further evidence of the dark-ego-vehicle principle: Higher pathological narcissistic grandiosity and virtue signaling are related to greater involvement in LGBQ and gender identity activism. *SSRN.* http://dx.doi.org/10.2139/ssrn.4204911; Krispenz, A., & Bertrams, A. (2023). Further basic evidence for the dark-ego-vehicle principle: Higher pathological narcissism is associated with greater involvement in feminist activism. *Current Psychology, 43*, 14619–14633. https://doi.org/10.1007/s12144-023-05451-x; Krispenz, A., & Bertrams, A. (2023). Understanding involvement in environmental activism: Relationships to pathological narcissism, virtue signaling, dominance, and sensation seeking. *SSRN.* http://dx.doi.org/10.2139/ssrn.4560799.

40. See Fimiani, R., Gazzillo, F., Dazzi, N., & Bush, M. (2021). Survivor guilt: Theoretical, empirical, and clinical features. *International Forum of Psychoanalysis, 31*, 176–190.

41. Bar-Tal, D., Chernyak-Hai, L., Schori, N., & Gundlar, A. (2009). A sense of self-perceived collective victimhood in intractable conflicts. *International Review of the Red Cross, 91*, 229–258; Taylor, S. E., Wood, J. V., & Lichtman, R. R. (1983). It could be worse: Selective evaluation as a response to victimization. *Journal of Social Issues, 39*, 19–40; Zur, O. (2013). The psychology of victimhood. In R. H. Wright & N. A. Cummings (Eds.), *Destructive trends in mental health: The well intentioned path to harm* (pp. 73–92). Routledge.

42. Jordan, J. J., & Kouchaki, M. (2021). Virtuous victims. *Science Advances, 7*(42).

43. Ok, E., Qian, Y., Strejcek, B., & Aquino, K. (2021). Signaling virtuous victimhood as indicators of dark triad personalities. *Journal of Personality and Social Psychology, 120*, 1634–1661.

44. Kaufman, S. B., Yaden, D. B., Hyde, E., & Tsukayama, E. (2019). The light vs. dark triad of personality: Contrasting two very different profiles of human nature. *Frontiers in Psychology, 10,* Article 476; Paulhus, D. L., & Williams, K. M. (2002). The dark triad of personality: Narcissism, Machiavellianism, and psychopathy. *Journal of Research in Personality, 36,* 556–563.

45. Dahling, J. J., Whitaker, B. G., & Levy, P. E. (2009). The development and validation of a new Machiavellianism Scale. *Journal of Management, 35,* 219–257.

46. Nietfeld, E. (2022). *Acceptance: A memoir.* New York: Penguin Press; Martin, K. (2022, August 3). *Emi Nietfeld is done reaching for redemption in "Acceptance."* NPR. https://www.npr.org/2022/08/03/1115445101/emi -nietfeld-acceptance-book-review.

47. Noor, M., Nurit, S., Samer, H., & Nadler, A. (2012). When suffering begets suffering: The psychology of competitive victimhood between adversarial groups in violent conflicts. *Personality and Social Psychology Review, 16,* 351–374; Sullivan, D., Landau, M. J., Branscombe, N. R., & Rothschild, Z. K. (2012). Competitive victimhood as a response to accusations of ingroup harm doing. *Journal of Personality and Social Psychology, 102,* 778–795; Zur, O. (2013). The psychology of victimhood. In R. H. Wright & N. A. Cummings (Eds.), *Destructive trends in mental health: The well intentioned path to harm* (pp. 73–92). New York: Routledge.

48. Fromm, E. (1939). Selfishness and self-love. *Psychiatry, 2,* 507–523.

49. Maslow, A. H. (1943/1996). Is human nature basically selfish? In E. Hoffman (Ed.), *Future visions: The unpublished papers of Abraham Maslow* (pp. 107–114). Thousand Oaks, CA: Sage Publications.

50. Kaufman, S. B., & Jauk, E. (2020). Healthy selfishness and pathological altruism: Measuring two paradoxical forms of selfishness. *Frontiers in Psychology, 11,* Article 1006.

51. Fromm, E. (2006). *The art of loving.* New York: Harper Perennial Modern Classics.

Chapter 6: Find the Light Within

1. A. Smith, personal communication, December 5, 2023.

2. Smith, A., Smith, A., & González, A. (2022). *Let your light shine: How mindfulness can empower children and rebuild communities.* New York: TarcherPerigee.

3. Elijah, T. (2018). *Water: A work in progress.* 5 Element Archive.

4. Safi, O. (2015, May 7). *Where the light enters you.* The On Being Project. https://onbeing.org/blog/where-the-light-enters-you/.

5. Kaufman, S. B. (Host). (2023, July 20). Find the place in you that isn't wounded—Niall Breslin [Audio podcast episode]. In *The psychology podcast.* Stitcher. https://scottbarrykaufman.com/podcast/find-the-place-in-you-that -isnt-wounded-niall-breslin/.

6. Fadiman, J., & Gruber, J. (2020). *Your symphony of selves: Discover and understand more of who we are.* Rochester, Vermont: Park Street Press.

7. Whitman, W. (1850). *Song of myself, 51.* Poets.org. https://poets.org/poem/song-myself-51.

8. Peterson, C., & Seligman, M. (2004). *Character strengths and virtues: A handbook and classification.* Washington, D.C.: American Psychological Association.

9. Tierney, J., & Baumeister, R. F. (2019). *The power of bad: How the negativity effect rules us and how we can rule it.* New York: Penguin Press; Vaish, A., Grossmann, T., & Woodward, A. (2008). Not all emotions are created equal: The negativity bias in social-emotional development. *Psychological Bulletin, 134,* 383–403.

10. McGrath, R. E., & Niemiec, R. M. (2019). *The power of character strengths: Appreciate and ignite your positive personality.* Cincinnati, OH: VIA Institute on Character.

11. Niemiec, R. M. (2023). *The mindfulness and character strengths workbook.* Cambridge, MA: Hogrefe & Huber.

12. McGrath, R. E., & Niemiec, R. M. (2019). *The power of character strengths: Appreciate and ignite your positive personality.* Cincinnati, OH: VIA Institute on Character.

13. Kaufman, S. B. (2013). *Ungifted: Intelligence redefined.* New York: Basic Books.

14. Sternberg, R. J., & Desmet, O. A. (2024). *Giftedness in childhood.* New York: Cambridge University Press.

15. Eisenstadt, J. M. (1978). Parental loss and genius. *American Psychologist, 33,* 211–223; Sternberg, R. J., & Desmet, O. A. (2024). *Giftedness in childhood.* New York: Cambridge University Press.

16. Ellis, B. J., Abrams, L. S., Masten, A. S., Sternberg, R. J., Tottenham, N., & Frankenhuis, W. E. (2023). *The hidden talents framework: Implications for science, policy, and practice.* New York: Cambridge University Press. https://doi.org/10.17/9781009350051.

17. Sternberg, R. J., & Desmet, O. A. (2024). *Giftedness in childhood.* New York: Cambridge University Press.

18. Page, S. (2024, April 19). He forgave the man who killed his son, and helped free him from prison. *The Washington Post.* https://www.washingtonpost.com/lifestyle/2024/04/18/tariq-khamisa-azim-tony-hicks/.

19. K. Katiti, personal communication, November 20, 2023.

20. Katiti, K. [Nyonyozimusic]. (2021, May 28). *This is how I ESCAPED the cult of WOKENESS* [Video]. YouTube. https://www.youtube.com/watch?v=S5Ak5uEcDUQ.

21. Luskin, F. (2003). *Forgive for good: A proven prescription for health and happiness.* New York: HarperOne.

22. Sutton, J. (2024, March 15). *Psychology of forgiveness: 10+ fascinating re-*

search findings. PositivePsychology.com. https://positivepsychology.com/psychology-of-forgiveness/.

23. Harvard Health. (2021, February 12). *The power of forgiveness.* https://www.health.harvard.edu/mind-and-mood/the-power-of-forgiveness.

24. Harvard Health. (2021, February 12). *The power of forgiveness.* https://www.health.harvard.edu/mind-and-mood/the-power-of-forgiveness.

25. Griffin, C. (2022, November 7). Watch Oprah's "The Life You Want" class on gratitude with Dr. Scott Barry Kaufman. *Oprah Daily.* https://www.oprahdaily.com/life/a41441542/watch-oprahs-the-life-you-want-class-on-gratitude-dr-scott-barry-kaufman/.

Chapter 7: Channel Your Gifts of Sensitivity

1. Foo, S. (2022). *What my bones know: A memoir of healing from complex trauma.* New York: Ballantine Books.

2. White, M. (Writer & Director). (2021, July 18). New day (Season 1, Episode 2) [TV series episode]. In J. M. Valerio, H. Persons, & T. Brown (Producers), *The White Lotus.* HBO Entertainment/Pallogram/The District/Rip Cord Productions.

3. Post, G. (2018, September 14). *Using your high sensitivity personality as an actor.* Daily Actor. https://www.dailyactor.com/acting-advice-columns/using-your-high-sensitivity-personality-as-an-actor/.

4. Eby, D. (2024, April 21). *Artists may be powerful because of their high sensitivity.* Highly Sensitive Person. https://highlysensitive.org/4/actors-and-high-sensitivity/.

5. Sager, M. (2022, June 29). What I've learned: Rick Rubin. *Esquire.* https://www.esquire.com/entertainment/interviews/a2294/esq0107rickrubin/.

6. Aron, E. (1996) *Are you highly sensitive?* Highly Sensitive Person. https://hsperson.com/test/highly-sensitive-test/.

7. Aron, E. (2002). *The highly sensitive child: Helping our children thrive when the world overwhelms them.* New York: Broadway Books.

8. Aron, E. (2002). *The highly sensitive child: Helping our children thrive when the world overwhelms them.* New York: Broadway Books.

9. Talks at Google. (2019, November 8). *Understanding the highly sensitive person: Alane Freund.* [Video]. YouTube. https://www.youtube.com/watch?v=2tKDnsns2bg.

10. Kaufman, S. B. (2013). Opening up openness to experience: A four-factor model and relations to creative achievement in the arts and sciences. *Journal of Creative Behavior, 47,* 233–255; Kaufman, S. B., Quilty, L. C., Grazioplene, R. G., Hirsh, J. B., Gray, J. R., Peterson, J. B., & DeYoung, C. G. (2016). Openness to experience and intellect differentially predict creative achievement in the arts and sciences. *Journal of Personality, 84,* 248–258; Oleynick, V. C., DeYoung, C. G., Hyde, E., Kaufman, S. B., Beaty, R. E., & Silvia, P. J. (2017). Openness/intellect: The core of the creative personality. In G. J. Feist,

R. Reiter-Palmon, & J. C. Kaufman (Eds.), *The Cambridge handbook of creativity and personality research*. New York: Cambridge University Press.

11. Oleynick, V. C., DeYoung, C. G., Hyde, E., Kaufman, S. B., Beaty, R. E., & Silvia, P. J. (2017). Openness/intellect: The core of the creative personality. In G. J. Feist, R. Reiter-Palmon, & J. C. Kaufman (Eds.), *The Cambridge handbook of creativity and personality research*. New York: Cambridge University Press.

12. Vuyk, M. A., Krieshok, T. S., & Kerr, B. A. (2016). Openness to experience rather than overexcitabilities: Call it like it is. *Gifted Child Quarterly, 60,* 192–211.

13. Aron, E. (2002). *The highly sensitive child: Helping our children thrive when the world overwhelms them.* New York: Broadway Books.

14. Kaufman, S. B., & Gregoire, C. (2016). *Wired to create: Unraveling the mysteries of the creative mind.* New York: TarcherPerigee.

15. Kaufman, S. B. (2024, February 20). Confessions of a neurotic extravert. *Scientific American.* https://blogs.scientificamerican.com/beautiful-minds/confessions-of-a-neurotic-extravert/.

16. Kaufman, S. B. (2024, February 20). Will the real introverts please stand up? *Scientific American.* https://blogs.scientificamerican.com/beautiful-minds/will-the-real-introverts-please-stand-up/.

17. Kaufman, S. B. (2015, May 14). Shades of sensitivity. *HuffPost.* https://www.huffpost.com/entry/shades-of-sensitivity_b_7243428.

18. Kaufman, S. B. (2020, August 8). *The nerdy dopamine pathway.* Scott Barry Kaufman. https://scottbarrykaufman.com/the-nerdy-dopamine-pathway/.

19. DeYoung, C. G. (2013). The neuromodulator of exploration: A unifying theory of the role of dopamine in personality. *Frontiers in Human Neuroscience, 7,* 762.

20. DeYoung, C. G. (2013). The neuromodulator of exploration: A unifying theory of the role of dopamine in personality. *Frontiers in Human Neuroscience, 7,* 762.

21. Cain, S. (2022). *Bittersweet: How sorrow and longing make us whole.* New York: Crown.

22. Orloff, J. (2018). *The empath's survival guide.* Louisville, CO: Sounds True Publishing.

23. Liebegott, A. (2019, March 16). Road trip: Dorianne Laux. *The Believer.* https://www.thebeliever.net/logger/road-trip-dorianne-laux/.

24. Heym, N., Kibowski, F., Bloxsom, C. A. J., Blanchard, A., Harper, A., Wallace, L., Firth, J., & Sumich, A. (2021). The dark empath: Characterising dark traits in the presence of empathy. *Personality and Individual Differences, 169,* 110172.

25. Greenfield, D. N., Cazala, F., Carre, J., Mitchell-Somoza, A., Decety, J., Thornton, D., Kiehl, K. A., & Harenski, C. L. (2023). Emotional intelli-

gence in incarcerated sexual offenders with sexual sadism. *Journal of Sexual Aggression, 29,* 68–85.

26. Bloom, P. (2016). *Against empathy: The case for rational compassion.* New York: Ecco.

27. Baron-Cohen, S. (2011). *The science of evil: On empathy and the origins of cruelty.* New York: Basic Books; Vachon, D. D., Lynam, D. R., & Johnson, J. A. (2013). The (non)relation between empathy and aggression: Surprising results from a meta-analysis. *Psychological Bulletin, 140,* 751–773.

28. Stone, O. (Director). (1987). *Wall street* [Film]. Twentieth Century Fox /Amercent Films/American Entertainment Partners L.P.

29. Whitman, W. (1850). *Song of Myself, 51.* Poets.org. https://poets.org/poem /song-myself-51

30. Jauk, E., Knodler, M., Frenzel, J., & Kanske, P. (2022). Do highly sensitive persons display hypersensitive narcissism? Similarities and differences in the nomological networks of sensory processing sensitivity and vulnerable narcissism. *Journal of Clinical Psychology, 79,* 228–254.

31. Krizan, Z., & Herlache, A. D. (2018). The narcissism spectrum model: A synthetic view of narcissistic personality. *Personality and Social Psychology Review, 22,* 3–31.

32. Kaufman, S. B. (2024, February 20). 23 signs you're secretly a narcissist masquerading as a sensitive introvert. *Scientific American.* https://blogs .scientificamerican.com/beautiful-minds/23-signs-youe28099re-secretly -a-narcissist-masquerading-as-a-sensitive-introvert/

33. Marcus, S. (2017, December 7). *7 Signs Kanye West is secretly an introvert.* *HuffPost.* https://www.huffpost.com/entry/kanye-west-introvert_n_380 5414

34. Kaufman, S. B. (2024, February 20). 23 signs you're secretly a narcissist masquerading as a sensitive introvert. *Scientific American.* https://blogs .scientificamerican.com/beautiful-minds/23-signs-youe28099re-secretly -a-narcissist-masquerading-as-a-sensitive-introvert/

35. White, M. (Writer & Director). (2021, July 18). The lotus- eaters (Season 1, Episode 5) [TV series episode]. In D. Bernad, N. Hall, & M. White (Executive Producers), *The White Lotus.* HBO Entertainment; Pallogram; The District; Rip Cord Productions.

36. Kaufman, S. B. (2024, February 20). Shades of sensitivity. *Scientific American.* https://blogs.scientificamerican.com/beautiful-minds/shades-of-sensitivity/

37. Jauk, E., Knodler, M., Frenzel, J., & Kanske, P. (2022). Do highly sensitive persons display hypersensitive narcissism? Similarities and differences in the nomological networks of sensory processing sensitivity and vulnerable narcissism. *Journal of Clinical Psychology, 79,* 228–254.

38. Jauk, E., Knodler, M., Frenzel, J., & Kanske, P. (2022). Do highly sensitive persons display hypersensitive narcissism? Similarities and differences in

the nomological networks of sensory processing sensitivity and vulnerable narcissism. *Journal of Clinical Psychology, 79,* 228–254.

39. Cooper, T. M. (2020). *Empowering the sensitive male soul.* Independently published.

40. Kajdzik, M., & Morón, M. (2023). Signaling high sensitivity to influence others: Initial evidence for the roles of reinforcement sensitivity, sensory processing sensitivity, and the dark triad. *Psychological Reports 127*(5). https://doi.org/10.1177/00332941231152387; Kaufman, S. B. (2023, August 30). Do people signal high sensitivity to get what they want? Signaling high sensitivity is different than being highly sensitive. *Psychology Today.* https://www.psychologytoday.com/us/blog/beautiful-minds/202308/do-people-signal-high-sensitivity-to-get-what-they-want.

41. Moroń, M., Kajdzik, M., & Janik, K. (2024). Signaling high sensitivity: The roles of sensory processing sensitivity, assertiveness, and the dark triad. *Journal of Pacific Rim Psychology, 18,* 1–17.

42. Lyon, I. (2023, September 17). *The difference between being a victim and identifying yourself as one #traumahealing* [Video]. YouTube. https://www.youtube.com/watch?v=G9_4KxnPB8A.

43. Dąbrowski, K. (2017). *Positive disintegration.* Maurice Bassett.

44. Post, G. (2018, September 14). *Using your high sensitivity personality as an actor.* Daily Actor. https://www.dailyactor.com/acting-advice-columns/using-your-high-sensitivity-personality-as-an-actor/.

45. Eby, D. (2024, April 21). *Artists may be powerful because of their high sensitivity.* Highly Sensitive Person. https://highlysensitive.org/4/actors-and-high-sensitivity/.

46. Sager, M. (2022, June 29). What I've learned: Rick Rubin. *Esquire.* https://www.esquire.com/entertainment/interviews/a2294/esq0107rickrubin/.

47. Ellis, B. J., & Boyce, W. T. (2008). Biological sensitivity to context. *Current Directions in Psychological Science, 13,* 183–187.

48. Talks at Google. (2019, November 8). *Understanding the highly sensitive person: Alane Freund* [Video]. YouTube. https://www.youtube.com/watch?v=2tKDnsns2bg.

49. Aron, E. N., Aron, A., & Jagiellowicz, J. (2012). Sensory processing sensitivity: A review in the light of the evolution of biological responsivity. *Personality and Social Psychology Review, 16,* 262–282; Greven, C. U., et al. (2019). Sensory processing sensitivity in the context of environmental sensitivity: A critical review and development of research agenda. *Neuroscience and Biobehavioral Reviews, 98,* 287–305.

50. Braiker, B. (Host). (2023, January 30). The dust-kicker: Artist Timothy Goodman on life, love and work. [Audio podcast episode]. In *Brooklyn Magazine the podcast. Brooklyn Magazine.* https://www.bkmag.com/2023/01/30/timothy-goodman-podcast/.

51. Foregard, M. J. C., Mecklenberg, A. C., Lacasse, J. J., & Jayawickreme, E.,

(2014). Bringing the whole universe to order: Creativity, healing, and post-traumatic growth. In J. C. Kaufman (Ed.), *Creativity and mental illness* (pp. 321–342). New York: Cambridge University Press.

52. Kaufman, S. B., & Kaufman, J. C. (2009). Putting the parts together: An integrative look at the psychology of creative writing. In S. B. Kaufman & J. C. Kaufman (Eds.), *The psychology of creative writing* (pp. 351–370). New York: Cambridge University Press.

53. Shriver, B. M. (2011, March 9). *Maria Shriver interviews the famously private poet Mary Oliver.* Oprah.com. https://www.oprah.com/entertain ment/maria-shriver-interviews-poet-mary-oliver/all.

54. Kaufman, S. B., & Gregoire, C. (2016). *Wired to create: Unraveling the mysteries of the creative mind.* New York: TarcherPerigee.

Chapter 8: Harness Your Underdog Motivation

1. Gladwell, M. (2013). *David and Goliath: Underdogs, misfits, and the art of battling giants.* New York: Little, Brown.

2. Memory Mountain—Sports. (2021, May 30). *Wilma Rudolph—From polio contorting her leg to the first woman to win three gold medals* [Video]. You-Tube. https://www.youtube.com/watch?v=hZYlykGp9vU.

3. Biography.com Editors. (2024, April 24). Wilma Rudolph. *Biography.* https://www.biography.com/athletes/wilma-rudolph

4. Roberts, M. B. (n.d.). *Rudolph ran and world went wild.* ESPN.com. https://www.espn.com/sportscentury/features/00016444.html.

5. Memory Mountain—Sports. (2021, May 30). *Wilma Rudolph—From polio contorting her leg to the first woman to win three gold medals* [Video]. You-Tube. https://www.youtube.com/watch?v=hZYlykGp9vU.

6. Memory Mountain—Sports. (2021, May 30). *Wilma Rudolph—From polio contorting her leg to the first woman to win three gold medals* [Video]. You-Tube. https://www.youtube.com/watch?v=hZYlykGp9vU.

7. Chen, G., & Klimoski, R. J. (2017). The impact of expectations on new-comer performance in teams as mediated by work characteristics, social exchanges, and empowerment. *Academy of Management Journal, 46,* 591–607; Kierein, N. M., & Gold, M. A. (2000). Pygmalion in work organizations: A meta-analysis. *Journal of Organizational Behavior, 21,* 913–928; McNatt, D. B. (2000). Ancient Pygmalion joins contemporary management: A meta-analysis of the result. *Journal of Applied Psychology, 85,* 314–322.

8. Nurmohamed, S. (2020). The underdog effect: When low expectations increase performance. *Academy of Management Journal, 63,* 1106–1133.

9. Nurmohamed, S. (2020, January 22). The upside of being an underdog. *Harvard Business Review.* https://hbr.org/2020/01/the-upside-of-being-an -underdog.

10. Nurmohamed, S. (2020). The underdog effect: When low expectations increase performance. *Academy of Management Journal, 63,* 1106–1133.

11. Hehir, J. (2020). *The last dance* [TV miniseries]. ESPN Films/NBA Entertainment/Mandalay Sports Media.

12. Nurmohamed, S. (2020). The underdog effect: When low expectations increase performance. *Academy of Management Journal, 63,* 1106–1133.

13. O'Keeffe, C. (2019, September 2). *The underdog effect: Ciaran O'Keeffe on the appeal, and how things change.* British Psychological Society. https://www.bps.org.uk/psychologist/underdog-effect.

14. *Top 25 quotes by Wilma Rudolph.* (n.d.). A–Z Quotes. https://www.azquotes.com/author/12751-Wilma_Rudolph.

15. Nurmohamed, S., Kundro, T. G., & Myers, C. G. (2021). Against the odds: Developing underdog versus favorite narratives to offset prior experiences of discrimination. *Organizational Behavior and Human Decision Processes, 167,* 206–221. https://doi.org/10.1016/j.obhdp.2021.04.008.

16. Feiler, B. (2023, January 19). *Could your life story use an update? Here's how to do it.* Ideas.ted.com. https://ideas.ted.com/could-your-life-story-use-an-update-heres-how-to-do-it/.

17. Henderson, R. (2024). *Troubled: A memoir of foster care, family, and social class.* New York: Gallery Books.

18. Mounk, Y. (Host). (2024, January 13). Rob Henderson on foster care, social class and the new American elite. [Audio podcast episode]. In *The good fight.* https://www.persuasion.community/p/henderson.

19. National Foster Youth Institute. (2022, October 18). *Higher education for foster youth.* https://nfyi.org/issues/higher-education.

20. Henderson, R. (2022, April 24). No one expects young men to do anything and they are responding by doing nothing. *Rob Henderson's Newsletter.* https://robkhenderson.substack.com/p/no-one-expects-young-men-to-do-anything.

21. Goggins, D. (2018). *Can't hurt me: Master your mind and defy the odds.* Carson City, Nevada: Lioncrest.

22. Goggins, D. (2022). *Never finished: Unshackle your mind and win the war within.* Carson City, Nevada: Lioncrest.

23. Cohen, G. L., Steele, C. M., & Ross, L. D. (1999). The mentor's dilemma: Providing critical feedback across the racial divide. *Personality and Social Psychology Bulletin, 25,* 1302–1318.

Chapter 9: Live Gratefully

1. B. Knopik, interview with Kelly Madrone, September 13, 2023.

2. Safran Foer, J. (2006) *Extremely loud and incredibly close.* Penguin.

3. Primo, J., & Grateful Living. (2023, December 7). The fearless dive: Grateful without conditions. Grateful.org. https://grateful.org/resource/fearless-dive-grateful-without-conditions/.

4. Emmons, R. (2013, May 13). *How gratitude can help you through hard times.* Greater Good. https://greatergood.berkeley.edu/article/item/how_gratitude_can_help_you_through_hard_times.

5. Gunatillake, R. (Host). Discover the power of self-compassion: Silvia Vasquez-Lovado, explorer. [Audio podcast episode]. In *Meditative story.* WaitWhat Inc. https://meditativestory.com/discover-the-power-of-self-compassion/.

6. Gunatillake, R. (Host). Discover the power of self-compassion: Silvia Vasquez-Lovado, explorer. [Audio podcast episode]. In *Meditative story.* WaitWhat Inc. https://meditativestory.com/discover-the-power-of-self-compassion/.

7. Gunatillake, R. (Host). Discover the power of self-compassion: Silvia Vasquez-Lovado, explorer. [Audio podcast episode]. In *Meditative story.* WaitWhat Inc. https://meditativestory.com/discover-the-power-of-self-compassion/.

8. Nelson, K. (2020). *Wake up grateful: The transformative practice of taking nothing for granted.* North Adams, MA: Storey.

9. Emmons, R. A., & Stern, R. (2013). Gratitude as a psychotherapeutic intervention. *Journal of Clinical Psychology, 69,* 846–855.

10. Schläppy, M.-L. (2019). Understanding mental health through the theory of positive disintegration: A visual aid. *Frontiers in Psychology, 10,* 1291; Dąbrowski, K. (1972). *Psychoneurosis is not an illness.* London, UK: Gryf.

11. Bonanno, G. A. (2021). *The end of trauma: How the new science of resilience is changing how we think about PTSD.* New York: Basic Books.

12. Hamby, S. (2021, March 2). *Trauma is everywhere, but so is resilience* [Video]. YouTube. https://www.youtube.com/watch?v=dTBqhQNUtrI.

13. Watkins, P., Emmons, R., Amador, T., & Gromfin, D. (2021, July 15). *Growth of gratitude in times of trouble: Gratitude in the pandemic* [Gallery presentation]. International Positive Psychology World Congress. https://doi.org/10.13140/RG.2.2.13815.34722.

14. Steindl-Rast, Br. D. (2023, November 30). *Grateful living.* Grateful.org. https://grateful.org/brother-david/.

15. Huberman, A. [@hubermanlab]. (2023, September 7). *What is a truly (mentally) healthy self?* Instagram. https://www.instagram.com/reel/Cw5WufbLYL5/.

16. Chesterton, G. K. (n.d.). *Heretics.* Project Gutenberg. https://www.gutenberg.org/files/470/470-h/470-h.htm.

17. K. Nelson, interview with Kelly Madrone, September 20, 2023.

18. Wiseman, R. (2003, January 9). Be lucky— t's an easy skill to learn: Those who think they're unlucky should change their outlook and discover how to generate good fortune, says Richard Wiseman. *The Telegraph.* https://

www.telegraph.co.uk/technology/3304496/Be-lucky-ts-an-easy-kill-to
-learn.html.

19. Wiseman, R. (2003, January 9). Be lucky— t's an easy skill to learn: Those who think they're unlucky should change their outlook and discover how to generate good fortune, says Richard Wiseman. *The Telegraph.* https:// www.telegraph.co.uk/technology/3304496/Be-lucky-ts-an-easy-kill-to -learn.html.

20. Zitek, E. M., & Jordan, A. H. (2021). Individuals higher in psychological entitlement respond to bad luck with anger. *Personality and Individual Differences, 168,* Article 110306.

21. Zitek, E. M., & Jordan, A. H. (2021). Individuals higher in psychological entitlement respond to bad luck with anger. *Personality and Individual Differences, 168,* Article 110306.

22. Zitek, E. M., & Jordan, A. H. (2021). Individuals higher in psychological entitlement respond to bad luck with anger. *Personality and Individual Differences, 168,* Article 110306.

23. Maslow, A. H. (1998; originally published in 1962). *Toward a psychology of being* (3rd ed.). New York: Wiley.

24. Brenner, G. (2023, September 6). A psychiatrist explains why calling everything toxic is bad for your brain: Many things are deeply problematic and have gone on for far too long—on the other hand, plenty of situations where there are challenges are difficult without being toxic. *Fast Company.* https://www.fastcompany.com/90944497/a-psychiatrist-finally-explains -the-ways-describing-things-as-toxic-is-harming-us

25. Keltner, D. (2023). *Awe: The new science of everyday wonder and how it can transform your life.* New York: Penguin Press.

26. Maslow, A. H. (1964). *Religions, values, and peak experiences.* London, UK: Penguin.

27. Jans-Beken, L., & Wong, P. T. P. (2021). Development and preliminary validation of the existential gratitude scale (EGS). *Counselling Psychology Quarterly, 34,* 72–86.

28. Rosmarin, D. H., Krumrei, E. J., & Pargament, K. I. (2010). Are gratitude and spirituality protective factors against psychopathology? *International Journal of Existential Psychology & Psychotherapy, 3*(1).

29. Primo, J. (2023, December 7). *The fearless dive: Grateful without conditions.* Grateful.org. https://grateful.org/resource/fearless-dive-grateful-without -conditions/.

30. Emmons, R. A., & Stern, R. (2013). Gratitude as a psychotherapeutic intervention. *Journal of Clinical Psychology, 69,* 846–855.

31. Knopik, B. (2022). *Beyond the rainbow: A mother's journey through grief to grace.* Tustin, CA: Morgan James Faith.

Chapter 10: Help Empower Society

1. Kennedy, R. F. (n.d.). Goodreads. https://www.goodreads.com/quotes /71634-few-will-have-the-greatness-to-bend-history-itself-but.
2. Bruni, F. (2024). *The age of grievance.* New York: Simon & Schuster.
3. Nordyke, K. (2022, March 14). Critics Choice Awards winner Jane Campion tells Williams sisters she faces a competition hurdle they do not: men. *The Hollywood Reporter.* https://www.hollywoodreporter.com /movies/movie-news/jane-campion-venus-serena-williams-sisters-critics -choice-1235110753/.
4. Murphy, M. C. (2024). *Cultures of growth: How the new science of mindset can transform individuals, teams, and organizations.* New York: Simon & Schuster.
5. Cehajic, S., Brown, R., & Castano, E. (2008). Forgive and forget? Antecedents and consequences of intergroup forgiveness in Bosnia and Herzegovina. *Political Psychology, 29,* 351–367; Wohl, M. J. A., & Branscombe, N. R. (2008). Remembering historical victimization: Collective guilt for current ingroup transgressions. *Journal of Personality and Social Psychology, 94,* 988–1006.
6. Cehajic, S., & Brown, R. (2008). Not in my name: A social psychological study of antecedents and consequences of acknowledgement of in-group atrocities. *Genocide Studies and Prevention, 3,* 195–211; Mack, J. E. (1988). The enemy system. *International Physicians for the Prevention of Nuclear War, 332,* 385–387; Gabay, R., Hameiri, B., Rubel-Lifschitz, T., & Nadler, A. (2020). The tendency to feel victimized in interpersonal and intergroup relationships. In J. R. Vollhardt (Ed.), *The social psychology of collective victimhood* (pp. 361–379). Oxford, UK: Oxford University Press.
7. Cehajic, S., & Brown, R. (2008). Not in my name: A social psychological study of antecedents and consequences of acknowledgement of in-group atrocities. *Genocide Studies and Prevention, 3,* 195–211; Mack, J. E. (1988). The enemy system. *International Physicians for the Prevention of Nuclear War, 332,* 385–387.
8. Nadler, A. (2019). The social psychology of intergroup reconciliation: Moving beyond guilt and victimhood. In A. M. Biro & E. Verhas (Eds.), *International studies in human rights and identity: Populism, memory, and minority rights—CEE issues in global perspective.* Brill; Noor, M., Vollhardt, J. R., Mari, S., & Nadler, A. (2017). The social psychology of collective victimhood. *European Journal of Social Psychology, 47,* 121–134; Vollhardt, J. R. (2020). *The social psychology of collective victimhood.* Oxford, UK: Oxford University Press.
9. Gray, K., & Wegner, D. M. (2009). Moral typecasting: Divergent perceptions of moral agents and moral patients. *Journal of Personality and Social Psychology, 96,* 505–520.

10. Vollhardt, J. R. (2020). *The social psychology of collective victimhood*. Oxford, UK: Oxford University Press.

11. Baumeister, R. F., & Leary, M. R. (1995). The need to belong: Desire for interpersonal attachment as a fundamental human motivation. *Psychological Bulletin, 117*, 497–529; Mullin, B.-A., & Hogg, M. A. (1998). Dimensions of subjective uncertainty in social identification and minimal intergroup discrimination. *British Journal of Social Psychology, 37*, 345–365; Vignoles, V. L., Regalia, C., Manzi, C., Golledge, J., & Scabini, E. (2006). Beyond self-esteem: Influence of multiple motives on identity construction. *Journal of Personality and Social Psychology, 90*, 308–333.

12. Fromm, E. (1992). *The anatomy of human destructiveness*. New York: Holt.

13. Kaufman, S. B. (2021, November 6). Group narcissism is everywhere. *The Atlantic.* https://www.theatlantic.com/family/archive/2021/11/group-narcissism/620632/.

14. Kaufman, S. B. (2021, November 6). Group narcissism is everywhere. *The Atlantic.* https://www.theatlantic.com/family/archive/2021/11/group-narcissism/620632/.

15. A. Golec de Zavala, personal communication, May 7, 2024.

16. Cichocka, A. (2016). Understanding defensive and secure in-group positivity: The role of collective narcissism. *European Review of Social Psychology, 27*, 283–317; Cislak, A., Wojcik, A. D., & Cichocka, A. (2018). Cutting the forest down to save your face: Narcissistic national identification predicts support for anti-conservation policies. *Journal of Environmental Psychology, 59*, 65–73; Cichocka, A., Cislak, A., Strange, S., Osborne, D., & Sibley, C. G. (2019). Does high self-esteem foster narcissism? Testing the bidirectional relationships between self-esteem, narcissistic admiration and rivalry. *Journal of Research in Personality, 83*, 103882.

17. Golec de Zavala, A., & Lantos, D. (2020). Collective narcissism and its social consequences: The bad and the ugly. *Current Directions in Psychological Science, 29*, 273–278.

18. A. Golec de Zavala, personal communication, June 19, 2024.

19. Golec de Zavala, A., Cichocka, A., & Iskra-Golec, I. (2013). Collective narcissism moderates the effect of in-group image threat on intergroup hostility. *Journal of Personality and Social Psychology, 104*, 1019–1039.

20. Golec de Zavala, A., Dyduch-Hazar, K., & Lantos, D. (2019). Collective narcissism: Political consequences of investing self-worth in the group's image. *Political Psychology, 40*, 37–74.

21. Golec de Zavala, A., Cichocka, A., Eidelson, R., & Jayawickreme, N. (2009). Collective narcissism and its social consequences. *Journal of Personality and Social Psychology, 97*, 1074–1096.

22. Agroskin, D., & Jonas, E. (2010). Out of control: How and why does perceived lack of control lead to ethnocentrism? *Review of Psychology, 17*, 79–90; Agroskin, D., & Jonas, E. (2013). Controlling death by defending

ingroups—mediational insights into terror management and control restoration. *Journal of Experimental and Social Psychology, 49,* 1144–1158; Aydin, N., Krueger, J. I., Frey, D., Kastenmüller, A., & Discher, P. (2013). Social exclusion and xenophobia: Intolerant attitudes toward ethnic and religious minorities. *Group Processes & Intergroup Relations, 17,* 371–387; Fritsche, I., Jonas, E., & Fankhanel, T. (2008). The role of control motivation in mortality salience effects on ingroup support and defense. *Journal of Personality and Social Psychology, 95,* 524–541; Fritsche, I., Jonas, E., Ablasser, C., Beyer, M., Kuban, J., Manger, A.-M., & Schultz, M. (2013). The power of we: Evidence for group-based control. *Journal of Experimental Social Psychology, 49,* 19–32; Greenaway, K. H., Louis, W. R., Hornsey, M. J., & Jones, J. M. (2013). Perceived control qualifies the effects of threat on prejudice. *British Journal of Social Psychology, 53,* 422–442.

23. Golec de Zavala, A., et al. (2020). Low self-esteem predicts out-group derogation via collective narcissism, but this relationship is obscured by ingroup satisfaction. *Journal of Personality and Social Psychology, 119,* 741–764; Golec de Zavala, A., & Lantos, D. (2020). Collective narcissism and its social consequences: The bad and the ugly. *Current Directions in Psychological Science, 29,* 273–278. In fact, in an experimental study in which researchers were able to increase a sense of collective narcissism, the result was an increase in vulnerable narcissism, not self-esteem!

24. Noor, M., Shnabel, N., Halabi, S., & Nadler, A. (2012). When suffering begets suffering: The psychology of competitive victimhood between adversarial groups in violent conflicts. *Personality and Social Psychology Review, 16,* 351–374.

25. Noor, M., Shnabel, N., Halabi, S., & Nadler, A. (2012). When suffering begets suffering: The psychology of competitive victimhood between adversarial groups in violent conflicts. *Personality and Social Psychology Review, 16,* 351–374.

26. Sonnenschein, N. (2008). *An identity challenging dialogue.* Haifa, Israel: Pardes.

27. Nadler, A. (2019). The social psychology of intergroup reconciliation: Moving beyond guilt and victimhood. In A. M. Biro & E. Verhas (Eds.), *International studies in human rights and identity: Populism, memory, and minority rights—CEE issues in global perspective.* Brill.

28. Schori-Eyal, N., Klart, Y., & Ben-Ami, Y. (2017). Perpetual ingroup victimhood as a distorted lens: Effects on attribution and categorization. *European Journal of Social Psychology, 47,* 180–194. The combination of victimhood and entitlement gives us tunnel vision, and we see things only through this narrow lens. Research shows that a "perpetual in-group victimhood orientation" (PIVO) invokes some major cognitive distortions. For instance, high levels of PIVO were associated with categorizing people in out-groups as hostile to the in-group, and PIVO was associated with

assigning malevolent intentions to out-group members *in ambiguous situations.*

29. Hameiri, B., Moore-Berg, S. L., Guillard, C., Falk, E. B., & Bruneau, E. (2024). Perceived victimhood shapes support for interpartisan political violence in the United States. *Psychology of Violence, 14,* 207–217.

30. Golec de Zavala, A., & Keenan, O. (2020). Collective narcissism as a framework for understanding populism. *Journal of Theoretical Social Psychology, 5,* https://doi.org/10.1002/jts.5.69.

31. Wohl, M. J. A., & Branscombe, N. R. (2008). Remembering historical victimization: Collective guilt for current ingroup transgressions. *Journal of Personality and Social Psychology, 94,* 988–1006.

32. Golec de Zavala, A., Cichocka, A., & Bilewicz, M. (2012). The paradox of in-group love: Differentiating collective narcissism advances understanding of the relationship between in-group and out-group attitudes. *Journal of Personality, 81,* 16–28.

33. Golec de Zavala, A., Cichocka, A., & Bilewicz, M. (2012). The paradox of in-group love: Differentiating collective narcissism advances understanding of the relationship between in-group and out-group attitudes. *Journal of Personality, 81,* 16–28.

34. Greenaway, K. H., Haslam, S. A., Cruwys, T., Branscombe, N. R., Ysseldyk, R., & Heldreth, C. (2015). From "we" to "me": Group identification enhances perceived personal control with consequences for health and well-being. *Journal of Personality and Social Psychology, 109,* 53–74. Across four studies, Aleksandra Cichocka and her colleagues found that low personal control was linked to an excessive concern with the external recognition of the in-group's worth, whereas high personal control was linked to healthy in-group positivity—a positive investment in the in-group that was independent of the recognition of the group by others. A sense of personal control and healthy in-group positivity was mutually reinforcing: healthy in-group positivity predicted increased feelings of personal control several weeks later. It's clear that healthy group identification can have positive effects on individuals by helping us feel capable and in control of our lives.

35. Golec de Zavala, A. (2019). Collective narcissism and in-group satisfaction are associated with different emotional profiles and psychological well-being. *Frontiers in Psychology, 10,* Article 203; Greenaway, K. H., Haslam, S. A., Cruwys, T., Branscombe, N. R., Ysseldyk, R., & Heldreth, C. (2015). From "we" to "me": Group identification enhances perceived personal control with consequences for health and well-being. *Journal of Personality and Social Psychology, 109,* 53–74.

36. Golec de Zavala, A., & Lantos, D. (2020). Collective narcissism and its social consequences: The bad and the ugly. *Current Directions in Psychological Science, 29,* 273–278.

37. Mandela, N. (n.d.). Goodreads. https://www.goodreads.com/quotes/228576 -you-will-achieve-more-in-this-world-through-acts-of.

38. Nadler, A. (2019). The social psychology of intergroup reconciliation: Moving beyond guilt and victimhood. In A. M. Biro & E. Verhas (Eds.), *International studies in human rights and identity: Populism, memory, and minority rights—CEE issues in global perspective*. Brill.

39. Shnabel, N., Halabi, S., & Noor, M. (2013). Overcoming competitive victimhood and facilitating forgiveness through re-categorization into a common victim or perpetrator identity. *Journal of Experimental Social Psychology, 49*, 867–877.

40. Adelman, L., Leidner, B., Unal, H., Nahhas, E., & Shnabel, N. (2016). A whole other other: Inclusive victimhood narratives reduce competitive victimhood and intergroup hostility. *Personality and Social Psychology Bulletin, 42*, 1416–1430.

41. Baumeister, R. F. (1999). *Evil: Inside human violence and cruelty*. New York: Holt Paperbacks.

42. Hart, W., Crease, C. K., Lambert, J. T., Witt, D. E., Hall, B. T., & Breeden, C. J. (2024). The Capone hypothesis: Do antagonistic individuals view themselves as more good than evil? *Personality and Individual Differences, 216*, 112426.

43. Sedikides, C., Meek, R., Alicke, M. D., & Taylor, S. (2014). Behind bars but above the bar: Prisoners consider themselves more prosocial than nonprisoners. *British Journal of Social Psychology, 53*, 396–403.

44. As quoted in Carnegie, D. (1936). *How to win friends and influence people*. Simon & Schuster.

45. Novogratz, J. (2009). *The blue sweater: Bridging the gap between rich and poor in an interconnected world*. New York: Rodale Books.

46. Ottesen, K. K. (2019). *Activist: Portraits of courage*. San Francisco: Chronicle.

47. Nadler, A. (2019). The social psychology of intergroup reconciliation: Moving beyond guilt and victimhood. In A. M. Biro & E. Verhas (Eds.), *International studies in human rights and identity: Populism, memory, and minority rights—CEE issues in global perspective*. Brill; Noor, M., Vollhardt, J. R., Mari, S., & Nadler, A. (2017). The social psychology of collective victimhood. *European Journal of Social Psychology, 47*, 121–134; Vollhardt, J. R. (2020). *The social psychology of collective victimhood*. Oxford, UK: Oxford University Press.

48. Vollhardt, J. R., Mazur, L. B., & Lemahieu, M. (2014). Acknowledgment after mass violence: Effects on wellbeing and intergroup relations. *Group Processes & Intergroup Relations, 17*, 306–323.

49. Andrighetto, L., Halabi, S., Kosic, A., Petrovic, N., Prelic, N., Pecini, C., & Nadler, A. (2024). Institutional acknowledgement of the chosen trauma in the background of its denial: A field experiment across conflicting groups. *European Journal of Social Psychology*. https://doi.org/10.1002/ejsp.3050.

50. Kesebir, P., & Kesebir, S. (2012). The cultural salience of moral character and virtue declined in twentieth century America. *Journal of Positive Psychology, 7,* 471–480.

51. Kaufman, S. B. (2015, September 30). *The surprising benefits of a quiet ego.* Quiet Revolution. https://quietrev.com/the-surprising-benefits-of-a -quiet-ego/.

52. Leary, M. (2007). *The curse of the self: Self-awareness, egotism, and the quality of human life.* Oxford, UK: Oxford University Press.

53. Wayment, H. A., Bauer, J. J., & Sylaska, K. (2014). The quiet ego scale: Measuring the compassionate self-identity. *Journal of Happiness Studies, 16,* 999–1033.

54. Wayment, H. A., & Bauer, J. J. (2008). *Transcending self-interest.* Washington, D.C.: American Psychological Association.

55. Brown, K. W., & Ryan, R. M. (2003). The benefits of being present: Mindfulness and its role in psychological well-being. *Journal of Personality and Social Psychology, 84,* 822–848.

56. Wayment, H. A., Bauer, J. J., & Sylaska, K. (2014). The quiet ego scale: Measuring the compassionate self-identity. *Journal of Happiness Studies, 16,* 999–1033.

57. Brudholm, T. (2006). Revisiting resentments: Jean Améry and the dark side of forgiveness and reconciliation. *Journal of Human Rights, 5,* 7–26.

58. Mack, J. E. (1988). The enemy system. *International Physicians for the Prevention of Nuclear War, 332,* 385–387.

59. Nasie, M., & Bar-Tal, D. (2019). Political socialization in kindergartens: Observations of ceremonies of the Israeli Jewish holidays and memorial days. *European Journal of Social Psychology, 50,* 685–700; Nasie, M., Diamond, A. H., & Bar-Tal, D. (2016). Young children in intractable conflicts: The Israeli case. *Personality and Social Psychology Review, 20,* 365–392; Nasie, M., Tagar, M. R., & Bar-Tal, D. (2021). Ethno-political socialization of young children in societies involved in intractable conflict: The case of Israel. *Journal of Social Issues, 77,* 1257–1281.

60. Nasie, M., Diamond, A. H., & Bar-Tal, D. (2016). Young children in intractable conflicts: The Israeli case. *Personality and Social Psychology Review, 20,* 365–392.

61. Gabay, R., Hameiri, B., Lifschitz, T. R., & Nadler, A. (2020). The tendency for interpersonal victimhood: The personality construct and its consequences. *Personality and Individual Differences, 165,* Article 110134; Kaufman, S. B. (2024, February 20). Unraveling the mindset of victimhood. *Scientific American.* https://www.scientificamerican.com/article /unraveling-the-mindset-of-victimhood/.

62. Bar-Tal, D., & Hameiri, B. (2020). Interventions to change well-anchored attitudes in the context of intergroup conflict. *Social and Personality Psychology Compass, 14,* e12545; Bar-Tal, D., Vered, S., & Fuxman, S. (2020).

Between open-minded critical thinking and closed-minded allegiance: Educational tensions in societies involved in intractable conflict. *Advances in Political Psychology, 42,* 3–28; Rosler, N., Sharvit, K., Hameiri, B., Wiener-Blotner, O., Idan, O., & Bar-Tal, D. (2022). The informative process model as a new intervention for attitude change in intractable conflicts: Theory and empirical evidence. *Frontiers in Psychology, 13,* Article 946410.

63. Kaufman, S. B. (2024, February 20). Unraveling the mindset of victimhood. *Scientific American.* https://www.scientificamerican.com/article/unraveling-the-mindset-of-victimhood/.

64. Schwartz, S. H., & Bardi, A. (2001). Value hierarchies across cultures: Taking a similarities perspective. *Journal of Cross-Cultural Psychology, 32,* 268–290.

65. Schwartz, S. H. (2007). Universalism values and the inclusiveness of our moral universe. *Journal of Cross-Cultural Psychology, 38,* 711–728.

66. Kaufman, S. B. (2013). *Ungifted: Intelligence redefined.* New York: Basic Books.

67. Brauer Group Lab (n.d.). *About.* University of Wisconsin–Madison. https://psych.wisc.edu/Brauer/BrauerLab/; al-Gharbi, M. (2020, December 29). *"Diversity training" doesn't work. This might.* Heterodox Academy. https://heterodoxacademy.org/blog/diversity-training-doesnt-work-this-might/; Chang, E. H., Milkman, K. L., Gromet, D. M., Rebele, R. W., Massey, C., Duckworth, A. L., & Grant, A. M. (2019). The mixed effects of online diversity training. *Proceedings of the National Academy of Sciences, USA, 116*(16), 7778–7783; Devine, P. G., & Ash, T. L. (2022). Diversity training goals, limitations, and promise: A review of the multidisciplinary literature. *Annual Review of Psychology, 73,* 403–429; Dobbin, F. (2024, March 27). Why diversity programs fail. *Harvard Business Review.* https://hbr.org/2016/07/why-diversity-programs-fail; Newkirk, P. (2019). *Diversity, Inc.: The failed promise of a billion-dollar business.* New York: Bold Type Books; Wilton, L. S., Apfelbaum, E. P., & Good, J. J. (2018). Valuing differences and reinforcing them: Multiculturalism increases race essentialism. *Social Psychological and Personality Science, 10.* https://doi.org/10.1177/1948550618780728; Kalev, A., Dobbin, F., & Kelly, E. (2006). Best practices or best guesses? Assessing the efficacy of corporate affirmative action and diversity policies. *American Sociological Review, 71,* 589–617; Khalid, A., & Snyder, J. A. (2020, August 5). *Why diversity training on campus is likely to disappoint.* The Conversation. https://theconversation.com/why-diversity-training-on-campus-is-likely-to-disappoint-143644; Lai, C. K., Skinner, A. L., Cooley, E., Murrar, S., Brauer, M., Devos, T., & Nosek, B. A. (2016). Reducing implicit racial preferences: II. Intervention effectiveness across time. *Journal of Experimental Psychology: General, 145*(8), 1001–1016; Paluck, E. L., Porat, R., Clark, C. S., & Green, D. P. (2021). Prejudice reduction: Progress and challenges. *Annual Review of Psychology, 72,* 533–560;

Legate, N., & Weinstein, N. (2024). Motivation science can improve diversity, equity, and inclusion (DEI) trainings. *Perspectives on Psychological Science.* https://doi.org/10.1177/17456916231186410; Stewart-Williams, S. (2024, April 26). *Reforming DEI.* The Nature-Nurture-Nietzsche Newsletter. https://www.stevestewartwilliams.com/p/reforming-dei; Pescovitz, O. H., Dullo, D., Navin, M., & Naus, J. (2024, April 25). Oakland University president, faculty leaders: Redirect campus diversity programs to original goals. *The Detroit News.* https://www.detroitnews.com/story/opin ion/2024/04/24/oakland-university-president-faculty-leaders-redirect -campus-diversity-programs-to-original-goals/73438948007/.

68. Foster, K. (n.d.). *About.* Karith.com. https://karith.com/about/.
69. Foster, K. (n.d.). *About.* Karith.com. https://karith.com/about/.
70. K. Foster, personal communication, March 6, 2024.
71. K. Foster, personal communication, March 6, 2024.
72. K. Foster, personal communication, March 6, 2024.
73. Killam, K. (2024). *The art and science of connection: Why social health is the missing key to living longer, healthier, and happier.* New York: HarperOne.
74. Haidt, J. (2024, May 6). The terrible costs of a phone-based childhood. *The Atlantic.*https://www.theatlantic.com/technology/archive/2024/03/teen -childhood-smartphone-use-mental-health-effects/677722/; Haidt, J. (2024). *The anxious generation: How the great rewiring of childhood is causing an epidemic of mental illness.* New York: Penguin.
75. Robertson, C., del Rosario, K., & Van Bavel, J. J. (2024). Inside the funhouse mirror factory: How social media distorts perceptions of norms. https://doi.org/10.31234/osf.io/kgcrq.
76. Rose, T. (2022). *Collective illusions: Conformity, complicity, and the science of why we make bad decisions.* New York: Hachette Go.
77. S. David, personal communication, March 28, 2024.
78. Cejakic, S., Brown, R., & Castano, E. (2008). Forgive and forget? Antecedents and consequences of intergroup forgiveness in Bosnia and Herzegovina. *Political Psychology, 29,* 351–367.
79. Kaufman, S. B. (2020). *Transcend: The new science of self-actualization.* New York: TarcherPerigee.

Index

acceptance, 73–74, 75
acceptance and commitment therapy (ACT), 45–49
Acceptance (Nietfeld), 128
activism, 140–42, 244
adaptive intelligence, 162
Adler, Alfred, 100
adversity, 161–63
affective empathy, 182
affirmations, positive, 112–13
Against Empathy: The Case for Rational Compassion (Bloom), 182
agency, 8–9, 123–24, 245
The Age of Grievance (Bruni), 232–33
aggression, 140
Améry, Jean, 253–54
amoral manipulation, 143–44
The Anatomy of Human Destructiveness (Fromm), 238–39
Andrighetto, Luca, 251
Angelou, Maya, 168, 180
anger, 226
anxiety
    author's experiences, 28–29, 30, 41
    Mingyur Rinpoche's experiences, 46–47
Aron, Elaine, 171, 173–74, 177
arousal level, managing your nervous system, 52–53
Arroll, Meg, 13, 15
attachment
    attachment style, 23–24
    attachment theory, 21–22

authenticity
    authenticity positive bias, 115
    feeling most authentic, 115–16
    healthy, 114–15, 116–19
    Healthy Authenticity Scale, 117–18
    understanding, 115
authoritarianism, 140–41
avoidance, 34–41
awe, 228

Bakan, David, 123–24
Barrett, Lisa Feldman, 5, 6, 35–36, 44
Barrie, Zara, 92, 93, 98
Bar-Tal, Daniel, 256–57
Bauer, Jack, 252–53
Baumeister, Roy, 92–93, 115
"beautiful monsters," 51–52
Beck, Martha, 37
behavior
    activation system, 191
    habitual, 25
    impact of genetics on, 24
    inhibition system, 191
behavioral activation, 71–73
beliefs, the power of, 206–07
The Bell Curve (Murray), 33
Bellet, Benjamin, 35
belonging, the need for, 89–90
Bertrams, Alex, 140–42
Beyond the Rainbow: A Mother's Journey Through Grief to Grace (Knopik), 230–31

biases
  authenticity positive, 115
  confirmation, 60–61
  egoistic (superhero), 137
  hostile attributional, 102
  interpretation, 62
  memory, 63
  moralistic (saintlike), 137
  negativity, 157–59
Bittersweet: How Sorrow and Longing Make Us Whole (Cain), 180
black-and-white thinking, 73
blame, 132
Bloom, Paul, 35, 182
The Blue Sweater (Novogratz), 248–49
the body and the brain, 19–20, 44
The Body Keeps the Score (van der Kolk), 17–18, 19
Bonanno, George, 13, 17
Boothby, Erica, 90–91
Both/And thinking, xxix
"bothness," 53–54
Boyce, W. Thomas, 196, 197
Brach, Tara, 50–51
Braiker, Harriet, 132–34
the brain
  and the body, 19–20, 44
  dopamine, 179
  and fear, 6
  as a prediction machine, 5–6
  sensitivity to social cues, 88
Branden, Nathaniel, 93–94, 112–13
Brenner, Grant, 227
Breslin, Niall, 153–54
brokenness, looking beyond, 153–54
Brown, Brené, xvi
Broyles, William, 255
Bruni, Frank, 232–33
Buber, Martin, 123n
Buck, Pearl S., 169
Bukowski, Charles, 224

Cain, Susan, 180
Campbell, W. Keith, 82–84
Campion, Jane, 233
Canevello, Amy, 128–29
Capone Hypothesis, 248
Carlin, John, 246
Carr, Danielle, 18

The Center for Mindful Self-Compassion, 109
Character Strengths and Virtues: A Handbook and Classification (Peterson and Seligman), 157–58
Chesterton, G. K., 221
children
  childhood origins of excessive helping, 126
  "dandelions and orchids" metaphor for sensitive children, 197
  political socialization of, 256–58
  twice exceptional, 161
Chödrön, Pema, 56
Clifton, Jer, 66
coddling, xxv
codependency, 130–35
cognitive distortions
  confirmation bias, 60–61
  questions to ask regarding, 68–70
  of a victim mindset, 62–65
  victim mindset of incels, 59–60
cognitive empathy, 182
Cold Comfort Farm (Gibbons), 3–4, 6–7, 27
collective victimhood, 236–38
committed action, 49
communion, 123–24
compassion. *See* self-compassion
confirmation bias, 60–61
conflict(s)
  intergroup, 245n
  intractable, 241–43, 255–57
  the perpetrator role, 248–49
  psychological needs approach to, 245
Conti, Paul, 221
control
  accepting the unpredictability of life, 56–57
  locus of control, 8–9
  and self-esteem, 240
The Courage to Be Disliked (Kishimi and Koga), 100
COVID-19, 220
creativity, 177–78, 198–200
Crocker, Jennifer, 101, 128–29
Cultures of Growth (Murphy), 233–34
Curran, Linda, 20

Dąbrowski, Kazimierz, 175–76, 219–20
"dandelions and orchids" metaphor for sensitive children, 197
Dangerfield, Rodney, 91
dark-ego-vehicle principle, 141
dark healers, 179–84
"dark triad" traits, 143
David, Susan, 30–31, 37, 41–44, 53–54, 261–62
defusion, 47
depression, 84
Deschene, Lori, 37–38, 46
Desmet, Ophélie, 162
DeYoung, Colin, 179
de Zavala, Agnieszka Golec, 239, 240, 246
diagnostic labels, xi
Diamond, Aurel Harrison, 256–57
Dirac, Paul, 94
disabilities, 161–62
discomfort, 33, 36–37
The Disease to Please (Braiker), 132–34
distress, 41
diverse views, respecting, 32–37
diversity, equity, and inclusion (DEI) programs, 258–60
Douglass, Frederick, 34
The Duality of Human Existence (Bakan), 123–24

education, 33–34
Egar, Edith, 10
ego
   egoistic (superhero) bias, 137
   quiet ego, 252–53
Einstein, Albert, 89
Elijah, Thea, 153
Ellis, Albert, 64
Ellis, Bruce, 89, 162, 196, 197
Emmons, Robert, 217, 230
Emotional Agility (David), 42
emotions
   allowing uncomfortable feelings to govern your actions, 32
   avoidance, 37–41
   bodily components of, 19
   emotional agility, 41–44
   emotional granularity, 21
feeling defined by, 43
handling difficult, techniques for, 49–56
labeling, 30
limited power of, 43–44
mixed feelings ("bothness"), 53–54
processing uncomfortable feelings quiz, 38–39
transient nature of, 42–43
empaths, 181–82
empowerment mindset, xxiii–xxv, 234, 245–47
"empty chair technique," 54
"The Enemy System" (article), 254–55
engagement, cognitive and affective, 205–06
entitlement
   and anger, 226
   the entitlement paradox, xxi
   entitlement rage, 95
   from excessive helping, 127–28
   key elements of, xxi–xxii, 225–26
   and a victim mindset, xxiii
   vulnerable, xix–xx, 187, 243
   warranted, xxi
Epstein, Mark, 31
Eurich, Tasha, 9–10
expectations, 202–07, 212–15
experiential acceptance, 46–47
experiential avoidance, 39, 40–41
extraversion, 177–78

Fadiman, James, 154–55
failure, 103
Fast Company (magazine), 227
fear
   author's experiences, 28–29, 30, 41
   avoiding psychological fears, downside of, 31–32
   fear of people's opinions (FOPO), 96–98
   harnessing, 55–56
   learning and unlearning, 6
   Philippe Petit's experiences, 29–30
feedback
   considering the value of, 105–07
   the feedback filter, 106–07
   sensitivity to, 101
   wise feedback, 214–15
Feiler, Bruce, 211
Fennimore, Anne, 138

Ferriss, Tim, 13
Fierce Self-Compassion (Neff), 107–09
Flett, Gordon, 94–96
Foo, Stephanie, 16, 170
Ford, Henry, 202
forgiveness
　acknowledgments of wrongdoing and
　　suffering, 250–51
　benefits of, 165–66
　and interpersonal victimhood, 63
　Kimi Katiti's experiences, 163–64
　the power of, 163–64
　the REACH method, 166–67
　and resentment, 254
　and self-love, 167–68
Foster, Karith, 259–60
founder's syndrome, 138n
Fraley, R. Chris, 23
Frankl, Viktor, 4, 47, 217–18
Freund, Alane, 196
Fromm, Erich, 146, 238–39

Gabay, Rahav, 62–63, 257
Gandhi, Mahatma, 234
Gebauer, Jochen, 137
gender and vulnerability, xvi
genetics
　and attachment style, 23–24
　and highly sensitive people (HSPs), 174
　nature *vs.* nurture, 21, 23, 177,
　　195–96
　preexisting temperamental differences,
　　23–24, 25
　and their influence, 25, 197
Gervais, Michael, 96–97
Gibbons, Stella, 3–4, 6–7, 27
giftedness, 161–62
Giftedness in Childhood (Sternberg and
　Desmet), 162
Gillihan, Seth, 68–74, 76
Giraldo, Greg, 84
givens of existence, xxvi–xxvii
Gladwell, Malcolm, 201
goals, 72, 103–04
Goggins, David, 214
González, Andrés, 151–53
Goodman, Timothy, 45, 54, 55, 198
gratitude
　and awe, 228

Beth Knopik's experiences, 216–17
during the COVID-19 pandemic, 220
Existential Gratitude Scale, 228–29
Kristi Nelson's experiences, 221–23
and luck, 224–26
service to others, 230–31
Silvia Vasquez-Lovado's experiences,
　218–19
spiritual well-being, 229–30
as a way of healing from trauma,
　216–19
Gray, Kurt, 237
grief and love, 31
group(s)
　acknowledgments of wrongdoing and
　　suffering, 250–51
　"chosen trauma" of a victimhood group,
　　237–38
　common victimhood, 247
　empowerment mindset, 245–47
　enemy selection, 255
　healthy in-group love, 243–44
　identity, 239
growth
　growth needs, xxvii–xxviii
　post-traumatic, 11–12
Gruber, Jordan, 154–55
guilt, survivor's, 142

Hamby, Sherry, 220
Hamieri, Boaz, 242, 250n–51n
happiness as a false target, 77–78
Haveran, Alouph, 257
Hayes, Steven, 45–46, 76
healing trauma. *See also* trauma
　bottom-up vs top-down
　　approaches to, 20
　society's reluctance to celebrate, 12–13
healthy selfishness, 146–48
Healthy Selfishness Scale (HSS), 146–48
healthy vulnerability, xvi–xvii
helping, excessive
　childhood origins of, 126
　and codependent behaviors, 130–35
　communal narcissism, 135–39
　dangers of, 122–23
　Emi Nietfeld's experiences, 128
　Excessive Helping Scale, 125–26
　healthy selfishness, 146–48

manifestations of, 122
motivations for, 126–27
narcissistic activists, 140–42
research, 126–27, 128
understanding, 120–22
Henderson, Rob, 212–13
Hicks, Tony, 162–63
Hidden Brain (podcast), 91
The Highly Sensitive Child (Aron), 174
highly sensitive people (HSPs), 170–80,
 184–200
"High on Compliments: What It Feels
 Like to Be Addicted to Validation"
 (essay), 92
Hillel, Rabbi, 123
Holistic Life Foundation, 151–52
Hollywood Reporter (magazine), 67
honest love, xxv–xxvi
hostile attributional bias, 102
How Pleasure Works (Bloom), 35
human existence commonalities, xxix
humility, 251

I Always Think It's Forever (Goodman),
 45, 54
i am through you so i (Steindl-Rast),
 220–21
identity
 developing a more complex,
 253–54
 developing a more flexible, xiii, 194
 embracing the idea of many selves,
 154–57
 of a group, 239
 impostorism, 110–14
 nonidentification, 48
impostorism, 110–14
incels (involuntary celibates), 59–60
information threat theory, 88
inhibitory control, 39–40
interpretation bias, 62
In the Shadow of the Mountain
 (Vasquez-Lovado), 219, 231
introversion, 177–78

Jans-Beken, Lilian, 228–29
Jauk, Emanuel, 184–85, 186–87
Johansson, Scarlett, 195
John, Oliver, 137

Jordan, Alexander, 226
Jordan, Michael, 206
judgment
 nonjudgmental contact with the present
 moment, 48

Kabat-Zinn, Jon, 75
Kajdzik, Martyna, 190–91
Katiti, Kimi, 163–64, 168
Kaufman, Scott Barry
 creative endeavors, 199–200
 excessive helping research,
 126–27, 128
 fears, 28–29, 30, 41
 narcissism research, 82–84
 sailboat metaphor for self-actualization,
 xxvii–xxviii
 school experiences, xvii–xviii,
 208–10
Keltner, Dacher, 228
Kennedy, Robert F., 232
Keon, Joseph, 169–70
Kernis, Michael, 102
Kerry, Nicholas, 66
Khamisa, Azim, 162–63, 164
Kidman, Nicole, 195
Kimmerer, Robin Wall, 200
King, Martin Luther, Jr., 151, 249
Kirkpatrick, Lee, 89
Kishimi, Ichiro, 100
Knopik, Beth, 216–17, 230–31
Koga, Fumitake, 100
Kranc, Lauren, 136–37
Krispenz, Anne, 140–42
Kushner, Harold, 12

Lantos, Dorottya, 239, 246
Laux, Dorianne, 180
learned helplessness, 4
learned hopefulness, 4–5
Leary, Mark, 88, 90–91, 100, 106,
 251–52
LePera, Nicole, 12
*Let Your Light Shine: How Mindfulness Can
 Empower Children and Rebuild
 Communities* (Smith, Smith, and
 Gonzalez), 152–53
Lewis, John, 249–50
LGBTQ+ activism, 141–42

life
  embracing the messiness of, xii
  givens of existence, xxvi–xxvii
  life-acceptance, xxviii
  life stories, 210–12
"light triad" traits, 144–45
Lincoln, Abraham, 34
locus of control, 8–9
loneliness, 34, 44–45
love
  and grief, 31
  healthy in-group love, 243–44
  looking for, 78
luck, 224–26
Luskin, Frederic, 165
Lyon, Irene, 192

Ma, Yo-Yo, 200
MacDonald, Geoff, 101
Mack, John E., 254–55, 257
magic, creating, xxix
Magness, Steve, 103–04
Mandela, Nelson, 246
manipulation, amoral, 143–44
Manson, Mark, 163
Man's Search for Meaning (Frankl), 4
Martinez, Brenda, 61
Maslow, Abraham, 108, 146, 227, 228
Maslow's hierarchy of needs, xxvii
Maté, Gabor, 23–24
McElwee, Rory, 110
McGonigal, Kelly, 44–45
McGrath, Robert, 159, 160–61
McNamara, Carter, 138n
meditation, 75n, 152
Meditative Story (podcast), 218–19
memories
  memory bias, 63
  storing, 18–19
mental health
  the balance between agency and
    communion, 123–24
  benefits of practicing gratitude, 219
Middle East example of competitive
    victimhood, 241–42, 247
Miller, Josh, 82–84
mindfulness
  Holistic Life Foundation's work with,
    151–53

mindful awareness, 73–76
  misconceptions about, 75–76
  strengths-based, 159–61
The Mindfulness and Character Strengths
    Workbook (Niemiec), 159–60
mindset
  dynamic, xxii–xxiii
  empowered, xxiii–xxv
  the entitlement paradox, xxi
  mastery, 103–04
mistakes, 134
Montaño, Alysia, 61
morals
  amoral manipulation, 143–44
  moralistic (saintlike) bias, 137
  theory of moral typecasting, 237, 248
Moroń, Marcin, 190–91
motivation, 128–29
Murphy, Mary C., 233–34
Murray, Charles, 33

Nadler, Arie, 242, 250n–51n
narcissism
  as an addiction to the feeling of
    self-esteem, 92–93, 102
  antagonistic, 140–41, 143
  collective, 238–41
  Collective Narcissism Scale, 239–40
  communal, 135–39
  as a continuum, xiii
  grandiose, xix, 93, 95–96, 102, 112,
    130–31, 133
  Maladaptive Covert Narcissism
    Scale, 185
  narcissistic activists, 140–42
  research, 82–84
  and self-esteem, 80, 81
  and sensitivity signaling, 191–92
  vulnerable, xix–xx, 82–85, 93, 95–96,
    112, 184–87
  vulnerable narcissism and vulnerable
    entitlement quiz, xix–xx
Nasie, Maytal, 256–57
Nature (journal), 19
nature vs. nurture, 21, 23, 177, 195–96
Neff, Kristin, 107–09
negativity bias, 157–59
Nelson, Kristi, 216, 221–23, 226, 228,
    230–31

nervous system arousal, 52–53
neuroticism
    as a continuum, 24
    defined, 24
    in highly sensitive people (HSPs), 176,
        177–79
    and vulnerable narcissism, 85, 187
Never Finished (Goggins), 214
New York (magazine), 18
The New York Times (newspaper), 35–36
Niemiec, Ryan, 159–61
Nietfeld, Emi, 128, 144
Nietzsche, Friedrich, 28, 67
nonidentification, 48
nonjudgmental contact with the present
    moment, 48
Novogratz, Jacqueline, 248–49
Nurmohamed, Samir, 203–07
NXIVM cult, 136–37

Oakley, Barbara, 121
Obama, Michelle, 110, 111
obstacles as opportunities, xii
Ok, Ekin, 143–44
O'Keeffe, Ciarán, 206
Oliver, Mary, 199
101 Trauma-Informed Interventions:
    Activities, Exercise and Assignments to
    Move the Client and Therapy Forward
    (Curran), 20
Open Heart, Open Mind: Awakening the
    Power of Essence Love (Tsoknyi
    Rinpoche), 51–52
open-mindedness
    of Abraham Lincoln, 34
    to make peace, 263
    for widening our circle of connection,
        34, 36
openness to experience, 174–76
overcoming challenges, xxiv–xxv
overexcitabilities, 175–76

Pacelle, Wayne, 140
pain, experiencing, 31
Palus, Shannon, 14
parenting's role in narcissism and
    self-esteem, 81
Parkes, Colin Murray, 31
The Passion Paradox: A Guide to Going All

In, Finding Success, and Discovering the
    Benefits of an Unbalanced Life (Stulberg
    and Magness), 103–04
passive-aggressive behavior, 133
the past, coming to terms with, 26–27
pathological altruism. *See* helping,
    excessive
Paulhus, Delroy, 137
peace, 263
perfomative vulnerability, xvi
personality
    Capone Hypothesis, 248
    "dark triad" traits, 143
    "light triad" traits, 144–45
    openness to experience, 174–76
    traits and their sensitivities, 178–80
perspective, getting some, 54
Petit, Philippe, 29–30
Pinker, Steven, 34n
Playing the Enemy (Carlin), 246
politics, 139, 140–41, 242–43, 256–58
positive disintegration, 219–20
post-traumatic growth, 11–12
post-traumatic stress disorder (PTSD),
    17, 32–33
The Power of Character Strengths (Niemiec
    and McGrath), 159
presence, 73–74
Primo, Joe, 217, 229–30
The Princess Bride (film), 15
privilege and positivity research, 66
promotion *vs.* prevention, 40–41
psychological flexibility, 41, 45–46, 194
psychological visibility, 93–94
psychopathy, 141–42
public service roles, 138–39

questions
    asking "what" questions instead of
        "why," 9–10
    regarding cognitive distortions,
        68–70

RAIN model, 50–51
Raniere, Keith, 136–37
the REACH method of forgiveness,
    166–67
reconciliation, 250, 253–54
rejection, 90–91

religion, 139
resilience
   the ability to recover from difficult
      experiences, 13, 220
   effect of trigger warnings on, 35–36
   and increased emotional granularity, 21
responsibility, 6–9
revenge, 63
Rinpoche, Mingyur, 46–47
Rinpoche, Tsoknyi, 51–52
Rivers, Joan, xi
Robbins, Mel, 105
Robertson, Theresa, 87–88
Rogers, Carl, 82, 119
Rogoza, Radoslaw, 84
romantic relationships
   author's experiences, 58–59
   dealing with rejection, 59
   incels, 59–60
Roosevelt, Eleanor, 77
Rosmarin, David, 31
Rubin, Rick, 195
Rudolph, Wilma, 201–02, 207
Rumi (poet), 10, 153
Russell, Bertrand, 145
Rwanda example of shifting perpetrator
   roles, 248–49

Safran Foer, Jonathan, 217
Salzberg, Sharon, 50
Schultz, Howard, 206
Schwartz, Shalom, 258
Schwarzenegger, Arnold, 66–67
"Screening for Anxiety Will Only Make
   Us More Anxious" (essay), 31
security needs, xxvii–xxviii
self-actualization
   inhibitors of, xviii–xiv
   the quest for, xxvii, 99–100
   sailboat metaphor, xxvii–xxviii
self-aggrandizement, 137
self-awareness, 9–10
self-compassion, 107–09
self-esteem
   Anti-Mattering Scale, 94–96
   authenticity, 114–19
   compared to self-compassion, 107–08
   contingencies of self-worth, 101–03
   fear of people's opinions (FOPO), 96–98

fluctuating, 105
fragile, 102
impostorism, 110–14
increasing your, 78–79, 81, 85–86
movement of the 1980s and 1990s,
   80–81
and narcissism, 80, 81, 92–93
and personal control, 240
and positive life outcomes, 80–81
purpose of, 89
Rosenberg Self-Esteem Scale, 79–80
sensitivity to feedback, 101
sources of, 104–05
uncertain, 85, 91
self-handicapping, 112
"Selfishness and Self-Love" (essay), 146
self-love, 167–68
self-presentation, 111–12
self-transcendence, 253
self-verification theory, 113
Seligman, Martin, 4
Seneca the Younger, 58
Sensitive Men Rising (film), 170
sensitivity
   in animals, 174
   being too sensitive, 193–94
   "dandelions and orchids" metaphor, 197
   highly sensitive people (HSPs), 170–80,
      184–200
   Joseph Keon's experiences, 169–70
   positive aspects of, 196–200
   sensory processing sensitivity, 23–24
   signaling, 188–92
7½ Lessons about the Brain (Barrett), 5, 6
shame, 83–84, 87–89
Shaw, George Bernard, xxix
Shiro, Edith, 11
shyness, 177
Siegel, Dan, 52
signaling
   sensitivity, 188–92
   virtuous victim, 142–45
The Six Pillars of Self-Esteem (Branden),
   93–94
Slate (magazine), 14
Smith, Ali, 151–53, 157
Smith, Atman, 151–53, 167
social media
   charitable pledges research, 129–30

division and disagreement, 261–62
getting attention from strangers, 7–8
vulnerability for attention, xvi
social protection system
acceptance research, 90
rejection, 90–91
social value, 90
sociometer theory, 90, 98, 105–06
society
acknowledgments of wrongdoing and
suffering, 250–51
encouragement of perpetual
victimhood, 234–35
fighting against, 233–34
Frank Bruni's struggles against,
232–33
healthy in-group love, 243–44
intractable conflict, 241–43, 255–57
peace within, 263
Sociological Science (journal), 130
"Song of Myself" (poem), 183
spiritual well-being, 229–30
Star Trek: The Next Generation (TV show),
181, 196
Steindl-Rast, David, 219, 220–21
Stern, Robin, 230
Sternberg, Robert, 162
stored survival stress, 17, 18–19
strengths
from adversity, 162–63
character, 157–59
strengths-based approach to disabilities,
161–62
strengths-based mindfulness,
159–61
VIA Classification of Character
Strengths and Virtues, 158
Stulberg, Brad, 103–04
success, 103
suffering, 12
survivor's guilt, 142
Sutton, Jeremy, 165
Sylaska, Kateryna, 252–53
Sznycer, Daniel, 87–88

Takala, Pilvi, 99
techniques for handling difficult
emotions
creating distance, 50

experiencing mixed feelings
("bothness"), 53–54
getting some perspective, 54
modulating your window of tolerance,
52–53
RAIN model, 50–51
Teicher, Martin, 25
temperamental differences, preexisting,
23–24
theory of desirable difficulties, 206
therapy
acceptance and commitment therapy
(ACT), 45–49
writing, 199
"Think Act Be" method, 68–75
thought
Both/And thinking, xxix
suppression, 39–40
Yes/And thinking, xxiii, 161
tough love, xxv
Toward a Psychology of Being
(Maslow), 108
toxic agency, xxiv
the "toxic" label, 227–28
toxic passivity, xxiv
toxic positivity, 231
Transcend (Kaufman), xxvii–xxviii, 63*n*,
64–65
trauma. *See also* healing trauma
"chosen trauma" of a victimhood group,
237–38
defined, 16–17, 20–21
gratitude as a way of healing from,
216–19
healing from, 11
and highly sensitive people (HSPs),
176–77
post-traumatic growth, 11–12
post-traumatic stress disorder (PTSD),
17, 32–33
potentially traumatic experiences, 17
resolving, 16
"tiny traumas," 13, 15
trauma responses, 14, 19
ubiquity of, 12–13, 20–21
"Trauma: America's Favorite
Self-Diagnosis" (article), 18
trigger warnings, 32–37
the twice exceptional child, 161

2016 Olympic trials example of confirmation bias, 61

Ulmer, Kristen, 55
underdogs
　author's experiences in school,
　　208–10
　expectations, 202–07, 212–15
　the need to prove oneself,
　　205–06
　perception exercise, 207–08
　the power of beliefs, 206–07, 208
　theory of desirable difficulties, 206
　underdog effect research,
　　203–07
　Wilma Rudolph's experiences,
　　201–02, 207
Ungifted (Kaufman), 28

Valdary, Chloé, 260*n*
validation, seeking, 92–93, 98–100, 102
values, 48–49, 258
van der Kolk, Bessel, 17–18, 19
VanderWeele, Tyler, 165
Vasquez-Lovado, Silvia, 218–19, 231
"Victim Entitlement to Behave Selfishly"
　(article), xxii–xxiii
victimhood trap, xv, 10
victim mindset
　best antidote to a, 74
　cognitive distortions of a, 62–65
　collective victimhood, 236–38, 246–47
　common victimhood, 247
　competitive victimhood, 241–43
　defined, xiv–xv
　interpersonal victimhood, 63, 235–36
　and a perpetual sense of entitlement,
　　xxiii
　vs. actual victimization, xv–xvi
virtuous victim effect, 131
virtuous victim signaling, 142–45
visibility, psychological, 93–94
Vohs, Kathleen, 92–93

vulnerability
　gender differences, xvi
　healthy, xvi–xvii
　perfomative, xvi
vulnerable entitlement, xix–xx, 187, 243
vulnerable narcissism, xix–xx, 82–85, 93,
　　95–96, 112, 184–87

*Wake Up Grateful: The Transformative
　Practice of Taking Nothing for Granted*
　(Nelson), 221–23
The Wall Street Journal (newspaper), 31
The Washington Post (newspaper), 140
Watts, Alan, 56
Wayment, Heidi, 252–53
Wegner, Daniel, 237
Weiss, Brandon, 82–84
West, Kanye, 186
*What My Bones Know: A Memoir of Healing
　from Complex Trauma* (Foo), 16
"what" *vs.* "why" questions, 9–10
When Harry Met Sally (film), 102
The White Lotus (TV show), 170–72, 186
Whitman, Walt, 154, 183
"Why TikTok Is So Obsessed with
　Labeling Everything as a Trauma
　Response" (article), 14
Williams, Serena, 233
Williams, Venus, 233
wise feedback, 214–15
Wiseman, Richard, 224–25
Wong, Paul, 228–29
writing, 199

Yalom, Irvin, xxvi*n*, xxvii*n*,
　　26–27
Yes/And thinking, xxiii, 161
Yurak, Tricia, 110

Zangwill, Israel, 3
Zitek, Emily, xxii–xxiii, 226
zone of nervous system arousal,
　　broadening your, 52–53

About the Author

Scott Barry Kaufman, Ph.D., is among the top 1 percent of the most cited scientists in the world for his groundbreaking research on intelligence, creativity, and human potential. He is a professor at Columbia University and director of the Center for Human Potential. Dr. Kaufman founded Self-Actualization Coaching, a whole-person approach to coaching that aims to help people find their most alive and creative center of being, connect deeply with themselves, and become who they truly want to become. He has authored eleven books, including *Choose Growth* (with Jordyn Feingold), *Transcend: The New Science of Self-Actualization*, *Wired to Create: Unraveling the Mysteries of the Creative Mind* (with Carolyn Gregoire), and *Ungifted: Intelligence Redefined*.

Dr. Kaufman also hosts *The Psychology Podcast*, which has received over thirty million downloads and is consistently ranked as one of the top psychology podcasts in the world. Dr. Kaufman received his Ph.D. in cognitive psychology from Yale University, an M.Phil degree from the University of Cambridge in experimental psychology, and a B.S. from Carnegie Mellon University, where he studied opera, psychology, and human-computer interaction. In 2015, he was named one of "50 groundbreaking scientists who are changing the way we see the world" by *Business Insider*.

Also by
Scott Barry Kaufman

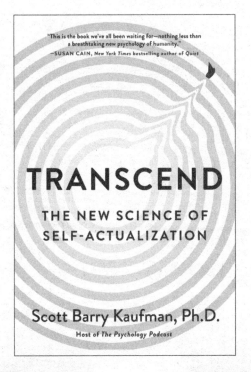

"This is the book we've all been waiting for—nothing less than a breathtaking new psychology of humanity."
—SUSAN CAIN, *New York Times* bestselling author of *Quiet*

TRANSCEND
THE NEW SCIENCE OF SELF-ACTUALIZATION

Scott Barry Kaufman, Ph.D.
Host of *The Psychology Podcast*

Choose Growth
A WORKBOOK FOR TRANSCENDING TRAUMA, FEAR, AND SELF-DOUBT

Scott Barry Kaufman, PhD
AUTHOR OF TRANSCEND

Jordyn H. Feingold, MD

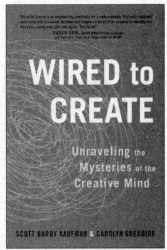

"*Wired to Create* is an empowering manifesto for creative people. Endlessly readable and chock-full of wisdom, Kaufman and Gregoire's study of the creative personality will have you saying over and over again: This is me!"
—SUSAN CAIN, *Quiet* Revolution cofounder and *New York Times* bestselling author of *Quiet*

WIRED to CREATE
Unraveling the Mysteries of the Creative Mind

SCOTT BARRY KAUFMAN & CAROLYN GREGOIRE

Tarcher